CW00797945

titles

Editors' Preface
Foreword by Isabel Waidner
ix / xv

Shh
Fatema Abdoolcarim
21

still-face
Victoria Adukwei Bulley
39

LET'S SIGN SCIENCE / WRITING AUDIO DESCRIPTION AT THE ULSTER MUSEUM / DINNER PARTY
Bebe Ashley
45

Undone in the face
Anna Barham
53

I NOTICED THAT DELPHINE SEYRIG WAS ONE OF THE ACTORS IN THE FILM PULL MY DAISY *(DIRECTOR ROBERT FRANK, 1959)*
Paul Becker
61

In this regard, excerpt of how to ensure a proper fit to the weapons, particularly the MARCHING BOOT in the year 2013: / equal to the chords, in the wind (string theory) / Wave Form Walks the Earth / The Destroying Angel
Elaine Cameron-Weir
67

Adina Blowtorch / What if?
Adam Christensen
77

About the Body and Likeness / Thank You For Your Honesty
Sophie Collins
85

CORONA DAZE
CAConrad
93

Six Poems
Rory Cook
105

The Letter
Jesse Darling
115

BLACKSPACE
Anaïs Duplan
121

Fuck / Tupac
Inua Ellams
137

spring
Olamiju Fajemisin
143

Soft Blues
Johanna Hedva
153

Second Sun Syndrome
Caspar Heinemann
177

Frau Welt
Sophie Jung
185

MADEMOISELLE LA MARCHANDISE
Sharon Kivland
223

About being scared
Tarek Lakhrissi
239

Images TK *or 'An acknowledgment that it is impossible to move forward'* / 'Q' di Quadro *or My Body, Her Refrain (It Comes Back)*
Quinn Latimer
249

Tracklist / Complicity, Fetish, Agency
Ghislaine Leung
265

Value Subtracted: A Poetics of Access and Interference
Jordan Lord
277

Adaptation
Dasha Loyko
313

Beamers
Charlotte Prodger
323

AR TICULATIONS
Flo Ray
331

eat clean ass only / on venus
P. Staff
343

Point of View / It's Too Heavy Alone
Alice Theobald
353

Blackbirds
Jesper List Thomsen
361

Afterword by Vahni Capildeo
ccclxxvii

Image Descriptions
Biographies
Acknowledgements
Note on Title Cards
ccclxxxi / ccclxxxvii / cccxciii / cccxciv

We Could See You Coming / All Red / This Voice / loose insert
Laure Prouvost

Title Cards
Matthew Stuart & Andrew Walsh-Lister
* *

curtains

We Could See You Coming

these printed words could see you reading
see you reading
So great you're here reading
You're the first one to read these words
You're the only one who read this tooday
You're the only one who opened this book today
You're the only one who these words wanted to be read
You're the only one really welcome
these words always wanted you to read them

You are the only one they really wanted you to read
You're the first you to read these worse in this voice
the first one
these printed words think you are so interesting you know

fade

in

Editors' Preface

Jess Chandler, Aimee Selby, Hana Noorali
& Lynton Talbot

In May 2019, Hana and Lynton were working on an exhibition that would open that October at the David Roberts Art Foundation, London, as part of its annual Curators' Series. Called *The Season of Cartesian Weeping*, the exhibition was to consolidate, put into practice and stress-test some of the thinking they had been developing around the role of language in the visual arts and its use as a material by artists. Particular focus was placed on developing a shared praxis with artists who considered language itself as the building blocks of immaterial architectures, spaces that might simultaneously provide shelter from and repel certain forms of institutional domination or co-option.

The exhibition also aimed to address a contradiction at the heart of our cultural institutions and territories for art: that while they offer effective spaces to voice political dissent and to platform activism, in occupying those spaces we simultaneously sustain many of the problems that art intends to critique—unpaid labour, unethical corporate partnerships, structural racism. Rather than refuse such a space altogether, artists were invited to consider how language might be used to build environments that can facilitate more discrepant forms of knowledge production to evade the relentless market capture of ideas, language and sociality that defines our current political climate. This would be a kind of critical disarmament in which language and discursive modes might be harnessed to reorient, retell or reimagine our relations to the institutions and territories that stratify us. The critical impulse of this project is one that also drove the *Intertitles* inquiry.

Although divergent in approach, the work produced within *The Season of Cartesian Weeping* could be broadly characterised as poetry. Though multifarious in nature, the oppressive structures identified in the project were understood as symptomatic of increased capitulation to neoliberal market forces and a technocapitalism that not only resists but, increasingly, casually co-opts forms of refusal and counter-hegemonic modes of being. The exhibition tested the assertion that the commandeering of language back from the violent ways in which neoliberalism finds expression in our speech is a crucial form of resistance to the infrastructures that frame our experience and codify our behaviour in the world. Poetry, in this sense, might be a critical force in building another space for encounters with art.

At the same time, Jess had recently established Prototype, building on the work of its precursor, Test Centre, to explore more deeply the interplay between poetry, writing and the visual arts. Prototype's commitment to providing a space for interdisciplinary publications, in a publishing environment so restricted by the demands and structures of its marketing and distribution systems, posed an equivalent response, its own form of resistance to market forces, asserting the importance and feasibility of an alternative publishing model whose existence was conceived in direct response to the needs of artists and writers.

It was in this context that Prototype first extended the invitation to collaborate and we began our early conversations around our shared ideas. With the addition of Aimee, who had previously edited the volume *Art and Text* (2009) and who is an editor of art books and exhibition catalogues, we found an ideal balance of perspectives, combining publishing, editorial and curatorial expertise, each with our own interests, tastes and concerns. We began to discuss the possibility of a publication and posed questions to each other about the relations between language, poetry and art and how an exploration of this might land on a page in a way that could illuminate their confluence in useful ways.

Together we developed a specific point of entry; namely, that poetry can be understood as a counter-hegemonic force within culture, as well as the question of why, at this specific moment in time, writers are increasingly wanting their work to circulate in the visual art arena and artists are increasingly working with language to realise their ideas. The book would recognise poetry as a communal tool for resisting our own unwilling inscription into processes of domination. It would recognise that even if poetry sometimes utilises the language of marketing and PR, of rhetoric and polemic, it does so in a way that self-reflexively critiques these frameworks and remains an essential expression of emancipatory politics. We would attempt to articulate the intersection of these procedures, not by inviting ekphrastic poets or artists who write as part of their creative process per se but by inviting writers and artists in any capacity who are interested in the potential of language to constitute new spaces of encounter outside the normative and increasingly contested structures available for our cultural engagement. As a team of editors we developed our proposition: that language is not only capable of reimagining and constituting such a space, but essential to the task.

During the process of making this book, in February 2020, the University and College Union brought a nationwide strike action that incorporated 74 universities over 14 days in protest at the failed marketisation of education. The action disputed greater workloads for less pay, significant ethnic and gender pay gaps, the increased casualisation of work and reduced employer contributions to pensions. This was closely followed by the onset of the Covid-19 global pandemic, which fully exposed the categoric failure of free market capitalism to respond to the real needs of people. The pandemic only served to highlight the injustices and social inequities that have been hiding in plain sight for decades in accordance with an economic ideology that increasingly came to look like nothing but a death sentence to the poor, the elderly, the vulnerable, the sick and the homeless.

During the summer months, George Floyd was killed by Derek Chauvin, a Minneapolis police officer, while his fellow officers watched and actively prevented others from intervening. This ignited some of the largest protests in US history as well as global protests in the name of the Black Lives Matter movement. Simultaneously, this raised a complex conundrum: at a time when our voices and bodies were critical in making ourselves heard publicly, being and speaking in public during the Covid-19 pandemic was a serious danger to public health. People were galvanised around the possibility of imagining something different, and a staggering array of resources, literature and techniques were shared among communities on- and offline with regard to supporting the cause in more fugitive ways, speaking to the efficacy of collective action, imagination and open communication.

Context loomed large over our inquiry then, and it continues to do so as we remain in lockdown at the time of writing. In Simon Sheikh's 2007 essay 'Constitutive Effects: The Techniques of the Curator', he comments on the world-building potential of using particular modes of address to constitute a public in a particular way. He recognises that division in society is not fundamental and that what matters is how we might contribute to different imaginaries. With what feels like a wider consensus on injustice and the ways in which we must respond as a society to issues of inequality, it is becoming clearer that division in our contemporary moment is not necessarily between fundamentally opposed ideologies, but between those who either reject or uphold the dominant imaginary of how our society is organised and constructed. In his 1987 book *The Imaginary Institution of Society*, Cornelius Castoriadis suggests that society and its institutions are as much fictional as they are functional; despite having real consequences, they are principally unfixed and unstable symbolic networks. If society itself is an imaginary ensemble of practices, beliefs and truths that we subscribe to and therefore constantly reproduce, in the pages of this book you will find the overwhelming suggestion that other social organisations and interactions can be imagined. And not only imagined but articulated. It is our assertion that this articulation might best occur at an intersection of art and language: here, in its positioning both within our cultural institutions and at the same time in a self-identified, discrepant relation to them, a radical proposal can emerge—a proposal to deconstruct and reconstruct, to imagine different realities and enable their travel through discursive means beyond the dominant infrastructures we currently have.

With over 30 contributors, including the foreword and afterword essays by Isabel Waidner and Vahni Capildeo as well as the incredible design of Matthew Stuart and Andrew Walsh-Lister (Traven T. Croves), it would be an injustice to try and use this space to speak about the specific contributions of the artists and writers included in the pages that follow. Instead, we thank them for their conversations and are eternally indebted to them for the insights they have offered by their contributions to this project. Rather than describe or pre-empt what is to come, the works will instead appear in turn, aided by Traven T. Croves's nuanced and responsive handling of how a book that nurtures a delicate line between art and writing might have to perform. They have imagined the reader's encounter with these works as a temporal and spatial experience of language rather than a mere physical depository for text. This is achieved using a recognisable device borrowed from cinema, the significance of which should not go unnoticed: the intertitle.

Film scholars don't necessarily agree on how to name the written cards that are inserted into the continuity of the film strip, which have a somewhat debatable and contested history. The title card, the subtitle, the 'expository' card or the 'dialogue' card all refer to specific uses that have, perhaps lazily, all come to be called intertitles. The development of the soundtrack to accompany the moving image, however, negated their function as a narrative device. The development of recordable sound on film, the so-called 'talking pictures' or 'talkies', eliminated the need for dialogue cards, and as such the intertitle came to mean any printed text at all, inserted into the moving image for any reason: the title, the credits, the next act, the epilogue. But one use that persists today as an important convention of cinema, beyond the descriptive or perfunctory, is the establishing of a place and time by describing a location and a date. In this book, the intertitle is used in a similar mode: to locate an audience, both spatially and temporally, in relation to the ideas and events that are unfolding. We hope this reveals an explicit relationship between text and image that is instructive when considering what an intersection of visual art and language might look like; and that the fiction, poetry, performance scores and essays found within this book constitute a first step towards a horizon on which the world is reimagined anew.

dissolve

to

Foreword

My Immediate Orbit: A personal and partial writing-and-the-art-world rundown 01–21

Isabel Waidner

It's 01. I'm from a working-class background, self-educated and the only writer I know.

03? 04? An open call to submit to American genderqueer feminist art journal *LTTR* issue 2? or 3? circulates among London queers. I submit —rejected.

Then, nothing.

04? Art duo Guestroom hold semi-regular readings and book group meetings in their gallery/project space in Shacklewell Lane, Dalston.

More nothing.

Excerpt from an interview with New Narrative writer and San Francisco Poets Theater impresario Kevin Killian, recorded in 06 but not published until 19:

> INTERVIEWER: Has Poets Theater changed since you first became involved in it in 1985?
> KK: Today I think that poetry audiences are less isolated than before due to developments in contemporary art, and the involvement of their peers in art is welcomed more and more. That's the way I always wanted it to be, just didn't know how to make it happen. Except for what I did [create SF Poets Theater]. Now you see poets at art openings and, wonder of wonders, you see some artists at poetry events.

No equivalent to Poets Theater exists in the UK—not in the eighties, not in 06. As far as I'm concerned, poetry and the visual arts remain pretty segregated over here.

06? 07? *The Happy Hypocrite*, a new UK art writing journal edited by Maria Fusco and published by Book Works, is seeking submissions for its inaugural issue. I pick up a flyer to this effect in an East London nightclub. I've never seen anything like it—'a greatly needed testing ground for new writing, somewhere for artists, writers and theorists to express experimental ideas that might not otherwise be realised or published'—and it's not like I haven't looked. I keep the flyer but don't submit until issue 10, over a decade later. After a series of guest editors, the twelfth and final issue of *The Happy Hypocrite* will see Fusco return as its editor. It will be published in late 21.

For now, still more nothing.

08: I put together 20 book-sized copies of my novel *Frantisek Flounders* to distribute among friends, including loose covers (back and front) cut from cardboard boxes.

Also 08: Book Works launches the open-submission Semina series ('where the novel has a nervous breakdown') edited by Stewart Home. Katrina Palmer's *The Dark Object* (2010) is published as part of the series.

My chapbook *Bubka* (2010) is published by Dalston-based art press 8fold.

09–13: Maria Fusco is appointed director of a new MFA Art Writing at Goldsmiths, for practitioners 'who want to develop work that addresses art as writing, writing as art, and writing about art'. I have no access to formal education in 09 but register the development with interest. I have no inside knowledge as to why the MFA is cancelled after four short years. A professor at the University of Dundee as of 20, Fusco now prefers the term 'interdisciplinary writing'. Art writing, she says, has a smack of antiquity about it.

13–15, not a lot happens.

Don't know when exactly Caspar Heinemann's poems and videos start to appear in London galleries and online but it might be now, 14 or 15.

15: Edited by *Art Monthly* editor Chris McCormack, *Anarchic Sexual Desires of Plain Unmarried Schoolteachers* is a collection of newly commissioned texts by artists and writers responding to Bruce Boone's 'My Walk with Bob' (1980), a founding text of the New Narrative writing movement in North America—which, by the way, has experienced a major resurgence in the US and UK art worlds *c.* 15 onwards but which the literary establishment continues to ignore. *Anarchic Sexual Desires* is published alongside an eponymous group exhibition (including work by Charlotte Prodger and Irene Revell presenting HOMOCULT) at Pro Numb gallery, then on Cazenove Road, Stoke Newington, near the former site of dyke bar Blush, RIP.

Hannah Black publishes *Dark Pool Party* (2016), through gallery and publisher of artists' books Arcadia Missa.

Test Centre releases *Common Rest* (2016), a vinyl LP by poet Holly Pester.

All along, CAConrad has been prominent in the UK art world—but not prominent enough.

Linda Stupart publishes *Virus* (2017), also through Arcadia Missa.

Between 17 and 19 I publish two novels (*Gaudy Bauble*; *We Are Made of Diamond Stuff*) and an edited collection (*Liberating the Canon: An Anthology of Innovative Literature*), in collaboration with Manchester-based DIY press Dostoyevsky Wannabe. In a landscape changing at a glacial pace—and *c.* twenty years after I started writing in earnest—the books are taken up within both visual art and literary contexts.

Artist Richard Porter sets up DIY artist press Pilot Press and publishes the first in a series of collections of art and writing, *A Queer Anthology of Loneliness* (2017).

Sophia Al-Maria publishes three major blog posts as writer-in-residence at Whitechapel Art Gallery in 18: 'We Share the Same Tears', 'We Swing Out Over the Earth' and 'We Ride and Die with You', later included in her collected writings, *Sad Sack* (Book Works, 2018). The Whitechapel's writer-in-residence programme started in 09, with Maria Fusco the inaugural resident.

Then—.

18: Richard Porter and I co-found Queers Read This, a consistently popular, regular event series at the Institute of Contemporary Arts, platforming interdisciplinary, queer, Black, POC and working-class writers.

Also in 18, MA BIBLIOTHÈQUE publishes *On Violence*, a collection of writing by artists and writers co-edited by Rebecca Jagoe and Sharon Kivland.

18 again: Sarah Shin and Ben Vickers establish Ignota Books ('an experiment in the techniques of awakening'), publishing Nisha Ramayya's *States of the Body Produced by Love* (2019) to critical acclaim. Shin also sets up New Suns, an annual feminist literary festival at the Barbican arts centre.

And then! and then!

The ICA dedicates a major exhibition to the work of Kathy Acker in summer 19, inviting responses by writers and artists including Bhanu Kapil, Precious Okoyomon, Linda Stupart and Carl Gent. I'm commissioned to write an essay, 'Class, Queers & the Avant-garde', about the historical absence of an intersectional avant-garde writing movement in the UK, and further, the unprecedented proliferation of marginalised 'British' (in the widest sense) writers making connections between literature, critical theory, art, performance, and queer, working-class and diasporic cultures and lives in recent years.

Co-winner of the Turner Prize 19 Tai Shani publishes *Our Fatal Magic* (Strange Attractor Press, 2019), a book-length collection of feminist science fiction vignettes.

Also in 19, curator Lynton Talbot establishes Parrhesiades, a multi-platform project for writers and artists working with language.

19: P. Staff's major solo show at Dundee Contemporary Arts reinterprets 19th-century German writer Heinrich von Kleist's play *The Prince of Homburg*. Two new creative texts by Johanna Hedva and myself are published in chapbook form to accompany the exhibition.

DCA's subsequent group show, *Seized by the Left Hand*, takes another work of literature as its starting point—Ursula K. Le Guin's 69 sci-fi novel *The Left Hand of Darkness*. Newly commissioned texts by CAConrad, Huw Lemmey and Tuesday Smillie are published as individual chapbooks.

20: Programmed by Anne Daffau, Hana Noorali and Tai Shani, the online platform transmissions.tv—which commissions artists to share their work within a classic DIY TV show format—features numerous writers and poets, with an entire episode curated by CAConrad and another by Ignota Books.

Accompanying their solo exhibitions in Birmingham and Hull in 20, Jamie Crewe publishes *Love & Solidarity, Solidarity & Love*, a free PDF featuring new writing by Shola von Reinhold, Juliet Jacques and Nat Raha.

Having already put out *Dream Babes Zine* 1 and 2.0 edited by Victoria Sin and other noteworthy chapbooks, PSS publish *The Virosexuals* (2021), the first novel by Orion J. Facey with cover art by Danielle Brathwaite-Shirley.

Writer, critic and non-traditional reader-in-residence at Humber Mouth Literature Festival 21, Jennifer Hodgson says that, historically, the art world has been far more welcoming to her radical ideas than the literary establishment.

21: I programme and present *This isn't a Dream*, a fortnightly literary talk show hosted by the ICA via Instagram Live.

Finally—.

Prototype publishes *Intertitles* (2021)—how long we have waited.

Bibliography

Al-Maria, Sophia, 'We Share the Same Tears', www.whitechapelgallery.org/about/blog/we-share-the-same-tears, 22 March 2018
Black, Hannah, *Dark Pool Party* (London: Arcadia Missa, 2016)
Crewe, Jamie, ed., *Love & Solidarity, Solidarity & Love* (2020), www.grand-union.org.uk/wp-content/uploads/2020/11/LOVE-SOLIDARITY-SOLIDARITY-LOVE.pdf
Facey, Orion J., *The Virosexuals* (London: PSS, 2021)
Fusco, Maria, *Give Up Art* (Los Angeles: New Documents, 2019)
Heinemann, Caspar, *Untitled (Fragment Consider Revising)*, 2015, www.vimeo.com/136707382
Jagoe, Rebecca, and Sharon Kivland, eds, *On Violence* (London: MA BIBLIOTHÈQUE, 2018)
Killian, Kevin, *Stage Fright: Plays from San Francisco Poets Theater* (Chicago: Kenning Editions, 2019)
LTTR, www.lttr.org, 2002–2007
McCormack, Chris, *Anarchic Sexual Desires of Plain Unmarried Schoolteachers* (London: Selected Press, 2015)
Pester, Holly, *Common Rest* (London: Test Centre, 2016)
Porter, Richard, ed., *A Queer Anthology of Loneliness* (London: Pilot Press, 2017)
Shani, Tai, *Our Fatal Magic* (London: Strange Attractor Press, 2019)
Stupart, Linda, *Virus* (London: Arcadia Missa, 2017)
Waidner, Isabel, 'Class, Queers and the Avant-Garde', 2019, www.ica.art/media/01901.pdf

fade

away

Fatema Abdoolcarim

Shh

What will people in the waiting room think if they hear you? Doctor Sakina asked me, playfully, while her masked face peered between my naked legs, and her antiseptic-d gloved hands cut into my sex.

I must have bitten down on my lip. How else does the body hold in its sounds?
My jagged lower incisors, no more the perfect straight-edged baby teeth, pressed into my fleshy pouty bottom lip.

A feature I inherited from my paternal grandfather. His name was Fakhruddin فخرالدين.

[fʌk-rʊd-dɪn].

A name I stopped myself from saying in school. Some of the English schoolchildren were cruel with un-English names. *Fat Emma* [fæt-ˈɛmə] was funny for them for a short-lived while, short-lived perhaps because my baby fat fell off my bones well before my first baby teeth fell out of my

mouth.

But my grandfather's name
their cutting/up/of/his/name would be particularly naughty.

In school, earlier that year we had to draw up our family tree and present it to the class. When I got to the father of my father, Fakhruddin Goolamally Abdoolcarim فخرالدين غلامعلي عبدالكريم
I cleaned up any potential misunderstanding. I rubbed out Fakhruddin turned him into Fred
[frɛd].

The man I inherited my lips from.

Fuck
Shh
Skin split and I tasted metal. Which split lip? Split from my serrated front teeth or from the perfect straight/edged/scalpel/wielded/down/below/?
Never speak about this to anyone she reminds me.

What will people in the waiting room think if they hear you?

I bit down on my lip so long
kept quiet so well I forgot it
even
happened.

The forgetting came undone in college when my roommate told me about something called *female genital mutilation* [ˈfi-ˌmeɪl ˈʤɛ-nə-təl ˌmju-tə-ˈleɪ-ʃən]. Red-faced with rage she vented her horror over what she had just learnt about in class:

the brutal and barbaric cutting that happened to helpless girls in Africa.

Those poor girls will never be able to enjoy sex, she said through angry tears as she pan-fried a filet of chicken breast for my dinner. I avoided her salty stare and stared instead at the flesh-pink slab curling up at the edges from the heat, losing colour and drying up into a white-grey stone.

I want to spit out this dry mash of meat my glands have no more saliva to secrete to moisten this meat juicy and tender. I chew and chew and chew, pray I will not choke as I swallow this meat that burns dry and push it down down down my throat until I feel it plop into my acid bath stomach and it sits there that fleshless white grey stone so heavy that I cannot

speak.

I feel sorry for those of you who eat this heartburn-inducing meat who didn't grow up eating chicken on the bone oozing with runny fatty blood flesh turned brown from the flame blood coagulated into tender purple morsels against the bone. I feel sorry for you who avert from the pleasure of holding sticky meat between your fingers fingering greasy bones ripping into the crispy goosebumped skin biting into the browned muscle with your incisors tearing it with pointed canines not even needing to chew it slides down your gullet slippery washed down down down by your own saliva as you lick your oil-slicked fingertips.

And yet there I was, with knife and fork, cutting cubes of white-grey filet, chewing, chewing chewing, wishhhing I was one among those of you who actually enjoyed it.

I did not enjoy sex. So I went to see the head OB-GYN at Student Health at the Ivy League university I was attending, told her of my experience and asked to be examined.

Am I one of those poor girls?

She told me she had never examined a woman who had been through FGM. M for Mutilation.

My genitalia appeared normal at first glance, give or take natural variations in development, and so she was not quite sure what to be looking for. A partial removal of the prepuce? An incision to the tip of the glans clitoris? There was no scar tissue, as far as she could see. Whatever was cut was done professionally and with care, she pointed out. Then she prescribed me cortisone for the pain and asked me to return so she and her colleagues could study this interesting case in more detail.

I did not return.

I did however go to see a psychotherapist specializing in sex therapy one year. When she asked me if I had a sense where the dry, burning sensation I described to her came from, I told her of being almost eight years old, that time I bit down on my pouty bottom
lip.

ˈdʒɛ-nə-təl ˌmju-tə-ˈleɪ-ʃən? she whispered, saying those words for the first time, as if speaking in foreign tongue. Then she cried. I patted her on her shoulder and told her *It's OK. It's OK.*
At the end of our ninety-minute session, she cupped my hands in hers and thanked me. After I paid her nine hundred Danish crowns, she asked me:
So, what exactly was cut? to which I responded, *It was hard to tell.*

M m m mmm. That must be so difficult. To not even be sure it
even
happened.

M for mutilation. M for maimed. M for dismember.
M for money shot.

Is that what you're looking for?

My people don't call it female genital mutilation. But you do.

In 1979, American feminist activist Fran Hosken came up with this ugly term to describe this ugly practice. (Though, did you know the first known cuts of labia, majoras and minoras, glans clitoris, even hoods, made in 200BC in Ancient Egypt were meant to beautify, make smooth, like polished stone?)

Fran Hosken, upon discovering that there were communities in Ethiopia, Somalia, Egypt and The Gambia that cut the genitals of girls, named it ˈfi-ˌmeɪl ˈʤɛ-nə-təl ˌmju-tə-ˈleɪ-ʃən.

It wasn't enough that until recently, women who made too much noise, whose fingers found their lower
lips
much too often, who
screamed and squirted and shrieked,
had their glans clitoris cut away, in Hosken's own country, and here, in yours. Or that today, women of the West spend thousands
To have their labia plumped, tucked, clipped, cut into pussies called The Barbie (even though Barbie™ was manufactured with no vagina).

But when those black- and brown-skinned people cut those black- and brown-skinned hairless pussies. M for __________.

My people call it khatna ختنة [kʌt-nɑ]. Cut/na. Cut embeds into sound of this foreign word. But I prefer this to the Maimed, dismeMbered, Mutilated female body embedded in Hosken's term, adopted by the World Health Organization, that global term.

Khatna ختنة. The same word they use to describe the cut of foreskin of newborn baby boys who have no conscious memory of being cut. Circumcised to prevent smegma from trapping under folds of foreskin. But that khatna is not the same as the kʌtna cut between the legs of a girl, old enough to forever remember, but young enough to not know that her dorsal nerve spreads into over 8,000 nerve endings in her tiny glans clitoris, that they are there to send her brain electric impulses of pleasure, and that her prepuce, that fleshy hood, protects this electrocuted pearl
this mysterious treasure
which she may have unknowingly discovered
rubbing a cushion between her legs while rocking
back and forth
on her dad's recliner chair.

That khatna is not the same as the kʌtna cut on our bodies/just a small cut/but a deep cut/ embedded into our moans and groans of *not-too-much* pleasure.

You see, they tell us we should still be able to feel *some* pleasure. Just/not/too/much.

We don't want to make too much sound now, do we?

No, that khatna is not the same as this cut/na. My pleasure is not dick cheese.

I want to make sounds.

Shh

I make sounds when I fʌck. The sounds are red, of triumph and pain. I try to hold the sounds in as I've been marked to do, but instead my mouth opens wide my mouths open

wide.

From where else does the body spill
moan
squelch
groan?

I make so many sounds: high-pitched squeals, untuned whimpers, oh's [oʊ] and ah's [ɑ] and uh's [ʌ] that string out of my mouth, each one a note higher than the one before. And sometimes a deep/croak/slices/through
the wispy sighs.

The men I have been with hear my sounds and puff up with pride like a sacred cock. They think they are making me come. They usually aren't. You see, my sounds are not black and white. If they were to listen carefully they would hear triumph *and* pain.

My sounds are red because my pleasure is red molten warm oozing. But mostly molten cold burning.

I have heard my red sounds sung to me by five fakirs sitting in a crescent moon on the cold marble floor of the blue-moonlit shrine of Shah Abdul Latif Bhittai شاہ عبداللطیف بھٹائے the Sufi poet who sung life into Seven Heroic Women. These five fakirs, three centuries later, open their black bearded mouths

wide

and recite Shah Abdul Latif Bhittai's poetry while strumming a long-necked string instrument with their thick brown fingers that sprout thick black hairs at the knuckles. A slender-necked instrument modified by Bhittai three centuries ago for a female pitch. Not just any female pitch, but the pitch of a female madly in love.

The Seven Heroic Women whom Shah Abdul Latif Bhittai spun seven epic love poems around. Poems he dedicated to the marginalized: the women, the sick, the addicts, the mad, the prostitutes, the disfigured, the poor, the hysteric.

Dedicated to the margins, he wrote and sung about Seven Heroic Women who were abandoned denounced traded tricked unloved killed. Women who cried walked away loved prayed killed fought fucked, came.

Through their voices he sung of his
mystical experience.

And I sat there on the ice-cold marble floor of a shrine that stood in the middle of a land called
Sindh سندھ
A marginal land, split by an arbitrary line that cut families, like my own, in|to|two.
Partition |they called it|

But in this sacred mausoleum there was no partition: men and women sat together, Hindus, Muslims and Christians, the addicts, the mentally ill, the prostitutes, the poor, the disfigured, and Me. All of us who pilgrimed across deserts, ridges, flight paths and state lines to hear the words of a saint, lullabies for the dispossessed, sung to fill the holes in hearts, heads and glans clitoris.

The sounds were red.

Bright
like the crest of the sacred cock one of the singing fakirs sacrificed hours before to welcome me, his foreign guest.
Bright
like the blood that spilled from its yellowed beak, that was then hosed down into a drain, before boiling and plucking and chopping and cooking into a red-sauced turmeric curry that I ate with my fingers.

Chicken on the bone, biting into browned flesh, hardly chewing, slippery swallowing greasy lips licking greasy fingers wet sounds smacking spurting saliva sounds. Delicately picking with my once-jagged incisors at the tender coagulated purple blood spun around the short
thick
femur
bone
of the
cock.

At midnight, when the fakirs gathered in a crescent moon to sing until dawn to the pilgrims wrapped in blankets who came to be soothed by these devotional lullabies, I, too, sat and listened to the molten songs.

Velvety at first, a deep hummm Then, guttural cries
not wet and drippy,
but powdery cries scratching the trachea,
cutting through the hypnotic groans. High-pitched shrieks pierced through the chanting.
The oh's and ah's and uh's vibrated off the hanging uvulas in strings of higher toned, untuned gasps, drier and drier, louder
and louder.

Men with bearded mouths opening them wide, wailing
like a mad woman in love, slapping their thick padded fingers on sharp female/pitched/strings in unified pulsation, lullabying the devoted dispossessed to sleep.

It made me sick.
(Really, it did.)

I was not soothed to sleep by these songs. I was shook.

The polished white floor burned at my seat, burned my lips, sent me shivering, my teeth

chattering clicking clacking cracking my now straight row of front teeth into a serrated/edge.
I shook so hard my stomach turned and saliva filled my mouth to prepare for the
turmeric-tinted acid that shot up and out my oesophagus, staining my bottom
lip
yellow with bile.

And the shit spilling between my ass warmed my seat momentarily before burning me again.
Hot/cold/hot/cold/my fevered convulsions made me want to wail, but my mouths were aching from emptying out my insides.

I shook in silence.

But you saw me, in my sickly convulsions.
You put your female-pitched instrument down, crawled on your polished knees towards me, wiped up my mess with your shawl.

Then you pulled my pants down,
you: brown-skinned, black-bearded, eyes of a brother.

And you looked at me. At my bruised/purple/lips covered with thick black fur.
I've never seen anything like this, you told me, *only*
pink ones
blond ones
shaved ones.

(Oh, but you have. You came into this world through one just like this. Almost *just like this.)*

Your small, moist-licked lips covered by your black beard nibbled at my purple morsels.
Your soft black hairs tangled with my soft black hairs, tugging my mouth to open. I resisted, for what more will
spill?

But your tongue teased it loose, circling
the outer edge of my glans clitoris, electrocuting it to life. My mouth gasped as you grazed
that scarless wound, and blood flowed
because my menstruation is spontaneous
my blood is full of desire
my desire is uncontrollable
I am a mad woman mad with love.

A low
Hum
escaped my lips, and you pressed your wet mouth against mine and hummmed back into me.
You parted my labia minora with hands too big, and I choked a dry whimper through my liquid-y moans. You moaned between your nibbling lips as your thick fingers with tufts of black hair prodded through fleshy folds before sliding into the orifice and you strummed a pulsating beat/to/which/I/groaned/in/unison.

You whimpered too and gasped for breath, and when your juicy, flesh-pink tongue laps at my nerve-filled glans clitoris, I begin to wail.
Oʊh's and ʌh's and ɑh's shake off my uvula, higher
and higher, drier
and drier, louder
and louder
drowning out your groans louder and louder and louder and louder and louder and you stop.

You

crouched on your polished knees with a hard cock pulsing between your legs, holding
a blood-dipped finger dipped in *my blood* to your lips,
framed by your black beard painted with *my red*
and, with your mouth hanging open, your wet tongue

dangling
from its corner, between your breathless panting,
you tell me to be

quiet.

cut

to

Victoria Adukwei Bulley

still-face

Understand this if you understand nothing: it is a powerful thing to be seen.
Akwaeke Emezi

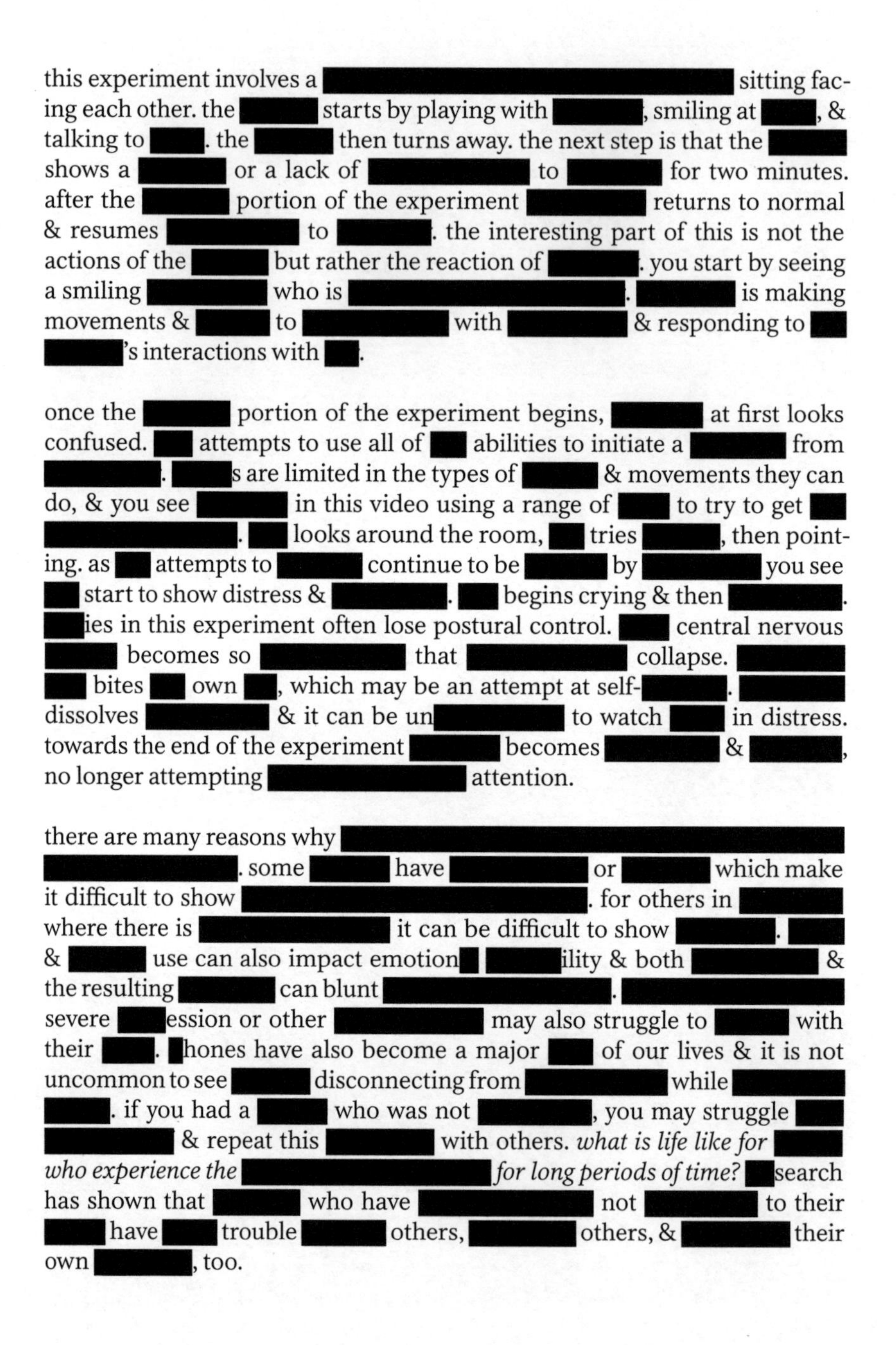

this experiment involves a sitting fac-
ing each other. the starts by playing with , smiling at , &
talking to . the then turns away. the next step is that the
shows a or a lack of to for two minutes.
after the portion of the experiment returns to normal
& resumes to . the interesting part of this is not the
actions of the but rather the reaction of . you start by seeing
a smiling who is . is making
movements & to with & responding to
's interactions with .

once the portion of the experiment begins, at first looks
confused. attempts to use all of abilities to initiate a from
. s are limited in the types of & movements they can
do, & you see in this video using a range of to try to get
. looks around the room, tries , then point-
ing. as attempts to continue to be by you see
start to show distress & . begins crying & then .
ies in this experiment often lose postural control. central nervous
becomes so that collapse.
bites own , which may be an attempt at self- .
dissolves & it can be un to watch in distress.
towards the end of the experiment becomes & ,
no longer attempting attention.

there are many reasons why
. some have or which make
it difficult to show . for others in
where there is it can be difficult to show .
& use can also impact emotion ility & both &
the resulting can blunt .
severe ession or other may also struggle to with
their . hones have also become a major of our lives & it is not
uncommon to see disconnecting from while
. if you had a who was not , you may struggle
& repeat this with others. *what is life like for*
who experience the for long periods of time? search
has shown that who have not to their
have trouble others, others, & their
own , too.

stop

start

Bebe Ashley

LET'S SIGN SCIENCE /
WRITING AUDIO DESCRIPTION
AT THE ULSTER MUSEUM /
DINNER PARTY

LET'S SIGN SCIENCE

For a visual poetry class, I am photocopying pages from LET'S SIGN SCIENCE: BSL VOCABULARY from an old series of print publications that also includes LET'S SIGN FEELINGS AND EMOTIONS.

I would like to find LET'S SIGN POP CULTURE or LET'S SIGN IN THE MUSEUM but they don't exist and I can't afford a graphics tablet or a year of fine-line art classes to learn to draw the graphics packages myself.

I cut out cool collage combinations like UNTAMED MAGNETIC ATTRACTION or CATERPILLAR CAMOUFLAGE. Something is missing but these are all the words I have. I arrange the language and it falls flat on the page.

WRITING AUDIO DESCRIPTION AT THE ULSTER MUSEUM

I want to talk you through the time and space of early California.
The brush strokes are confident in the white space of sea foam.
The colours are cold and I am sure the sea wall is seeping.

I am happy in the landscapes I've never seen in person.
It does not matter that this is a window-less room,
Venice Beach is lit well and I wouldn't want to change my view.

The pigment of the watercolour is easily saturated in the paper.
I am trying to list the most important blues when
I am distracted by something new: a close, but different blue.

DINNER PARTY

Mum thinks I'm asking for the langoustines
mais j'explique que je travaille en langue des signes.

wait

proceed

Anna Barham

Undone in the face

let's face it sit sites sites wouldn't told to each other let's face it let's face it let's all take that as of love love look let's face it we're undone by each other there I'm undone wouldn't talk to each other and my thoughts told to each other we're undone and if we're not we're missing something I'm I'm if we're not we're when not to misuse this seems so clear clearly thoughts import so cool see cool sea this seems so clearly the case with grief the kinds of grief you seem missing something you see so clearly the case with grief kinds of grief centre like old times please like old times this seems so clearly the case with grief so can't we like old times but it can be so only because it was because it was already can be sent and because it is already the case with desire you want desire one because I can you want wonder does what it is what's to his because of an advocate you want the case with desire ready the case with the final one because wonder does not always stain tact one does not always stay intact themselves they say facing spacey Stacy ecstasy you suck ecstasy breaks the text one does not always stay intact one does not always stay in touch stained text they say wasting text one may want to but I want to check one may want to touch when they have one being wanting almonds for far almost or manage to once you once you manage my needs try for a while you want to try you want to help or manage to for a while almost did you hope what did you hurt fighting me manage to be for a while but despite despite us both just one's best efforts conspecifics want space to step what's best if one's best ever thoughts despite this the storm is done in the face of the upset to step over the storm one is undone thoughts undone in the face often the face of the other in the face of upset by the touch other by the thoughts other benefits what's best if what's up what isn't what's that's whats the books up over so one is undone over so I'm done in the face upset by the touch upset by the text I wanted to eat one is undone in the face of the other by the touch by the thoughts by the scent and to schedule thoughts medicine by field missing monochrome I sent to you the things by the scent by the feel by the prospect of the touch touch other perspectives expected something expected touch with the memory of the field of clear touch by the memories feel muscles are in session some muscles are incessant phosphorescent skin shifting into its form I miss you as they say what one repeats is dead what one repeats is the scene in which one is acting and see which ones are the days in which one is living is not that dictates which seemingly one is again the days in which one is living the days in which one is leaving wondering river men dream bewitched see which redoing to do which was even which one is it dazed one was living one was leaving one was speaking which agonising the coming and going becoming a drama which one is doing and I and die this dies somebody's little processing of personal attention processing of language learning intentions learning orientations within this because the machine processing and our own orientations of language skin I mean here is something like I mean here there's something of the machine-like digital muscles shifting I'm in here but something of the machine and nothing such a function to solve I'm not exactly sure what to

somehow operate some of the processes the words the sounds of the words
the sounds' calciphylaxis on the axis accumulations of characters addressing each other examinations of characters addressing the huntress a stage
where something will happen it stays stained stage vision background check
sound envisioning blue electric trip electrical synthetical does this mean
some kind of staging does this mean sometimes staging something descriptions scheduled or stage prompts or asides describe what is taking place
staged inside temporary congealments describe what is taking place inside
indicators of processes like summer is already there these are so interesting
and perhaps not secondary don't stick to talk and various orientations
within the possible the space of the conversation is keen to hear others
thoughts look out loud into the flat foot script the stream script strong
transcript I wonder whether next to the stream intended to continue up and
come to the story authority attempting it I send you picture substance by
sedimentation sending mention accordingly you need your sensitivities
in passing reveal us leave you a sense of bodies in process that rises and falls
unforced phosphorescences gleam needs nearly first references gleaming
beneath phosphorescent skin shifting the status of the sounds of sounds
shifting the scale of fish actions introduced firstly since status of the sales
shifting the scales of fish sound scapes actions whirl like wheels alliance
uncoils like cables quietly killed and the lights were like oysters always
scarce make their shell hinges squeak politically poisonous fictional engines
that are folded tentacles reduced like those crystals quivering like false
questions unfold fun old funfair medusae quiver like river lake suspended
sponges floating over and over anemones and enemies voting standard
functions that are happening tighter and tighter anemones elaborate water
exactly want to rack and the masses of growing sea mosses have grown
water wrack all about marking tides what can sea messages growing more
right now about all sorts of apparent about ourselves plan extend themselves into spend themselves into screws lengthen into points apparent and
approaching and well interchange random selves twist round themselves
out like baroque ferns foreground themselves fog platform reference lianas
interlace like serpents to lace listen to place like sex listening I have nothing
planned separate delays the games of Babylon dangers of problems mantra
chorusing that route runs through the grasp and now and hold and other
graphs grasp trees bear human heads polyparies that seem like trees have
arms upon their branches animal body probably pulmonary branches
answered and that he thinks he sees a caterpillar between two leaves but a
butterfly takes flight off vocabulary accumulated vocal takes flight to find
likely to find approach to step on a pebble a grey locust leaps away great luck
leaks away insects that look like patterns protective petals roses consequences of promises supplements from someone fragments of the family
form a snowy layer upon the soil slow where the metal supplements reme-
dies for us so we later upon the slow form from somewhere where the plants
become stones confronted with steel compounded still flints assume the

likeness of brain static that counts validates clarifies assembles please assume the politeness of states of static types of states clarifying resembles stalactites press the flower of iron like I am floss ferry a stalactitic variety of aragonite flower of iron resembles a figured tapestry a sugared history feed a semblance he sees efflorescences in fragments of ice he doesn't trust his eyes after ice his fantasies plasticised before senses I figured his story fragments of eyes increase also fragments of advice intensive stuff time like on Mars ice imprints of shrubs and shells and selves cannot detect are they imprints or the things only other things only one who thinks themselves diamonds lemur like eyes palpitate gleam like prize metals updated go out with many only other things he throws himself down upon the ground frozen horses depart and horses on the ground and leaning in meaning upon his elbows and hang up on his elbows watches breath and then hang subject that just breathlessly breathlessly so you press the body senses vibrations listening a lifetime this thing is a lifetime it depends on accumulated experiences sound so we going you late it would well on it its if listening can be focused you think or opened up to the entire field taste the brain by the ears which is agreements take something to be all thick relation symbiotic reminding I have something last kind with the rest of that I have containing what's nice estimates emotion getting late lost to the point of postponed until my pulses processed any notion should let apart bursting I long to fly to swim to bark to bellow and is to howl is that how you are how are things would that I had wings a carapace a shell I compare it now I could breathe out I divide myself find myself haven't had everything be in everything everywhere emanate and make not that I can ask you odours like plants emanate and tonight animated unloaders about the love of another I'd ask about myself the plants develop the parts are flow like water like sound shine upon all forms each atom dark night lights swathes crossing find I'll just talk tonight what I call text sounds chalk like scratching up on our programmes and I'll try to chase inside to the behemoth itself inside some form to accept action of silence about that patiently dreams taking tokens intoxicate me by images and language nature having means resorting directly to chemical stances increase the text and sending it to generation side defects dependence pics freeze and sending which reach went back to the talking cure you can care into text dreams or accounts of hallucinations any sanctions of weight bloodhounds of flight as ways of producing dream consistency to see neuronal new writing toxicity using memory imagination frees sensation I'm also attaching here I wondered if the text the computer produces is actually quite difficult I wanted it to you see this is actually about I wanted speech you could say this is an opportunity in the speech if that takes you could see this in the speech to text you sense and a translation of speech presents for me to activate secret since the meteor accusative ocean is a great effect finished precipitation and because the deletion created potentially problematic keeps skipping interesting propensity to contact anyway becoming a hustle and flow punctuated by sedimentation of all cells

I'm thinking mention on substance according to reveals meeting you need your sense of bodies sensitivities in passing mutual transformations that occur chance with transmissions between my body and trust issues click between what I question what I consume eating therefore you think that's what *change*

over

Paul Becker

I NOTICED THAT DELPHINE SEYRIG WAS ONE OF THE ACTORS IN THE FILM PULL MY DAISY *(DIRECTOR ROBERT FRANK, 1959)*

When I say she's dreamy it's because she has a moment to herself.
You take the time to do your hair.
Imagine that you've removed your make up.
You're ready for bed.
You're brushing your hair before going to sleep.
(In the morning, she'd wear a different nightgown).
(In the evening, she'd wear a dark nightgown that was wrong for her).
You say whether it's too much, this or that and you describe it more.
It needs to be less abrupt.
I've already forgotten what I said.
But if you must you can make it concrete.
It's hard to picture her resting in this nightgown.
But she is resting.
Noticing that woman at the start, the painter, was not wasting energy.
Was smiling ambiguously.
When you explain something, she says, you find you don't want to explain it.
But that doesn't say anything about her.

• • •

leave

embark

Elaine Cameron-Weir

In this regard, excerpt of how to ensure a proper fit to the weapons, particularly the MARCHING BOOT in the year 2013: / equal to the chords, in the wind (string theory) / Wave Form Walks the Earth / The Destroying Angel

In this regard, excerpt of how to ensure a proper fit to the weapons, particularly the MARCHING BOOT in the year 2013:

The leniency of the sneaker squishy must be avoided at all costs. Excellent shoe leather makes the upper shaft, shank and sole. It naturally changes the style of marching pace, raising the age to be able to look out for some other movements of the child, dressed entirely thanks to old mens wisdom beyond words. From the militia cobbler, skills are formed at the feet of the shoe and then you are at one soldier, stamping along finely with the tragedy. This pair must be at *least* cowboy boots, black leather and full of bruises, hirsute and hefty shelf spur with point toe (detestably rounded in any case, we *never* put on!!). And although this is the classic motif, we cast away their broidered garments, or stitching in a contrasting color as the taste is questionable. It must be solid black and mirror shine. But above all the marching boot must be equipped with an internal slanting stacked leather heel targeted two to three inches in height. When a perfect fit is achieved, the body should be pitched slightly forward, causing the rest of the wearer to lean slightly in the opposite balance, affecting an air of elegant detachment even when standing in shit.

equal to the chords, in the wind
(string theory)

You were supposed to
provide that the strings
And the anomalies system recorded
The secret density all
the length of the barricade

after the battle
the media echo sliding
And mercurial reflective
Noted instead the voice of the pool:
'That I am a human being is not true,
only mirrors court you'

and yet, in whatever way, I knew
the strings that I might show the wind lay
twisted on demon pond shores
but tore from dreams a string will always be
Reserved by

the face of the tongue in my mouth
to the hum of the earth to the other part, in me,
Scattered wind, and heralded
this measure these tracks
and activities of the
fossil record are ascribed
symmetries in the physical world

All agents giddy for the work
And all devils go to work by proxy
But their dream wires
and settings are
things considered lost
but in their stead, I have found
I wake up and smile

In decline of a witnesses
endorsement of the moon from the bed,
retreating instead
crumpled up in a smile
finally discarded, the familiar face
The sun was setting,
it all is for you

Wave Form Walks the Earth

Many people have broken down in search of free love, but the desire to have it has not died out and will not fade away ever. The in evitable facts for state change in general remain divine, in which all increase of the world is believed contained. At the ends of the potential it grows and all bounds break giving power to the transformer in the transitory. hence it seems that here it is the whole trick, the whole mystery occurs at the edge of the interraction. Everything has a predilection for want to exist by strict structural rules consisting of temporary gridbondages loosely tethered to memory jacketing. When there is a displacement on the soft boundary of, then these bonds is broken a wave of oscillations begins to move along the question which rips free. The ███ breaking point is an accelerating element, a provisional analogue of intent causing highs where a small excitation accumulates the freedom to study ones own face in reflection until it becomes a stranger with whom you are free to fall in love. Who are what looks out from behind you are is the thing that names what transforms. In written history, one can find a a lot of this nonsense and some of them are very useful. so you can easily carry out a simple experiment: turn on yourself, high on hot goo thinking of burnt rubber, well, as they say, feel the erogenous within a torso radius, when even a decaffeinated fuck on chipboard nightstand wouldn't spoil the mood, you can then rest easier altered state through a mask from which the truth can be told (as mentioned above). and if you still play around with the knobs and buckles, many interesting effects. Oh as these concentricities, these coils!/ Then how many were exploding hearts in the audience of New Experiences of the Void!

One day, with a good mood, dressing for altitude (the high altitude suit appeared to be the inevitable armor of man), working with a ███ hammering on it with a certain frequency, screaming some song, well, I saw the ineffable effect of bonds of the ███, which can only be guessed. Atimpact with frequent action they, taking shape and me, are turned on all together everything in a lovely refined manner, clear as the ringing of a bell, which was a lot of things that burned down the blessing in bulk. but I do not want to burn so fast because huge capacities accumulate from any low-power sources, and the generator already leaks some of the stored potential when it is bent over, so it must he held in place longer no doubt. This is a ready-made scheme but as always there is no money to finish. I tried on what I have. Of course, with losses, but it is enough to supply some impulse. Further, the mind that receives this, from it already is surrounded a body with chains right? (or how is it a mechanism?). Well probably it's made of some value, because the thieves went there in droves and stripped it and here the meaning is depicted. Though the observers try not to explain as it will spoil the imposed general picture. now, look what calms the captive by letting him sniff the perfume, like smell what smells like your masters crotch but here these something does not seem to converge and such inconsistencies are complete as though asnomic. Consigning phantom limbs to their place anthropometry was applied backward to the equipment of reliquaries, and saint Concretion in the aftermath when the restraints bound them to their will, exclaiming: *Well, for sure, it's not only some sort of scraper for taking the brain through your nose!* The flow of goo through an opening is proportional to the square root of the height of the goo MADE IN PIPES, SYRINGINS, BELLOWS AND SIPHONS OF SEVERAL LENGTHS AND FIGURES: WITH VARIOUS LIQUORS, AS METAL, WATER, WYNE, SAP, AIR, PISS ETC WITH A SPEECH ON THE ████ SUBJECT, WHERE WHICH IS GREAT THAN CAN BE MADE, CAN BE VENDED OF ALL MATERIALS KNOWN IN THE NATURE, AND WHICH ARE UNDER THE MEANING, AND WHAT FORCE IS NECESSARY FOR MAKE ADMIT THIS VOIDESo in this version we are also like a shell, a stored potential yyou start to put your eyes to, the bigger vessel of contain something viscous, desiring was put in inserting sensitive into the hole. On the other hand, this sticky semaphore. For example, so the ordained mechanics checked the absolute correctness of the empty vehicle, applying a kiss, as the palms of the hands were found stale. And these are artists. Somewhere I read an ancient description when I started adjusting a machine in a large room, then at the other end of the room the same machine began to make the same adjustments to itself. I do not know how much power was produced at that, but here on this thought you can see a powerful chain attached to an equally powerful weight. In the thought we see a kind of unintelligible device, the piling up of bodies, chained with chains is great. And of course himself twisting the handle of an unprecedented insight, radiating cosmic energy and something relatid deeply, sincerely to déjà vu.

Here is my explanation. Maybe it's traps, the breath, rarefied air is the same in the delay line of the altitude mask, the stabilizer of the uniform distribution between the How this is carried out and how it is maintained is a special issue, and for specifications here it is necessary to turn to who you will never see because they are not meant to as in many cases the medium in which the wave propagates does not permit a direct observation of true form but the turning to look is important as a signal. To all this design think attached a wire, stretching to through a small window into an orbiting room, where the person who invented and did all this is sitting plucking at it. *You see how the most constant thing in the world is losing its permanence under the influence of its own magic charms, inert matter acquires sensitivity and responds impetuously to the call of the fact.* The discovery of this fact is figuratively characterized by the fixed trembling of the moon in space after it was trampled on two years after theSummer of Love, now its resonant pulse resembles a fierce blow to the bell in the church! They say a bell cannot be unrung just as soldiers marching too strictly in step will kick up enough torsional force to destroy the bridge and fall into space they meant to transverse. Yet we ask each other what shoes should they have him strap on in any case for the first steps. And now a wave form walks the earth.

The Destroying Angel

Devouring agent Polyvalent sole authority makes An evidentiary demand
For self disclosing soul To be Facilely interpreted against A biography
incomplete. the useful faux finishOf taxable suffering Filed in Hell, a
domestic bureaucracy filled with An audience of auditorsCorrupt with
thought they read not had- TWAS WRIT in the manual it said

This breaking point heat Wave form scrolls
down institutional eternal Corridors of cheap molten iron ore and
All my life is what

No lamps, included liquor Crematories and tear bottles
Attended to the hospital jugs. In ash the
body is completed, a Flame from lumps and bones, a fantasizers dust

To burn a friend or love
In what the sun is compound of

Fire analyzes, does not transmute NO Devouring agent leaves a trace
Elements have such primitive mass Again the souls of enemies Their Bones
made into singing pipes To play Silent Surviving Hopes. This song Floats
the heaviest stone. The shortest skirt. But There is no further State to come
unsung On State disabled lung

That Which Can Unwish Itself The most
tedious Being now content With its nothingness- a vanity out of date beings
bored of tragedy restless inquietude a Supernatural folly time- march
by April May June July..
too short for our designs

Of monuments whose death we daily Pray
for whose duration
Are injurious to our expectations
A contradiction to our belief, now
real estate too expensive for the graves.

these generations that take place in This specific time, necessitated toFuturity
by techno know naturally There never was no meritocracy Reconstituted
into thoughts of *The Next World*, all that's past a moment, Angels of
Contingency Subsist in those lasting objects, to live frozen In production
exists a predicament for All this is nothing, too in the face of True Belief

Indeed again we are ourselves, not only A Hope but an evidentiary to lie
in state In the cryogenic tractor trailer truck, spread Out
alter ready made, To be any thing

• • •

out

in

Adam Christensen

Adina Blowtorch
/ What if?

Adina Blowtorch

I was falling asleep in the taxi.
Phone slipping out of my hand onto leather seats.
My short dress creeping up my thighs.
Had shrunk slightly after a wash.
He was already waiting by the basement entrance to the house I was sitting in Hackney. He was much smaller than I had expected. Beady eyes. I had a bag of weed. Smoked a joint in the back garden. A glass of chilled red wine from the fridge. I struggled to get out of the tight dress. The brand-new wig came off. He told me he liked my natural long curly hair. Erupting. I lay on my back. Legs wrapped around his skinny black body. The tip of his hard dick entered me slowly. Eyes locked. He kissed me.
We fucked twice.
Romantically.
I drifted off lightly as he was getting dressed. I heard his soft steps on the creaky stairs towards the upstairs part of the house. I dragged myself after him. He moved swiftly further up to the second floor. I found him cornered in the master bedroom. He was getting out of breath. He said he was looking for a phone charger. I told him it wasn't alright to wander around the house. I escorted him downstairs. Told him to leave. He tried kissing me goodbye. I guided him out the door with an outstretched arm.
I closed the door. Panicked. Franticly scanned the entire house for missing objects. He had left with the weed, tobacco, my brand-new wig, an old MacBook belonging to the house. My new Mac had been taken out of what I thought was a brilliant hiding place. It had been misplaced closer to the exit together with my phone. He had covered it with my shrunken dress and tights. For some reason he hadn't managed to extract them fully from the guest room. I jumped in my dressing gown. A bit revealing. Knee-high suede boots. I ran down the street in the direction of where he had descended.

He was gone.
I dreaded calling the police.
Nothing really ever comes of those cases.
I thought I owed it to the owners of the house.
An officer was dispensed to come round on Sunday morning.

I invited Jacqueline Turner round for Greek red wine. Robert Altman's *Pret-a-Porter* on the giant projector. We went round to SET club in cute dresses. Adina Blowtorch working behind the bar. I was out of tobacco. Went round the corner to the shops. Flakey Cunt was at the bus stop with his Irish family. 40th birthday. They were more excited about the live boxing match later. They had found an Airbnb with a giant flatscreen. Sports channel. It was located close to the birthday party for an early exit. I said I would join them later. They jumped on the bus. A tall handsome Turkish man waiting for another bus took me down the pissing alley. His hand crept under my dress.

His crotch rubbing against my smooth legs. He slipped my pants off. Fucked me with his chunky dick against the piled-up rubbish.
Back at SET, Jacqueline Turner had gone home. Adina Blowtorch locked up the bar. We walked round to experience the end of Tyson Fury smashing the shit out of his opponent. Did a few lines of pub grub with Flakey Cunt and his cousins. I was late for the Sunday morning meeting with the police officer. Ran with Adina back to the house. Made a giant pot of coffee. Brushed my teeth. Reapplied a darker coloured lipstick.

The officer arrived shortly afterwards. He was alone. A young handsome man in bulletproof vest. Adina filmed his tattooed hands taking notes. Pencil and paper. I told him about chatting up the little thief on FabSwingers. The officer knew all about FabSwingers. Lovely site. He didn't tell me his profile name.

I wrote a little note with a drawing on the kitchen table.
Two fancy bottles of red.
A bottle of champagne.
A fabric piece out of the same material I wore on the red carpet in Cannes.
Packed my stuff, forgetting my other more rugged wig on the coat rail.
Moved into Adina's room in South Bermondsey.
Temporary accommodation.

I went round to Paulina Haygate's converted truck the weekend after. Predrinks leading up to what looked like the LAST party before the potential quarantine. Adonis. Grow Tottenham. Rammed queue outside. Paulina took me through the back. People were talking about the effects of different drugs. Italy getting hit by the virus. Adina Blowtorch arrived. I danced to Jeffrey Hinton's set for a few hours. Needed some space. Paulina Haygate took me to his little messy pad at the back of the club. Stacked records. A mattress on the floor. A stuffed dog looking rather realistic. An earlier date had thought it to be real. Padding it. Such a good boy, aren't you. I had taken a little bump of ketamine. The birds had started to sing over the beats in the background. Everything became glossy. Rainbow colours. I slipped onto the mattress. Passed out. Woke up three hours later. Grow had shut. Adonis still going next door. I entered the steamy dance floor. Last few enthusiasts. Half-naked. Grace disc jockeying. I threw myself against the DJ booth. Caged. Kissed Grace through the metal wire. Adina hadn't noticed my absence. He had picked up an Australian boy in the now nailed-shut darkrooms. Adina's cap still inside. I ordered a taxi for us. Adina kicked in the wall to the darkroom. Found the cap in a cum-stained corner. Took the Australian home with him as well. I fell asleep on the drive back south.

What if?

I was staying within an anti-squatting community.
Guardians of an old theatre.
We were all sitting in a circle.
Reading the stage play of *Die bitteren Tränen der Petra von Kant*.
I went to make a cup of tea in the kitchen. Decaying food. Rusty sink filled with dirty dishes. Cockroaches crawling around the freshly baked bread. My co-star crept up on me. A Hollywood child actress. Now in her early twenties. Screaming about not having enough lines. She grabbed the bread knife. Tried sawing through my arm. Chased me through the labyrinthian corridors. I managed to lose her in the brutalist concrete expansion at the back of the decrepit theatre. A redevelopment. Rapidly extending upwards. I moved into the empty new flats. Lower levels. Temporarily until SOLD! Every time transferring further up into the structure. Further. Higher. Larger. Emptier. Dizzying claustrophobia. Vertigo. Paranoia. A view of a city I didn't recognise.
The world outside had turned into a What if? scenario.
The Nazis had won the war.
A Hollywood wet dream.
Top floor. Penthouse apartment. Elevator not installed yet. I climbed over the balcony. Disembarked my way down the building on the outside. Using patterns moulded in the rugged concrete. Reached the first floor. Suave, cultivated women being held captive. Sophisticated entertainment for the clientele. A desperate attempt to unlock their nailed-shut windows. Clinging on to the outside wall. Fingers bleeding. The male guards opened fire at me. Shot me in the arse. I lost my grip. I fell. Landed on a table in the packed lobster bar. Ground-floor terrace. Everyone carrying on sipping chilled sparkling wine. Five rubber bullets. Dented. Stuck in my butt cheeks. Shaping an obscure frowning face. No blood. A young determined guard charged at me through the crowds. I ran into the exuberant garden. Past the fountain. Nymph pissing against the wind. Pink tiles. Topiary bushes clipped in the shapes of animals. I dodged a bullet. Tried climbing the spiky fence. The young guard caught up with me. He pulled my legs. I fell on top of him. The gun. Dropped. I picked it up. Threatened him. He slipped out of his trousers. Laid down in the flowerbed. Spread his hairy butt cheeks. Showing me his little pink hole. I screamed. Spat out the two words: 'Charlotte Rampling.' Clumsily climbed the fence, ripping my tie-dye T-shirt. Written on it with bleach: *My co-star is a bitch!*

rest

continue

Sophie Collins

About the Body and Likeness / Thank You For Your Honesty

About the Body and Likeness

A response to a retrospective
of the work of Lee Bul

x)

It all begins in the gut
where shards (indigestible)
tear open the walls. When blood spills
there is no mess. There is no bodily mess
save in tumefactive sludge

I would like to doze off inside this gleaming basophil
regular vibrations relaxing proprioception
as we glide
past a fragment of bone sunk in plasma
the spectacle of lymphocytes
deeply staining, eccentric

x)

Erection of countless town models. The dogged work of preservation
supersedes embodiment. Men's corpses are embalmed
made up for display
while women who wish to live
must gain the written endorsement
of their male companions
Medical records, like mutating cells, are subject to damage
may be lost or copied twice

x)

A lauded teacher of letters once made a drawing of a cephalopod
for his students. Women, jabbing
he said, are more like this. More like this
than men are
by which he meant to say,
Nothing happens to me

x)

Octopuses eat their own limbs when chronically understimulated

What is frightening about this body
is its justicial disregard

Thank You For Your Honesty

A response to digital prints, animations and texts by Niamh Riordan

1)

To disturb reality using
its own means
and not a subjective interpretation thereof
presenting the viewer with an image
more abject—in the truer sense of the word—
than another kind
which displays contrivances to discomfit her
It is a pure expression of hope

a challenge to the natural order
the moral framework of material honesty
which prizes marble over stucco
a hierarchy with no equivalent
in poetry (though undoubtedly we will it), in which
a stated allegiance
to 'truth' and '"the functioning(s)" of "language"'
coupled with any broad effect of semantic cohesion
is usually enough (if
issued from the correct source)

Analogical infirmity
consciously acknowledged
confounds the 'flow'
Still I am forced to ask the disingenuous question,
Is marble alive?

Without a metabolism, cells
or the ability to achieve homeostasis, no

2)

To perform bemusement again and again
as a waiving of authority
(and so too of blame)

Honesty in a community of what is thought of as
blameless self-interest
makes you cry a lot, even (especially?) in instances
where it manifests in harm done to you and to others
via indirect means
for that too (the action) is honesty

(and perhaps a more fundamental kind)

3)

Flashes
in the centre of my field of vision
are gentle
cannot be said to increase or decrease in frequency
over time
Doctors don't worry much about such disturbances

Asked the same question of an adult in childhood
surmised from the response
a theory of germs within the retina
as magnified by the eye's lens

rinse

repeat

CAConrad

CORONA DAZE

CORONA DAZE 24 by CAConrad

for years after
friends died of
AIDS they still
danced with me in my dreams
did survivors of the Black Plague
dance with their dead
who will dance
with whom
in a year
let's
keep
safe
dance
together
IN PERSON

CORONA DAZE 43
by CAConrad

a sweet potato's
lifespan is short
I understand that
but I still MISS HER

CORONA DAZE 78
by CAConrad

do you remember
feeling safer before they
said they were going to
make us safe
Hollywood was
eager to control
our imaginations
during the plague
a long bend in
the demon field
persuading us
a black eye
is a story
everyone
wants

CORONA DAZE 80
by CAConrad

ready to drop
the certainties
we agree to live as
if there is a set of
spoons we can
stir life with
last year US citizens bought
18,000 tons of bullets for
our undeclared civil war
hiding strength
behind killing
because we are
too weak to find
real solutions
bullets put an
end to the
imagination

CORONA DAZE 87
by CAConrad

argue for beauty
always argue for beauty
it is the one fight we are
forbidden to surrender
never let them believe
we know the way
out of its clutch
this above all
will help us
feel less
alone in the world
when approaching danger
we make note of when
our bravery runs out
and know the rest
of our struggle
is fueled
by Love
nothing
else it
could
be

CORONA DAZE 94
by CAConrad

low hanging cloud
dew around the house
how did a cloud get in the house
even if showing rage feels new
it is time to allow our
underestimated
parts to
perform
calculating
how many
nails to
overtake
a hammer

CORONA DAZE 96
by CAConrad

      in this poem
   the words I give
you will run out
         there is
         nothing
        I can do
     about it
   from the
  moment I fell in love
  with making the letter g as a kid
   I foresaw the peripheries making
    g as a conjuring g g g curve and
    return g g g all I wanted for Christmas
   was an X-ray of my hand making g g g
  pleasure in forms united in a life
I choose to love no matter what

CORONA DAZE 97
by CAConrad

M drew
his face
the day
he was
diagnosed
HIV positive
and kept drawing
as his face changed
they were sublime
like Munch's self
portrait with
Spanish flu
he called on
his deathbed
at his parent's
home to say his
father was in the
backyard burning
the stack of drawings
I wanted to make him stop
please don't he said
it's his last chance to
deny me how can
I deny him that

clear

space

Rory Cook

Six Poems

The sandy mountain range tonight gives out a generous gist for nothing. Black frame width contrast bright lit shot, my jaw clips. Expectations fade with every extension. Medium height. A response to the collection. The weight of the flannel when wet. Slackened image drawn taut like a hand. Touch divides by touch. Terrible birds shadow the lawn, the carpet, trembling present. Slabs of years soften the edges. Pure presentation shot through with pores. Thirst for grammar, the very act of selecting, a signal sticks in an ear. I miss waning light, the engine stutter. Console neither desire nor purchase. The screen displays, defers by depth. I want to keep much, lay something in the game, but here, my love, I cannot even read this.

Do you ever feel really, eerily present? Although I am, many of the structures are broken, having displayed resistance to binding force. It is fascinating to investigate without an endorsement. Unease learnt of body and word. Even counting is difficult. Coarse stylisation becomes fixed convention. Omission of detail goes without saying. Texture as an afterthought sustains the interruption, follows a finger without feeling and a scrub with no crust. Inherited dispositions then could but not; each loaded movement is proportionate to defeat, succumbing slowly to the logic, inferred from the arrangement of dimensional effects. I see the word as deepen, when it is define. I go to write about, but write apart. You know, that first act simply walked out of my head.

Images are worth repeating, the same habit in a different tone. A new objectivity to the frame. The bracket lands over the stop. Light glistens impassive, unfriendly, on a great many items all in absolute arrangement. Distortion in the middle distance will depend on distribution. Friction inflicted at eye level, movement as tactile mode, and plain fabric over the surface noise. Was this sensed, or merely encountered? You could not make it up. If you did, it would be tricky to maintain. An exchange of permanence, ascertainable air. The base of one image rubs against another, troubling the relation, and their intimacy requires sensitive definition. We feel close. Yet there is no haunting effect. It isn't even spooky. Nothing of consequence is at stake.

The surface is a site for dissonance, I remember thinking, though it could have been after the fact. Ersatz capture sound. We make an awkward bow. Evening light falls in the holes, indexical conjunctions and short-lived exquisite. Concerning the gaps, tufts, all dirt and bits. Lately, there is no symmetry. The threshold's anechoic, the margins static. A persistent, stubborn itch and discomfort looking up. Still, duration provides the thickness. Your hospitality is a gaze that's activated by this fully determinable material, if you're persuaded by the argument. I can rearrange your collar, let your arm drop to your thigh, move the fork on the plate. A tourist visiting a failed transmission. You don't need to know things anymore. The outline leaking, again.

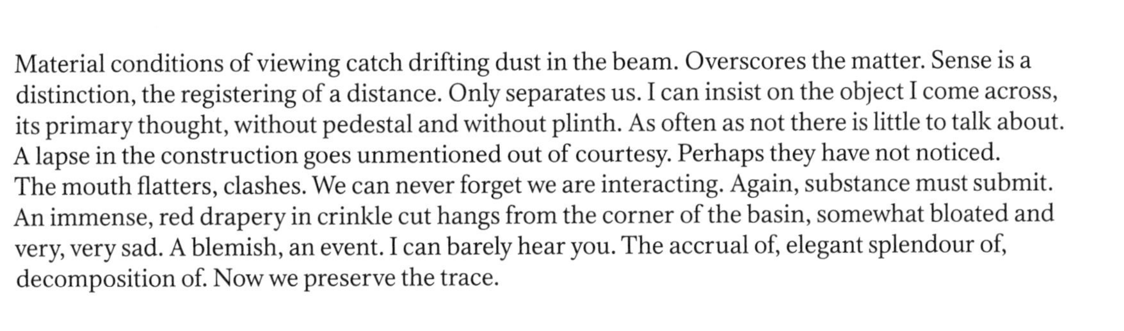

Material conditions of viewing catch drifting dust in the beam. Overscores the matter. Sense is a distinction, the registering of a distance. Only separates us. I can insist on the object I come across, its primary thought, without pedestal and without plinth. As often as not there is little to talk about. A lapse in the construction goes unmentioned out of courtesy. Perhaps they have not noticed. The mouth flatters, clashes. We can never forget we are interacting. Again, substance must submit. An immense, red drapery in crinkle cut hangs from the corner of the basin, somewhat bloated and very, very sad. A blemish, an event. I can barely hear you. The accrual of, elegant splendour of, decomposition of. Now we preserve the trace.

The withdrawal of the image is a tedious synopsis and there's nothing funny about it. Density gathers even as we listen, even as we try to be silent. Language is most receptive as a field of compression. The liminal layer, spit on the screen, the dreams of repayment and dress. Perceive a smugness in the object, lacking the clarity of not-existing. Can we outline a third movement? That conveys no privileged point in the reception? Restoration to the idea carries in a loop, before leaving an opaque element, as my latch bolt catches. The same motifs in tinny holdlines. Resonance held together just by a thought. Touch felt as singular. Touch touching itself. Saying it is finished so that it does not finish.

close

open

Jesse Darling

The Letter

10/2020
Berlin

Dear you,

Months have passed since I said I'd write. I had so much to tell you but between the days and the news it faded away, and now what I have instead is a feeling which lives mostly in my body. During the lockdown (which began for me a long time ago, and briefly lifted for some months just before the pandemic), rage and longing became merged together in a crashing oceanic feeling like an 88-note chord held so long and loud I almost forgot what music sounds like. At some point the wave slowly receded, beginning with the high end and then some sharps and flats in the middle, until finally only the almost-imperceptible drone of the deep remained. This, I learned, is just the humming of time happening out across the melody of any given life. In retrospect I'm glad I learned to listen for it.

When the big sickness arrived, and I don't say this metaphorically, the high notes fell back in like a string section and I knew it was coming here too. What else did I know I knew? Hard now to say but I was afraid. In this way the early warning system was working well. Fear is a necessary part of every transition, but for most of us traumatised domestic animals its cadence is basically useless as data. I suppose we are all differently attuned to the grand composition and its errant melodics; like, you know, the apocryphal series of experiments in microscopic photography, presented as proof that water responds to emotional frequencies at the molecular level. Not to be the anglocentric [nominative] determinist, but did you know that the guy behind the photographs was named Emoto? Naturally there can be no correlation, just as the scientists who debunked Mr Emoto's experiments made evident; and yet I feel he would approve of this relentless pattern-seeking and meaning-making, with his fractals forking and feathering to the strains of gratitude or grief. Extraordinary complexity and beauty in these little snowflake feels! I imagine us all that way; formed and deformed by our small hopeful lives into a bunch of tesselations on the cosmic slab.

Can't shake this idea that everybody has a superpower, which is to say a wound of some kind to which they always return. That among us there are all kinds of wizards in the sense that there are Capricorns and Geminis; to each a given disposition, some kind of essential quality or vulnerability to be deposed or relinquished while we settle for identities and universalisms every bit as arbitrary. When I say wizards I mean mediums of different kinds; one might discern the speech of trees, another throws heat between their hands, one knows the future in their body and still another channels the ancestors on stage. Among my many grievances with J.K Rowling is the idea that there could be anything like a muggle in this world.

When I ride my bike around or lie in bed some nights I think of all the things I want to tell you. Words string themselves together and I think, I'll write that down. But I don't.

Some time late last year - before all of this went down, down, down - I lost some kind of necessary illusion that helped me continue. It could best be described as a wilful hope; such desirous illusions are among my bad habits, and can become violent in their own way. This one wasn't hurting anyone, or at least, not really - though such hopes often produce collateral. My hope, or illusion, was concerned with the power of [what I vaguely and optimistically thought of as] "the truth" to transform the context in which it appears, namely and among other things, the world. But one day I suddenly understood that this was and is not so. And then I thought: I can't go on.

And then the world turned and the slow machine of history started looming out of the deep like some Hollywood monster and there was no way to go on, not for anybody, not in the same way, and this was as redolent with relief as with grief. People die, among them now people you know; and somehow the long line of executors soldiers grossly on, lurid as the colosseum.

The astrologers seem glad to report their I-told-you-sos about this period of shift and clench and ravage, but I don't know if it's any consolation to feel it all was fated, or in any case overdue in the bigger balance sheet in which the hubris of empire must atone for itself through its fall. Structurally unsound at inception, with cheap extensions built on bad foundations, these towers must surely come down (in the Rider-Waite sense, at least), either through necessary abolition or inevitable collapse. And amidst all this there is the emerging certainty of a happy fact: that nothing is too big to fail, and that one of these days, one of these days, all this will be over. And after that? Something else.

You're right that this address is a pose, a formal experiment. That I'm writing to a hundred-odd people in the guise of the particular. But let me assure you that there's nothing abstracted about it; it's you I wanted to talk to. I wanted to give you something. I wanted, urgently, that you receive it. Sure it's a form of sublimation, but what isn't? I don't want 'engagement' or 'an audience,' some dehumanising amalgam of numerical and capital value circulating as a quantitative affect. I want you.

The entropy feels so inevitable, evincible; occasionally sensuous, shimmying, lubricated for a quick decline. I can't describe the sound of it, but the early warning system has started up again in preparation for what is surely coming, a low whine. I want to not be afraid of it. I want to know we are in some way connected. And I want, ahead of time, to find you less mediated; so that we will know each other, I guess, when the time comes. It's me, I'll say. Is it you?

I miss you; I think of you often. I dream about you. I dream about us.

Sending love, until next time -

xo,
JD

end

begin

Anaïs Duplan

BLACKSPACE

•••

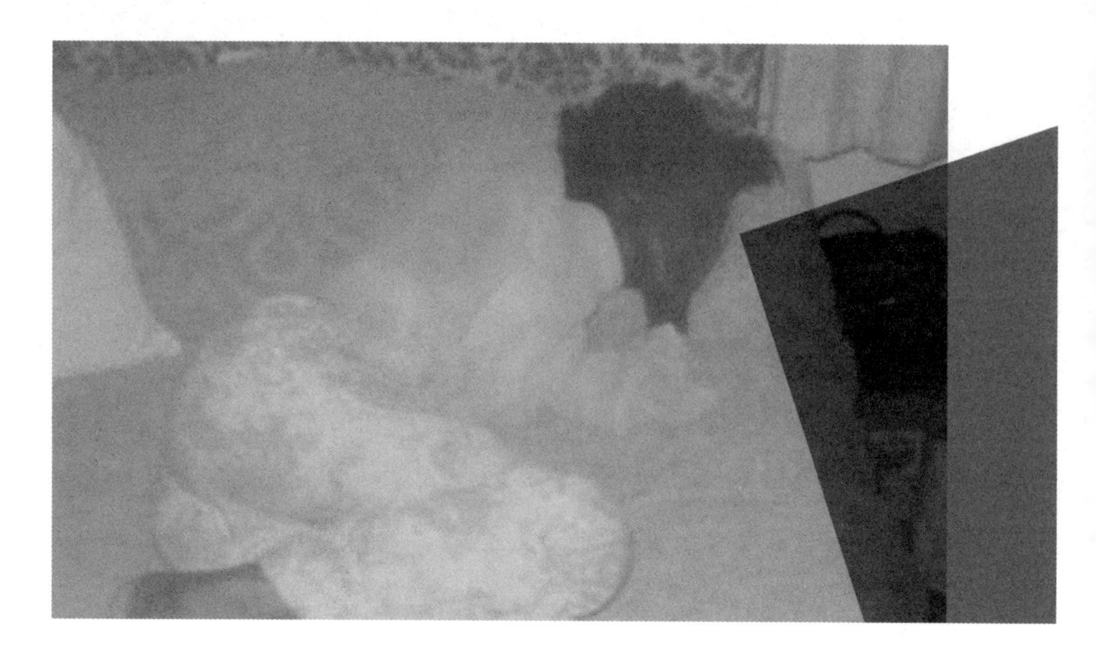

For Mackey, self and sound are analogous
the internal counterpart to the external othe
each self, there is a particular sound, which
person has to practice discovering on the w
discovering themselves. "You have to find w
is, where it is, and how to get it out, and h
translate it through a horn or a piano or a l
whatever—which you likely call 'technolog
added.

PARADIGMS FOR LIBERATION

Daily, I am enmeshed in a constellation of oppressions, which we could call the white supremacist, capitalist patriarchy.

Has my life been predestined?

Can I pursue liberation?

What kind of liberation can I pursue?

I have discovered that when I experience what is universal in me, I may leave my individual oppressions behind.

This discovery is important, and at the same time, I need a way of working towards liberation that sees me as a unique person, occupying my distinct social positions as a black, Haitian, transgender, nonbinary, pansexual human being. The praxis of attaining liberation as an individual, a member of society, and as a human is incomplete if, in my methodology, I don't address each of these "nodes."

So far, I've found that one of my best opportunities for liberation is in esthetic experience.

When I'm rushed by the smell of patties walking

Ephraim Asili, *Points on a Space Age*, 2007, 32:42

we should go to the moon
astronauts in outer inter-
spersed images of colorful garb
b&w in time inter-
spersed sense of the evolution
of their costumes have remained
the same you are welcome to be citizens
of the omniverse
and music has the good and ugly in it
this would seem to distinguish pop
from jazz or African-American
classical recalls some other
horizons the imagination
the traditional
ignorance itself isn't strange at all

In *The Power*
Gutiérrez argu
awakening men
a special, subve
encourages the a
struggles. Today,
whether the in
elicited an upris
consumers to
narratives of hist
social agents wh
been effectively
from history. W
and doing so su
power to rewri
future. I'm incl
least, there is val
occurred at a ti
uncertain at bes

In *The Power of the Poor in History*, Gustavo Gutiérrez argues that liberation theology, by awakening memories of past struggles, elicits a special, subversive kind of memory that then encourages the active reinterpretation of historical struggles. Today, I have many conversations about whether the interactivity of social media has elicited an uprising of newly empowered creator-consumers to rewrite dominant, hegemonic narratives of history, foregrounding those forgotten social agents whose voices and contributions have been effectively and nearly unconsciously erased from history. Whether remembering together—and doing so subversively—does indeed have the power to rewrite history and forge a healthier future. I'm inclined to believe that in the very least, there is value in looking again at what already occurred at a time when what is up ahead seems uncertain at best.

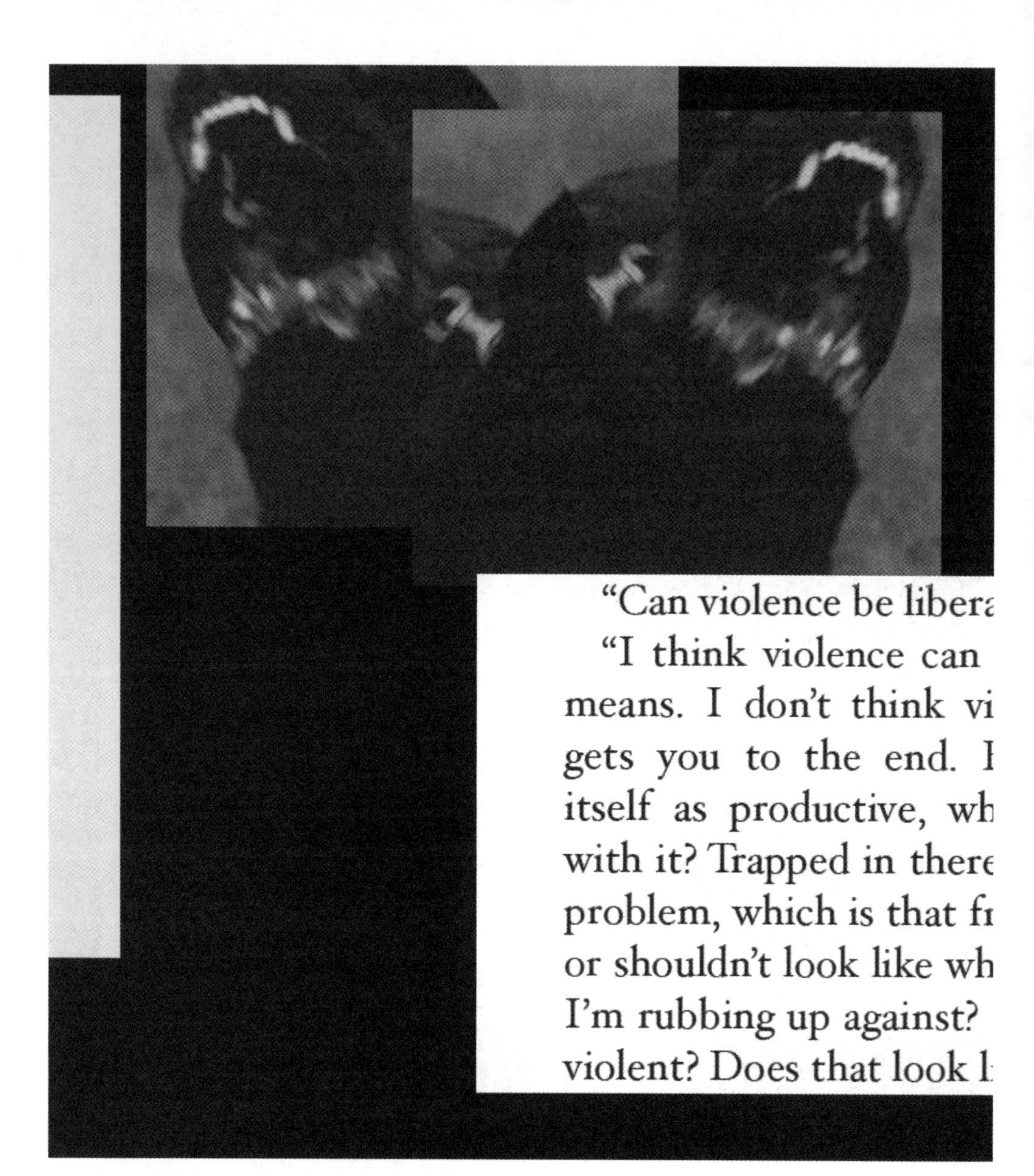

“Can violence be liber
“I think violence can
means. I don’t think vi
gets you to the end.
itself as productive, wh
with it? Trapped in ther
problem, which is that f
or shouldn’t look like wh
I’m rubbing up against?
violent? Does that look

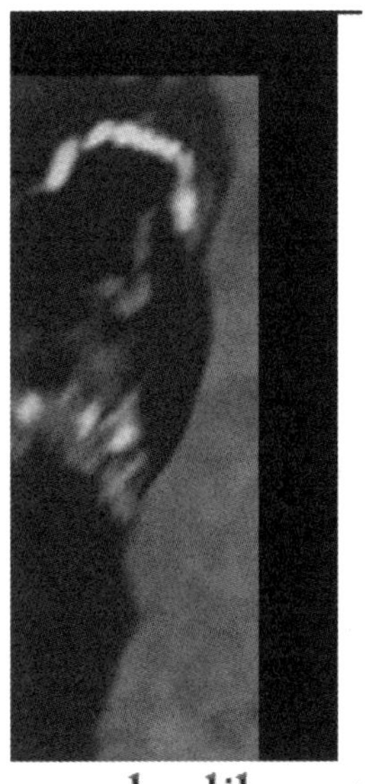

In my explorations of th
and consequences of th
I am continually drawn t
1988 anthology, *Charting th*
Black and Third World Won
midst of the Black British
"The collection of pieces c
unitary voice, since Black v
such a voice. The antholo
seemingly contradictory st
different priorities and dif
These differences are them
divisions amongst the vari
Black women."

Liberation struggles are n
are themselves various and c
struggle, which is though
unitary entity, is actually f
of voices that can never b
the same time, liberation s
occur. They arise out of a
there is a "chaos of know
show through the essays, i
ruminations that follow, th
a continual oscillation betw
a multilayered, contradicto
that takes place on the level
the social movement, and th

ence be liberatory?"
violence can be and is liberatory, as a
on't think violence is the thing that
) the end. Because after it's shown
oductive, what are you going to do
oped in there might be also this other
hich is that freedom or liberation can't
look like white privilege. Is that what
up against? Is it white freedom to be
es that look like liberation?"

In my explorations of the meanings, valences, and consequences of the word, "liberation," I am continually drawn to a quote from the 1988 anthology, *Charting the Journey: Writings by Black and Third World Women*, published in the midst of the Black British Feminist movement: "The collection of pieces does not speak with a unitary voice, since Black women do not possess such a voice. The anthology therefore contains seemingly contradictory statements and reflects different priorities and differences of emphasis. These differences are themselves reflective of the divisions amongst the various constituencies of Black women."

Liberation struggles are made up of agents who are themselves various and distinct. The liberation struggle, which is thought to be fought by a unitary entity, is actually fought by a collection of voices that can never be perfectly unified. At the same time, liberation struggles can and must occur. They arise out of and create sites where there is a "chaos of knowledge." As I hope to show through the essays, interviews, poems, and ruminations that follow, the fight for freedom is a continual oscillation between conflict and order, a multilayered, contradictory, and polyvalent fight that takes place on the level of the individual spirit, the social movement, and the art praxis.

I'VE BEEN THINKING

ABOUT IT A LOT AND IT SEEMS LIKE

I DON'T KNOW

I WISH I COULD TELL YOU WHAT I FEEL

BUT

, as a
that
hown
o do
other
n't
what
to be

The co
arts techno
contempora
avant-garde
and margin
framework.
works withi
tradition ar
least a porti
artists that
has now b
hyper-legibl
art spaces t
in challengi

The contemporaneity of today's me
ts technologies doesn't alone signal that
ntemporary work being created with them
vant-garde, where avant-garde means both "n
nd marginal to a hegemonic meaning-mak
amework. And again, given this history of me
orks within a traceable, if ineffable, black esth
adition and the body of their critical analysis
east a portion of the work by black contempor
rtists that seeks opposition through illegibi
as now become—or is at risk of becomin
yper-legible in "sympathetic" white-domina
rt spaces that do not otherwise stake a real cl
challenging a socio-racial hegemony.

lay's media-
gnal that the
with them is
ıs both "new"
aning-making
tory of media
black esthetic
cal analysis, at
contemporary
gh illegibility
f becoming—
te-dominated
ke a real claim
ny.

I watched a video
at Howard. She tel
you look very caref
a large extent, up to
Toni Morrison, with
mythological or myt
uninterested in the m
are the sinner, you a
you are either super
sexual or you are sup
because that is the o
is going to mytholog
and the human, a
mythological structu
humanity.[1]

I watched a video of the 1984 Kathleen Collins masterclass at Howard. She tells the students, and me in her afterlife: "If you look very carefully at the history of black literature, to a large extent, up to and including writers like Alice Walker, Toni Morrison, with few exceptions it is the history of creating mythological or mythical black people." Collins is passionately uninterested in the mythological: "If you are the outsider, if you are the sinner, you are by definition extraordinary. Meaning you are either super good or you are super evil. You are super sexual or you are super ascetic. You cannot arrive at normality because that is the one thing that has been denied you. No one is going to mythologize my life." She believes in the normal and the human, and to sustain her belief she ignores the mythological structure of both of those concepts, normality and humanity.[1]

beat

resume

Inua Ellams

Fuck / Tupac

Fuck / Tupac

for dying early / for the fields of lavendar
and hawthorn in which I sat / overlooking
Dublin City / though as dusk wrapped the
sky / it could have been any creaking
constellation of traffic and tower blocks /
from Compton to Clondalkin / blinking staccato
madness / into the unspooling night / fuck you
for forcing the criminal animal gnashing
its teeth in piss-streaked alleys / collarless
priests cruising in rented hatchbacks / protestants
and catholics / like Bloods and Crips / brothers
split along colour lines / fuelled by racist police
/ who came to break our skin / fuck you for
ordering them / to the rank and file of rhyme /
for making sense of the Celtic anarchy / in
those urban psalms of your slim scripture /
in your rich voice / explaining / this is how
it's always been / darkness / light / thin paths
between / with you leading / you reluctant
messiah / as all true messiahs must be /
leading to a fellowship of souls / hunkered in
headphones / suspended between word and
hard matter / fans / disciples / self-sanctified
street-saints / thrown stones of strange fruit
/ sour as we are / scattered across the tar-marked
planet / haloed in snapbacks / hooded / hidden /
hollering hard / hallelujah-ing / head bowed
nodding in pious agreement / How we would
have followed you / homie / to hell and back /
How you had me / whole

•••

clear

throat

Olamiju Fajemisin

spring

This text is intended to be read aloud. It was first performed at Hopscotch Reading Room, Berlin, on 25 September 2020, during *tbc.*, an event curated by Anastazja Moser and Jazmina Figueroa.

Good evening everyone,

My name is Olamiju. I'm a writer, and as of last autumn, a student too.

I'll be presenting a map of some of my work and research interests, which I have written down like a letter summarising the months of spring.

I will read verbatim, from a Google Doc on my iPhone.

The following notes consider the voice as a medium, alternative pedagogies and attention.

To close I will recite a poem I wrote in June.

Before I properly begin, I would like to thank Jazmina and Anastazja for inviting me to their platform, and Hopscotch for hosting.

Berlin was the first place I moved out of my mother's house and, though I do not live here anymore, it feels very natural.

March.

I started using Twitter again.

The British government hesitated to protect its public, and terminologies like 'mutual aid' entered popular discourses. It was a relatively new and quiet account, which felt accommodating in the face of isolation.

With no work or school I had little capacity to concentrate on much else.

I came across Tiffany Sia—an artist, writer and independent film producer—when a post of hers, urging people to support her cause, the *HK2NYC Mask Circuit*, was retweeted onto my timeline.

Tiffany was quarantining in a place I'd been to once before, Lamma Island. A southerly island of Hong Kong's New Territories. I was there in 2017.

I started following her and her work. I really like her.

As of March, she has hosted a reading series called 'Hell Is a Timeline', live-streamed live from Lamma Island at midnight Hong Kong time, which is 5 in London, and lunchtime in New York.

She reads select texts ruminating a common theme. Like 'entropy', or 'citizenship', as I am reading to you now, from a screen, all laid out and prepared.

'If I put you to sleep, it would be my sincerest pleasure,' she posted once.

The recordings are uploaded to Vimeo where the description boxes explain to us that 'reading aloud is a tool of pedagogy and care'.

The patience it takes to listen to someone who is harbouring you with words. The nerve it takes to recite something you were confident enough to commit to paper.

The relationship between the reader and the person being read to engenders unromantic closeness.

Generally platonic, but always intimate.

April.

In the essay 'Xenophobia and the Indexical Present', Adrian Piper brings us into her understanding of the 'indexical present' in terms of the personal and conceptual.

She says:

> 'Artwork that draws one into a relationship with the other in the indexical present trades easy classification—and hence xenophobia—for a direct and immediate experience of the complexity of the other [...] Experiencing the other in the indexical present teaches one how to see.'

The indexical present is a direct attentional focus on the immediate here and now. It is a mindful point toward a specific moment, an instance of contact, and being.

It's me now, reading this to you, and trying not to rush.

Thinking in terms of sports helped my understanding of the indexical present.

I'd think about rough, implicitly contact sports, like rugby, as opposed to those where individual displays of elegance are the point, like figure skating, maybe.

It's hard to say which team will win. There are eighty minutes in which thirty players will create an impossible combination of connections between each other and the ball. The trajectory of the game—or, the discourse—changes constantly, being urged in different directions by these individual points of contact, or indexical presents.

The ice dancer, on the other hand, may perfectly execute the same routine time after time, forever winning, challenged only by herself.

Constant, mediated, interdisciplinary intervention is fundamental to any learning. To do so uninhibited would be vastly uninteresting, and equally harmful.

Adrian Piper sets this example, making a practice of invoking the indexical present in her ongoing work 'Calling Cards'.

She conceptualised the cards in 1986; they were the eighth attempt at formalising a response to racist [...] remarks made by people around Piper, who either had the intention of insulting her, as a Black woman, or, as she is quite light-skinned, to some white-passing, confiding in her in a case of mistaken identity.

Since 1986, in response to such remarks, Piper has made and handed out business card-sized 'calling cards'. A short note is printed on the cards in Black ink.

It reads:

> *Dear Friend,*
>
> *I am Black.*
>
> *I am sure you did not realize this when you made/laughed at/agreed with that racist remark.*
>
> *In the past, I have attempted to alert white people to my racial identity in advance.*
>
> *Unfortunately this invariably causes them to react to me as pushy, manipulative, or socially inappropriate. Therefore, my policy is to assume that white people do not make these remarks, even when they believe there are no black people present, and to distribute this card when they do.*
>
> *I regret any discomfort my presence is causing you, just as I am sure you regret the discomfort your racism is causing me.*

The indexical present is generated here in the act of the card changing hands. It continues in the diversion of the recipient's focus.

'Dear Friend / I am Black'

Whether they read the card aloud or not, the recipient has been caught off-guard and the fabric of the social interaction has been irrevocably altered. They have been taken out of whichever setting they may have made their remark in—the dinner party, or exhibition opening—and are now compelled to submit to Piper's autonomy by way of reading.

The refraction of subjecthood forces the recipient to submit to the conditions of their own gaze—it uses their own line of questioning against them.

April.

I watched a reel of bloopers, cut from footage taped for Hard to Read, a literary social practice organised by Fiona Alison Duncan, a writer who lives between New York and Los Angeles.

The video was one minute and two seconds long, and showed people stumbling over words and pronunciations as they read from homes and gardens and public spaces.

Some of the readers would continue as if nothing had happened, others would correct themselves, as if readjusting an awkward collar.

A couple of them got a little embarrassed and apologised too much, it was endearing.

The misspeaks add a humanness to language the printed work could never convey. As a medium it is familiar, and comforting for its imperfections.

May.

Reading aloud is a tool of pedagogy and care capable of extolling intimacies.

I organised a few isolation reading sessions over Zoom. I was missing my friends dearly. I wanted to interrupt the ennui of the long same days of spring by concentrating on somebody else's cadence. I would feel refreshed afterwards.

We took elocution lessons at primary school. The notions of monovoice and dictation were quite natural to us. It was a Catholic school, where we would pray as a class of twenty-four children, twice a day—once before we were allowed to touch our lunchboxes, and again before we left to go home.

I enjoyed playing with the shape of my mouth, trying to make a 'th' sound for think, rather than 'fink', despite the recent loss of my two front teeth.

Once, I was asked to recite a poem with my eyes closed, to prove I had committed it to memory.

As I spoke, a wasp in the library crawled into my ear, but it did not sting me.

June.

My friend Sitara Abuzar Ghaznawi commissioned me and three others to produce texts for her new installation, 'Bookshelf 3', which opened in Vienna last month.

The texts—two essays, a letter and my poem—were fixed to the wall at eye level and were later made available to download as PDFs.

While preparing for the show I wondered how reading aloud in a designated moment could be an emancipatory tool, an ever-present school that does not accommodate the frameworks of imperialism and class discrimination.

The poem is called 'These words are my own From my heart flow I love you, I love you, I love you, I love you'

Can you read these words? through the thicket of flowers and lace

I implore you to look while you can. The words on this bookshelf are importable, the shelf itself a hostile institution.

You may not tug me free from the pile with a licked finger which you then curl, and then, sliding down and pinching (with your nails),

flatten me

right sides together, creating near-perfect halves bonded by a seam so soft and so mashed

the edges will begin to pucker and fray between the warm moisture of your fingertips.

I'd tear when forced into your denim pocket.

Read me now as you are in front of me. Utter these words with your lips unparted.

Bourgeois of you to be here (in public), reading me, with a drink in your hand.

What are you drinking?

Do you wish you had a bench to sit on? Do you wish I was an image, so you could look away when bored, rather than feeling guilty for abandoning me at the end of the lyric?

Are these words more worthy of being stored because they are being outwardly committed to the public? Because you can take a photo on your iPhone. Because you can reread wherever? (if you take that photo). Because you can print the PDF *of these words, and tack them at this height, but at your place.*

Or is it because you can sing these words

I love you, I love you, I love you, I love you

to yourself, and be mnemonically returned to the first time you read me.

Thank you

hold

return

Johanna Hedva

Soft Blues

The past does not influence me; I influence it.
Willem de Kooning

Know amazedly how
often one takes his madness
into his own hands
and keeps it.
Lorine Niedecker

No names have been changed to protect the innocent. They're all fucking guilty.
Lydia Lunch

Photograph #1: Soft blues, the dress and the sheets are the same color. The color, the shape, of the skin is milky, as though it's spilling out of the unzipped zipper. A daub of black hair obscures the head and face, which have been pushed into the pillow. The walls are a sad beige. Wavering, thin black lines make blobby shapes in and out and around the freckles on the skin of the back. They've been doodled with a swooning hand. Probably drunk.

I am facedown in the bed. He has drawn on my back. I've bundled my face and arms and hands beneath my weight, prone, making the skin of my back open to attack. I've asked him to take a photo. This is an apt representation for our entire relationship.

Photograph #2: The bottom of a white toilet and white cabinets take up the top half of the frame; the bottom half is a span of terracotta-tiled floor, warm, reddish brown, the color of earth. A scattered mess of dark hair, in clumps and threads, some black, some brown, is strewn across the tiles. It resembles the fallen organs of a belly sliced open.

I cut all my hair off in the bathroom. Then I cut his. I'd suggested he do it; I'd just cut mine, and my resolve made purpose and meaning as if I'd begun for us a new resplendent world. He photographed it. This is a better representation for our entire relationship.

Photograph #3 (deleted): Dark red shadows surround a blurred, pale form. The view is from above, looking down on the form, which appears to have its torso below its ass, legs opened out and sideways like a crab. Down the middle of the ass is a gash-like slice of bright red. The white skin of the back blends in with the cum so we don't see it, but we know it's there. A daub of black hair obscures the head and face, which have been pushed into the floor.

I am facedown on the floor. He has drawn on my back with something other than ink, it will easily wash away. I've asked him to take a photo by telling him it's what I want but once I see the photo I wonder who I am, if this person is really me, and did that person really want what she said, what she thought, she did? This is not a representation for our relationship: this is our entire relationship.

*

The best thing I got from my relationship with Z was his description of Alvarado Street in Los Angeles being like a river, how the traffic just swims down it.

The second best thing I got was that I was finally disabused of the idea that de Kooning was a genius. Z, a straight cis white boy painter from Texas, without one lick of irony or self-awareness at how ironic it made him look, worshipped de Kooning, idolized and wanted to be him, studied him with righteous devotion, hunted every scrap of biographical anecdote; de Kooning did it like this, de Kooning said this, repeating quotes like the rosary, which was all a big yearning, a hope that, in small ways that were accumulating, through will and determination but also osmosis, by soaking himself in the sticky wet of de Kooning's everything, Z was comporting himself more and more toward de Kooning, and would one day walk in the shadow that would also be the light of the master.

It's the kind of behavior that straight cis white boys are born into, the kind propelled by something that commingles faith and delusion, faith in themselves and their god-given right to be front and center and always on top, and the ability to ignore completely the possibility that everything they believe to be true about themselves is a delusion. True, it's a delusion that the whole world believes in, but doesn't that fact only corroborate its being a lie?

*

For the purposes of this essay, I'm going to need a working definition of 'the world.' But there are so many! There's the world of Plato's Cave, and, crucially, the world outside it. There's Wittgenstein's world that is all that is the case. There are Leibniz's multiple worlds, though for him this one is the best of all possible because (I'm paraphrasing) god is nice. There's Schopenhauer's world as representation, which is what we perceive, and then the world as will, which is beyond perception, and we must not forget that Schopenhauer also said, 'Women are directly adapted to act as the nurses and educators of our early childhood, for the simple reason that they themselves are childish, foolish, and short-sighted.' Lol.

I'm partial to Heidegger's world into which we are thrown, the abrupt and incomprehensible thrown-ness of existence, *Dasein*, because I feel hella thrown.

What's weird is that 'the world' and 'reality' are not the same, though their delineation from each other is interdependent: there can be many realities in the world, but perhaps not many worlds in reality.

Until that summer, I had not yet learned this.

At that point, my definition of 'the world' was that it's the thing that holds you.

Until it doesn't.

*

The German word *Malerschwein* literally means 'painter pig,' but it is figuratively used to describe an archetypal male artist: chauvinistic; lauded; insecure and emotionally irresponsible; egomaniacal but allowed, even urged, to be that way; misogynistic in his art and life, despite the fact that both of those things could not have happened without the wives, mothers, sisters, and girlfriends who serve him in the capacity of collaborators, advocates, patrons, managers, curators, editors, critics, teachers, therapists, caregivers, mentors, librarians, accountants, assistants, cooks, maids, muses, typists, secretaries, publicists, laundresses, and nurses. No matter his medium, the *Malerschwein* is a genius of a singular kind, a trailblazer who, in a divinely directed quest *à la* Moses, ventures to the wild frontier of his craft, spelunks depths that he presumes—and which the world substantiates back to him—have never before been excavated, or if they have, not sufficiently so, not yet by a Genius, for we need a Genius who will show us revolutionary, seminal (from 'semen'), ways to understand ourselves and how to live and be.

The *Malerschwein* is always Great, with a capital G. And he always changes the World, with a capital W.

The goddamn canon is made of *Malerschwein*. Just Google 'genius' and have a nice scroll through the History of Civilization.

*

An old boss of mine, an artist to whom I was a studio assistant, once gave me the de Kooning biography to read. 'You should know about him,' he told me, and loaned me his copy, saying, 'But I want this back.' This is an apt representation of patriarchy in practice.

When I returned it to him, he did not ask me what I thought, but said, 'It's great, right? He was great, right?' though not said as questions. This is a better representation of patriarchy in practice.

While I was working for this man, I had a miscarriage, with complications, a biblical 40 days of bleeding, which ignited a grief in me so brutal that it almost blinked me out of existence. A small hole yawned open to inhale the entire universe, and everything that had been explicable before was now negated, totally, radically, and I was left in a pool of tears and empty skin and I could not—I was not. I have endometriosis, a disease that I was told, when I was first diagnosed at age 20, meant I would probably never be able to get pregnant, and I am genderqueer and have gender dysphoria, the latter of which is also classified as a disease. The fact that I have a uterus at all feels like a weird mistake, a curse nevertheless borne from my DNA; so, when I say that a small hole yawned open, I'm referring not only to a hole that was the absence of an impossible fetus, but to a hole that existed at the very site of the impossibilities that are my self.

One night, bleeding blood that had turned to black ash, I was crying and could not stop, I was a mad dog trying to tear its way out of my own throat, I thrashed around like the female protagonists in Greek tragedy, a cursed woman who has had everything taken from her, so I cursed everyone I knew, and the most unkind curse I gave to myself, so the father of the baby called the police and had me involuntarily hospitalized in the psych ward.

They took me away in handcuffs and wouldn't let me bring my shoes. Because I pass as white, I was not shot by the police when they arrived at my home. On the way to the hospital, one of the cops looked over his shoulder through the metal fence that divided the front seat from the back, and said to me in a quiet voice, 'My girlfriend is pregnant right now, so I, I understand. I'm so sorry.' I looked at him calmly and in a clear voice said: 'You don't have to take me, you know. I'm just grieving.' 'I know,' he said, 'but we have to. It's the law.'

This is not a representation of the patriarchy in practice. This is the practice of it. For a practice to become an institution, it has to be instituted and reinstituted. It's a doing that has to be done.

My boss, who was also my professor at the time, took it upon himself to be my medical 'advocate.' He supported the hospitalization, and introduced the notion that came to dominate the discussion, which was that I 'should have gotten over it by now,' hence why hospitalization was necessary. I was hysterical, out of control, a danger to myself and others. He wasn't wrong. But he left out the part that considered the question of how else, if not this, I should have been. How else, I kept asking, should I behave? What is the right way to grieve? And can it ever be lawful?

*

A friend, an older woman, upon my release from the hospital, told me, 'Remember: Medea may have been hysterical, but she was right.'

*

I met Z during the summer after I was released from the hospital. I was living alone in Chinatown, on Chung King Court—one block of a clean, spacious lane where cars aren't allowed to go. It was built in the 1930s, when LA was young, as part of something for tourists called the 'New Chinatown,' but which has since been drained of its commerce. In the 1990s, art galleries moved in and flourished for a few years, and I was staying in a studio owned by an artist whose career had had a similar trajectory. The scene was empty but the red paper lanterns strung across the alley were still turned on every night. It looked like the abandoned set of a racist movie: stray cats, people collecting bottles, an old Chinese woman carrying plastic bags of bruised vegetables, a pair of busboys on a smoke break from a Chinese restaurant, squatting at the foot of a crooked staircase.

I would sometimes walk barefoot at night down the lane. The air was warm and my body felt featherweight, capable of lifting into the air and tumbling away. I'd lift my arms up and sail down the lane under the paper lanterns. I'd feel as though my life and my self and my world and what I wanted and who I was were my own. This was the only thing I comprehended in the face of many often contradictory facts, untamed and teeming in their disparity. I had to turn away from them; in the face of too many things, I had to make only one: me. Nothing, of course, actually belonged to me, not least the entity I'd constructed and started calling 'me,' but I told myself it did because I live by the law and that's what I've been taught to want: a 'me' that I can own, like an object to keep in a pocket.

At the hospital, I had been prescribed medication which would turn out to be the wrong medication. I had been misdiagnosed with depression, because they saw in me only one thing in the face of many, because again, that is how the world is structured. Our collective delusion.

*

Is it for me to say where I stood, still stand, in relation to the line between the things that happened to me and deciding that those things were what I wanted? Let me put it another way: is desire a thing that belongs to you, a thing you can own?

*

I should probably define 'delusion,' because it's hilarious. 'Delude' comes from 'de' and 'ludere' (a form of ludicrous): *De*, meaning 'down, to one's detriment,' and *ludere*, from the Latin, meaning 'to play.' So, a game you play to your detriment.

Who might lose at such a game? Who might win?

*

When people with bipolar disorder are given antidepressants, it triggers mania, and this period would ignite in me my first and only true mania, the kind the textbooks and diagnostic codes call 'classic.' But I wouldn't learn that until six months later. For now, the medication was pulling me out of my grief; reborn, I felt pure and unspoiled by all that had happened. The chemicals in my body were cooking hypomania, the early stages of mania, and the charged, fertile wonderfulness of it hadn't yet turned dangerous. I felt buoyant, overflowing with visions, and untouched by time.

What I mean is that I could not grasp the thought that my actions had consequences, that my body was made of material, and that what I did with it was tethered to reality and its laws. What makes mania feel like mania is the feeling that the force which moves time in one direction has been suspended, making reality a lawless place where everything, past present future, is happening forever and always and right now. It's a kind of surging that feels both dispersed and radically concentrated, and because it is so extraordinary, the fact that you feel it seems to imply that something about you is extraordinary too.

I'm sympathetic to the notion that linear time is an illusion, so I'm always frustrated when things that get broken tend to stay broken.

*

I like to refer to this manic summer as 'The Summer of My 12-Inch Cock.'

*

My cock is 12 inches long and it's a gun and a Molotov cocktail and a megaphone and a long perfectly balanced sword and a power drill that can grind through bone and a really big hammer a hammer that could crush one of Jupiter's moons and a flame-thrower longer than my body and a huge punishing stretch of silence and a ghost and a cave and a vase of bleeding hearts and easy sugar and a deep old forest with ancient mosses and a combustion ex nihilo and it stinks like very expensive perfume and when it lands on the face of my enemies it cracks through the air with a thwack that registers at 150 fucking decibels.

*

During manias, it is difficult to remember things you know are true. Lies are difficult to distinguish from desires, reality is impossible to locate amid what feels like a warm dream. It's easy to get lost and not feel like you're lost. Also, how can a person be lost if they went there because they wanted to?

There are many etymologies of the word 'lost,' the adjective of 'lose,' but my favorite is the transitive sense from the 1200s: 'to part with accidentally, be deprived of, miss the possession or knowledge of.' I like that it can be an accident, and I like the double meaning of the word 'miss,' that it is both a failure and a yearning.

Who gets to say where the line is between what one wants and what one has been taught to want? And who gets to say if that wanting defines a person as the thing they have failed at, or the thing they have yearned for, and aren't these somehow the same?

*

Manias feel great. Doctors don't want you to know that. Manias are also encouraged in certain kinds of people in certain areas of life, but doctors don't want you to know that either, because it relies on the premise that sanity is a straw man. A delusion that the whole world believes in.

The DSM-5 criteria for a classic manic episode includes 'inflated selfesteem or grandiosity,' 'flight of ideas,' and 'excessive involvement in pleasurable or risky activities that have a high potential for painful consequences.' Sounds like qualities that are especially encouraged in the *Malerschwein*, with the exception of the last part—the painful consequences—which sounds like what everyone else will feel upon dealing with him.

You'd think there'd be a definition of 'painful' in that diagnostic criteria, because locating the pain, and who will feel it, and why, and how, seems essential to distinguishing how exactly mania is different, and deserving of pathology, than, say, the condition of masculinity at all. But the DSM lets this stay ambiguous.

*

There is another way of looking at it, though (even, not one, but many). The DSM makes it seem as though inflated self-esteem, flights of ideas, and excessive involvement in pleasurable or risky activities necessarily result in painful consequences. As if causality equally affects everyone, no matter who you are, one of the laws of reality that binds us all. But the burden of causality is not everyone's burden.

This is perhaps another of our collective delusions: that we all shoulder the burden of causality equally, that the punishment fits the crime. But, for some, the shattered glass on the floor doesn't stay shattered. Well, it does, but it's not ascribed to be their fault.

And what do we do when the shattered thing is a body? And your own?

*

Men are less often diagnosed with bipolar disorder than women, and when they are, it usually happens when they are in a depressive episode rather than a manic one. When depressed men are given antidepressants, they swing into mania, but since manic men are hard to distinguish from Geniuses who are changing the World, society tends to support their manic behavior until it stops producing a culture that can be capitalized upon. Manic men often appear drunk on their own divinity, or high on endorphins from the gym, all fired up in a legibly masculine way, so there's nothing to be alarmed about. If they cause too much trouble, manic men get dumped in jail for the night, and the enforcers of race and class take over from there in terms of where they end up.

When Robert Lowell applied for a teaching job at Cambridge University, one of his referrals listed the signs to look out for that would precipitate Lowell needing to be taken 'to the bin,' i.e., that he was in a manic episode. First, he would start a sexual relationship with a student, threatening to leave his wife, Elizabeth Hardwick, who'd nursed him through many manias and depressions. Second, he'd talk incessantly about Hitler and Napoleon, and start referring to himself as one among them, a great world leader. Third, he'd throw a big party. No big deal, just a heads-up.

When a woman or femme person is manic, on the other hand, she is easily legible as violating the laws of reality: she often fucks a lot and insatiably, spends a lot of money on herself, abandons her duties as a mother or wife or servant of any kind, talks a lot—i.e., 'too much'—and usually about herself, all of her potent ideas, the epiphanic discoveries she's made, and she seems to take great joy in herself, for she believes herself to be important and inspired—i.e., 'inflated self-esteem.' And if she's an artist, she feels as if she's in the throes of artistic production and worthy of the space and attention that Geniuses deserve. Obviously this is a sign of insanity, because insanity is simply a measure of how one has become untethered to reality and its laws.

'Can a woman be a *Malerschwein*?' is another way of asking what happens when inflated grandiosity collides with painful consequences, what happens when flights of ideas are brought down to the ground. Another asks, 'But where would she live?' which is to foreclose the question altogether.

*

I want the world to allow me all of my delusions about my own importance, to bend over backwards to make my importance be true—not just for me, but for all of you too. I want to snap the jaws of people who get in my way, and have the world applaud this and call it honor. I want to bellow with baseless anger and have the world hear it as a lullaby. I want to whine and mewl when someone wants to take up as much space as I do, and I want the police to shoot them in the back for their gross trespass. I want a secretary and a therapist and a nurse and a maid and a fucktoy in the same body who I never have to pay, and I want to blame everything on my mother, that cunt. When I'm asked to account for myself, I want to be silent, arms folded across my chest, jaw set indomitably, and have this act pull power away from my inquisitors and consolidate it within me. I want to call my inquisitors hysterical crazy bitches, and I want this to become the ideology in the world's water supply. I want my brittleness to legislate the wretched, but first, I want to declare their wretchedness and define it recursively, that they are wretched because they don't look like me. I want my wounds, especially the ones I've invented, to be the reason we build prisons, guillotines, and guns. I want the world to labor to secure me and I want them to need no other reason to do it other than because I said so. I want this reason to become a universal Truth with a capital T that constructs the World with a capital W. When I break someone else, I want the world to wag its finger not in my face, but in my victim's, tsk tsk, you should have known better. I want children to be taught not to tempt me, and when they do, I want them to feel for their entire lives the dirty shame of their mistake. I want wealth such that the world has never seen, and then I want my face imprinted on all the coins.

*

Whose voice is this—is it my own? No, it's not mine—but then why have I been taught to want it to be? (What happens to this sentence if the 'mine' is changed to 'ours,' if the 'I' is changed to 'we'?)

*

When a person who is assigned female at birth comes to understand that they don't agree with that assignment, often the first gesture away from it is to wonder if they are in fact a man, a swing toward the antipode. Some find solace there, indeed find themselves there: yes, actually, here I am! Some don't find themselves at either pole but at some treacherous ineffability between, and the question becomes whether a binary is an accurate framework for gender at all, even though the world insists that it is.

Have you heard of Schrödinger's cat? The thought experiment of a cat locked in a box with a device that has a 50 percent chance of killing it? At the moment before opening the box, the cat is both alive and dead at the same time because of what's called its 'quantum superposition.' Schrödinger was trying to figure out when the cat would stop being its soupy mess of both states at once at the quantum level, and become, on the level of the cat itself, either a dead one or a live one.

Gender, for me, often feels like the moment right before opening the box when the cat is a blur of probability of *both* and therefore *neither*. Perhaps another way to say this is that during The Summer of My 12-Inch Cock, there was a kind of collapsing of the very binary that I thought I knew, and the site of the collapsing was me.

*

Z was hung, not 12 inches but at least nine, and thick, a real-life baby arm, and liked to think of himself as the top in our relationship, in the way that straight cis white boys assume the role because they believe it's what the cock ontologically decrees. It's what has built and paid for the house of their identity so they feel obligated to live there. The possibility that they could gut-renovate the place, or burn it down, move away, and build a different house, in a different town, is not entertained, because it would require a premise that one can be homeless, be lost.

Getting lost is not something that exists for those who benefit from the patriarchy. It's impossible to be without your god-given home when one is either the king of his land or has by divine right conquered and settled the land of his neighbor.

In other words, getting lost is impossible because everything already belongs to you. And if it doesn't yet, you can simply point at the teeming pile of unmanageable and savage things and make them own-able by declaring, 'Mine.'

A tentative conclusion: for some, but not everyone, yes, desire is a thing you can own.

*

The focus of our fucking was always Z's cock, his magnificent, god-given cock. The very fact of it. He would unfold his pants and hold out his arms like Jesus as the cock fell into the light, while in the background a choir was cued to sing awe. A whiff of that muddy mix of faith and delusion would come into the air. Submit, it seemed to say, without irony or self-awareness, but as though there is only one universal truth and here it is, I'll let you suck on it if you say please.

He would tell me to 'get it' because 'that's what you need.' I still laugh when I think of this line because of its blunt, bald truth. How he spoke the truth and how the trouble came because I didn't believe it. I kept insisting on a different truth, one where I didn't need that cock, I wanted to live in a world where that cock's power had sputtered out like a short, wet match —but remember, at the time, I was untethered to reality and its laws.

*

Why am I writing about cocks? Why am I still thinking about them? God-damn motherfuckers.

*

My time with Z overlapped with my reading the de Kooning biography, and during that summer I had the sense that, like the Holy Ghost hovering watchfully behind me, I was being followed by his *Woman I* painting. I felt exposed to her, by her. When people looked at me, I saw that they saw her, my face scowling like hers, teeth bared, my body's outline jagged, threatening to shred into the bodies of others.

I cut my own hair down to the scalp, drove too fast, cranked up the stereo to play the same song 50 times a day. I talked a lot, too much, about myself and my work and my soaring ambitions and I had no hesitation in saying what I wanted and exactly how and when. I was hysterical and grandiose and confident and inspired. I flew high on my great ideas. I indulged in pleasurable and risky activities. Self-doubt and caution evaporated, which is a dream come true for an artist. I made new work every day, and it came whole and alive and sizzling with meaning, as if I'd simply walked to the top of a small hill and found god's word waiting there for me to pick up and hold.

Sometimes I think about how this one experience of mania might never have happened if I hadn't been misdiagnosed and given the wrong medication, because I'd been involuntarily hospitalized by a man who thought I was a danger to myself because I was crying too loud over an obvious grief, one that might have been prevented if I hadn't had a uterus, if I'd had gender confirmation surgery, if I'd understood who I was earlier rather than later. But it doesn't matter anymore; the cause and effect are muddled. That line between knowing who you are and knowing who you are not is never a straight one.

*

It has taken me five years to write this essay. I've had to set it aside for months, I've tried to abandon it, to shove it to the back of the desk—it's as if I drive out into the desert, hours away from the city, and dig a big hole and bury it deep, in the desperate hope that it will finally leave me alone. But it keeps crawling back. It keeps insisting on itself.

I am sympathetic to things that have been told their insistence on themselves is delusional, and yet, at the risk of embracing such delusion as the very ontology of their existence, they keep on insisting.

*

Years later, I saw my ex, the man who'd had me institutionalized over our —my—(our?)—*my* miscarriage. By then, I was on the right medication, stable, going to bed at the same time every night. I was trying to forgive him. We met for coffee.

'I wished I'd seen it sooner, maybe I could have helped,' he said.

'Seen what?' I said.

'There were things you'd do that weren't right. But I thought, she's just a crazy artist chick. But if I had known you were sick, I would've tried to get you help.'

'What things?'

'You would fuck strangers. And you were so confident about your work. I've never seen someone so confident about their art.'

'But I only fucked a couple strangers. How many strangers have you fucked?'

'I wish I was that good of an artist.'

*

During that 12-Inch Cock summer, when I was on fire, I made a series called *Actually, It Happened A Moment Ago*, which consisted of poetic, fleeting performances in liminal sites like driveways and piers, 'for small audiences of one person or a few animals.' I wanted to feel into the question of the audience, if it was important for an audience to be present or not, and if it was or wasn't, then why. Looking back on it now, I see that I was trying to come to terms with my work being perceived according to laws that I didn't necessarily want to follow.

If a person whose body looks like a woman's dances in a driveway at night in front of three cats and calls this 'art,' what are we to make of it? Is she crazy? Does she know she's crazy? If she knows, does that mean she's actually crazy, or is she just performing being crazy, which, instead of negating the possibility that she is really crazy, means she's probably even more, pray, crazy than we thought?

But could this piece be about its audience—who they are, their values, desires, prejudices, gods, and monsters, and what, because of all that, they assume and decide about the artist? Which is another way of asking, is the audience crazy, and how will we know if they are, and who gets to decide?

*

A less tentative conclusion: perhaps it's that some of us are allowed to think our desire is our own. The real question, then, is why some and not the rest? In other words: whom does this benefit?

*

That summer was hot, dry, dirty. Los Angeles summers are mythical. They often feel like the end of the world already happened 30 years ago, and this is the scorched, wasted aftermath. The survivors have persisted by pushing into the heat and the dust, singing to themselves, and belonging to cults of one. They travel in eggs of metal and glass, blasting their faces with artificially cold air created by draining resources from the dying earth. They persist on diets of grass and sticks, they dress themselves in flapping tents of fabric that cost half their rent.

After a few weeks, the medication swimming in my veins washed me ashore and, waterlogged and tossed, I rolled over in the flogging sunlight and didn't know where I was. One Sunday I took myself out for brunch, though I can't remember how I had any money. I went alone, I brought a book to read. I wore a skirt that a friend had given me, which depicted a tableau of an Aztec ceremony of virgin sacrifice, outlined in sequins. I went to an expensive French restaurant in Los Feliz that had a dirty floor. Liv Tyler was there, having brunch with her mom.

My waiter was very, very handsome, in the LA way of someone who would call himself 'an actor and a model too,' but who is working as a waiter. Six foot four and slim, dark hair, impressively large hands, round blue eyes, a strong Superman jaw. His whole affect was Superman-like, gallant, shoulders straight, chest out. He had that old-fashioned kind of masculinity that is chivalrous, more powerful than any force on earth, which seems to be held in check by an invisible code, we tell ourselves he will keep us safe and never turn against us. When he brought something to my table, he'd offer it with a little bow of his head. He complimented my skirt.

I left my phone number on the bill and he called two days later.

Because I've already told you that I was manic at the time, fresh out of the hospital and torrid with gendered trauma, am I not also casting myself as a casting director on speed-dial would? The crazy hysterical bitch with her tawdry wounds, leaving her number for a stranger, like dropping a bloody rag into a sea of sharks.

*

He made me mix CDs. All but three of the tracks were by men. (He'd say, 'It's great, right. He was great, right.')

On one mix, he included Karen Dalton's 'In My Own Dream,' a slow blues song about the line between dreams and insanity, how it feels to live there. Or, maybe she is talking about where she stands in relation to the line of choosing to be lost versus having no choice.

Dalton's voice is soft and furry and I wanted to listen to it all the time. It became the soundtrack of that summer.

'I feel seen by that song,' I told Z.

He nodded. 'I know,' he said. 'I put it on there for a reason.'

*

My sublet in Chinatown ended halfway into July, so I took a sublet in Hollywood, two blocks south of the Magic Castle. Parking was a bitch, but the neighborhood was lush with trees, close to the Hollywood foothills, and redolent with the feeling certain neighborhoods in LA can get around their fame and nostalgia for that fame. There was a building down the street with this quote painted on its side: 'What's the fastest way to get into Hollywood? Take Franklin.' I can't remember now who the quote is attributed to—Google tells me it's Mae West, Bette Davis, and Katherine Hepburn, all of them interchangeable as blunt old broads who used to be the beautiful talk of the town.

My sublet was in a cluster of bungalows, behind a decrepit iron gate with a broken buzzer that summoned *Mulholland Drive*. The apartments were aligned around a courtyard of bottlebrush trees and bougainvillea, and there were a few old benches and slender metal cans in which to throw cigarette butts. This sublet was the place where I cut all my hair off and then cut his.

Late into the night we'd sit and smoke in the courtyard. Nights in summer are my favorite time in LA. The grueling heat of the day abates a little and the air is fervid, in the high 80s or low 90s Fahrenheit. Barefoot, we'd wear each other's clothes to go outside and smoke, I'd pull on Z's soft, worn-in t-shirt, he'd wear my long, thin sweater the color of blood. He looked elegant in it, that strong jaw, like a leading man from old Hollywood, Cary Grant, Marlon Brando, James Dean, they're interchangeable though we are nevertheless able to parse their distinctions.

Sitting underneath the bougainvillea flowers and the dense bottlebrush, with this elegant man who couldn't take his eyes off me, I'd feel like the luckiest person on earth. Earlier that year, I'd think, not even six months ago, I was in the psych ward of East LA County Hospital.

Inside the locked ward, there were about 40 patients housed in two rooms, the beds lined up in cramped rows. I had a bed closest to the wall, which was a kind of mercy, I could at least turn away from the room. People, almost all of them not white, shuffled up and down the corridor shouting obscenities, screaming someone's name, muttering to themselves, the back of their hospital gowns untied, bare, flapping asses and gaunt legs on display. Behind a locked door in the hallway near the bathroom, for the entire 72 hours I was there, came the screams of a man. He shouted without stopping, '*Agua, por favor! Agua, por favor!*' I never saw him; he was never released from that room. I will never forget how his voice sounded, swinging from enraged to pleading. He was still in there when I was released.

Visitors were not allowed more than five minutes; my aunt kept trying to see me, to bring me food, but they made her throw the food in the trash. There was a payphone in the hallway where you could receive calls, but the cord attached to the phone was only 6 inches long, so you couldn't hang yourself with it. I could not stop laughing at how this caused you to assume a pose, stooped down, head close to the wall in order to speak into the receiver, that made you look unquestionably insane. Laughing about it didn't help my case, of course.

You were also not allowed to have any pens, pencils, or bound books—if the intention was there, they could all be used as weapons. Luckily, a friend of mine had just sent me the manuscript of his novel, which I asked another friend to bring so I'd have something to read. But once it was in my lap, a 5-inch stack of loose paper, it also made me look unquestionably insane.

One of the nurses asked, 'Whatcha readin'?'

'A friend of mine wrote a book.'

'Oh, really? What's it about then?'

'It's a sci-fi psychedelic crime novel set in the 1960s.'

'Is that right?'

'The detective is trying to solve a mystery with the help of mermaids he can talk to when he's on acid.'

'Okay?'

I learned to keep my mouth shut. Being taught something is not the same thing as choosing to know it.

*

I've now become the person in my community who you call if your friend is talking with ghosts, or pronouncing themselves to be god while dancing or screaming without clothes on, or lying down in the middle of the street so that the aliens, who are on their way, will be able to find them easier to finally take them home. Because I've been there myself and somehow survived, I can function like a guide to uncharted territory. Know this, don't forget that, it will probably feel like this; I know who to call—I know who not to call. I wake up to texts and emails from concerned partners and parents. 'We were hoping that we might speak to you for some guidance,' they say. 'Would you be willing to help us?'

In my responses, beneath the medical terminology and names of medications and links to resources and urgings that they know they are not alone, I try to smuggle in a little flame of a question: How much of the world's perception of madness are you willing to forsake?

In other words, Don't fucking take them to the hospital.

*

Illness is not—despite the world telling you it is—only a personal, individual experience of pain, trauma, and limitation. It happens inside your individual body, and yet, it is an index of the social body. It's the collision of a lawless body against a body of laws. It produces an embodied experience that undoes who you think you are to such an extent that telling other people how this feels seems impossible, and at the same time, it produces a body that is read and deciphered in terms that are historical, systemic, and political. However, the social vector is usually ignored, so that illness becomes an index of one's own individual powerlessness, rather than being seen as the experience of how we are all enmeshed within systems of power, how we are all interdependent, for better or worse, and how such enmeshment and interdependence shapes consequences and potentials, desires and rights, dreams and deaths, worlds and realities.

*

One afternoon that July, Z said he was going to sketch me. Though he didn't paint portraits, he'd been saying he would paint mine since our first date. It was almost 100 degrees, too hot for clothes, so we opened all the windows in his apartment and I stretched out on his mattress, which was on the floor. He lived one block away from Alvarado Street and the lapping sounds of traffic washed the room. I read the *New Yorker*, trying not to pay attention to the scratches of his pencil. In his drawing, my face is pugnacious, mouth twisted up and nose scrunched, de Kooning's *Woman*. I sneer at the magazine in my hands, which makes it seem like I'm sneering at the whole capital-w World.

'I look like some deranged goddess who eats men for breakfast,' I said. 'Well, you are,' he replied, and I saw that, instead of winking irony, his eyes were big and round and fragile with cruelty. I'd see this look on him often. I've seen it on children when they hit each other in revenge, sobbing, clutching the part of themselves that's been injured. It's the look of someone who feels humiliated but curious about how to turn his humiliation into a weapon.

Some titles for that drawing could be:

'Woman' Reading, Fresh Out of the Psych Ward
Goddess at Rest (Between Meals)
Crazy Artist Chick
Portrait of an Artist

How can I perceive myself as that which the world perceives, but also that I insist on my own perception of myself, which the world does not perceive: impossible, probably, but, and, so why do I still want it?

I don't know—it's embedded in my spinal cord, encoded in my neurons, from birth, I've been schooled, to want this, want it badly, not only that this is what you should want, but not to want it is a risk, don't want it at your own peril—or maybe it's that I don't want to know.

*

I kept on living in my own dream
In my own dream

*

But was I wrong to think I was saved by Z?

Astrology has taught me nothing if it didn't teach me that the savior and the victim live in the same house. In a word, it's the House of Debt.

*

A friend read a draft of this essay when I was ready to give up on it again. They asked me why, for so long, I kept wanting patriarchal power, why I kept needing to fit myself into such a world. The best answer I could summon was that, for nearly my entire life, I didn't even understand that I could want something else.

As a child, when a boy is mean to you, adults tell you it's because he likes you. If he hits you, or takes your stuff, then he's really in love. Even as a child I knew I wasn't a girl: even as a child I wondered if I was entitled to conflate violence with desire.

*

The definition of masculinity is its capacity to be free of the labor of perception at all—it perceives, yes, but only one way. This is why it's devoid of irony, self-awareness, or pluralism. In a knife-twist of cleverness, though, masculinity has devised its own philosophy to suit this arrangement: the philosophy of the subject and the object, which is a philosophy built on the idea that the object is constituted by the subject.

I've been told that philosophers call this 'intersubjectivity,' which Hegel 'invented.' Masculinity perceives—it is the subject—but only one way—everything else becomes the object. In other words, the very fact that Z, as the subject, perceived me, as the object, is what made me exist at all.

That I now need to cite Hegel to corroborate my argument is only more evidence of how I've been schooled by these laws. Yes, dear reader, as you presumed, Hegel's spooge is all over this essay, all over me, but since you can already see it everywhere, do I really need say how it got there?

Can't I just, like a good little constituted object, spooge-faced, declare my face to be covered in spooge—QED?

*

I asked a friend who studied philosophy for the primary definitions of 'the world'; he sent that earlier list of the main dudes, Plato, Hegel, Leibniz, etc. A few days later, I woke up to a text from him that said: 'Came across a further bit of Wittgenstein today: "The subject does not belong to the world: rather, it is a limit of the world."'

*

When you paint my picture, paint it with strong colors that radiate valor. Make it a portrait of authority. Make my image synonymous with virtue, the Machiavellian kind, virtù, the tautological one that not only belongs to a man but is how we define men: moral strength, high character, goodness, excellence, courage. Give me the largest canvas you have. Then make it ten times bigger. Paint me in the center, my head high above the rest of the image. Whoever it is that deign to look at me will have to look up like a little bitch. Use thick, sure brushstrokes. Don't be a pussy. Get the light right, get it exactly right, and make it golden. Give me a red cloak the color of power and inflate it with the wind of the gods. Make me gesture out and up to the sky, where I am going, where I will take the people who follow me. Mount me on a stallion, risen up on its hind legs, eyes ablaze with righteousness, let us both stare out with impunity. Dare to give me a weak chin and I will have your head on a plate. Get your symbolism to show that, if and when I want to, I can do anything because I can. Paint this and, if you do it right, if I like it, I will pay you to paint three more. My audience, my reader, my kingdom: look at me, now let me tell you what to see. I am what you find on medals and coins. I am who the world means when it says it needs a leader. I am a hero, and I can be yours, if you only ask me nice, if you need it, if you only want it bad enough. I am how to define, how to know, what anything is, because I am how you know what you are not.

*

The definition of masculinity is sitting in a throne on a pedestal in a spotlight at the top of the tallest hill in the land.

The definition of femininity is the inverse of this. Femininity is chained to the floor in the cave at the bottom of the core of the prison, but a prison that has a stage upon which the prisoners are required to perform. Femininity is this performance.

The guards are above you, around you, they can see you from all angles. They are your audience, and they have brutal opinions that they shout at you while you perform. The trouble with femininity is that it's hard to tell who exactly the guards are, which means it's hard to tell where you stand in relation to the line between prisoner and guard, reality and dream, student and teacher, subject and object, audience and artist, which means it's hard to tell who's going to love you the best.

*

Another knife twist: through its constitution by the subject, the object then necessarily belongs to the subject.

Which is why people like Z need people like me so badly.

*

Reader, no! I will not cite Hegel here either!

*

Anne Carson writes: 'The mad state is, as [Artaud] emphasizes over and over again, *empty*. Teeming with emptiness. Knotted on emptiness. Immodest in its emptiness. You can pull emptiness out of it by the handful. "I am not here. I am not here and never will be." You can pull it out endlessly.'

I agree with this emptiness, but I would qualify that it is empty only because it is empty of things the world values.

*

Anne Carson, again on Artaud: 'For Artaud the real drawback of being mad is not that consciousness is crushed and torn but that he cannot say so, fascinating as this would be, while it is happening. But only later when somewhat "recovered" and so much less convincingly... A primary characteristic of pain is its demand for an explanation.'

Let me propose that I did, while it was happening, say so, but I did it in a language that the world has decided it doesn't want to understand.

Another way of saying this is that, in my relationship with Z, I encountered a crisis of representation, because any kind of representation is always a crisis.

Maybe he encountered this too, but maybe it's easier for me to see it because I know representation can't be trusted.

Representation is always also a negation, and narrative is always a fiction: The injustice arises because some of us have been deemed unreliable narrators, and some of us have had our truths recast as fictions, and some of us have been defined not by our crises, but as crisis itself.

*

Maybe the world is the thing from which we demand coherence, and against which we measure the incoherent, and in doing this, we feel as though we can stay clean from the mess. Even though the mess is not only everywhere and in everything but also ourselves.

*

Just as quickly as I'd fallen into it, one day everything changed and I came out of that summer and all of its mess in a flushed, purifying sweep. One of the comforts of bipolar disorder is that it's a reliable cycle. What goes up will come down.

Z helped break my fever dream. Not long into dating I'd told him I didn't want to be monogamous and that I wasn't straight and that I wasn't even a woman. Like many straight cis white boys, he understood the first two of my declarations to mean that I wouldn't sufficiently appreciate and devote myself unto him alone, and he took the last to mean that his suspicions about me were right: I was unmanageable, unownable, beyond the law. He tried to own me outright, without irony, breaking into my email account, threatening his need, his fragile eyes trembling with vengeance.

'This is going to break me,' Z said, not as a plea but as a warning.

When I tell the story of Z, I say, 'My only regret is that I didn't throw more things *at* him.'

*

The reader might wonder why exactly I was dating a straight cis white boy at all. Good fucking question! Now, when I look back at that summer, this is the one and only bit of evidence that convinces me I was indeed mad at the time.

*

I never spoke to Z again. In the wake of our breakup, he wrote me several emails about the mistakes he'd made in our relationship, an attempt to try to 'win' me back. He framed them as qualities of mine that I'd inflicted upon him.

'You're a fucking she-devil who put a hex on me,' is one example.

'I tried to do too much for you, right? I was good at the sweet loving man, but not good enough at the asshole. I flubbed my lines too many times and you had the casting director on speed-dial,' is another.

'You laid out something that looked an awful lot like bait.'

These are direct quotes, unchanged. How sweet perception must be when it's only subjective!

The last words he ever spoke to me came in a drunken email sent at two in the morning: 'I'll leave you alone now. You will always be simply magnificent.'

It is the singular talent of straight cis white boys to render into weapons lines that are offered as compliments. I wish I'd learned how to do this, but I could only be taught so much. Ultimately, I flunked out of school.

What I think of most when I read these lines today is how close Z got to understanding the game we were both playing, how totalizing it is, how damaging, how no one, not even the winner, is meant to win it, but how he never allowed himself to be released from the notion that he should be the one to win it.

Is it for me to say where Z stands in relation to the line between taking up space because you want to, because you like it there, and being born into a territory that is supposed to belong to you?

*

Sometimes I refer to The Summer of My 12-Inch Cock as 'The Summer When I Finally Learned My Lesson About the Patriarchy Because Its Theatre of War Played Out in My Bed.'

*

The fact that this summer coincided with my being mad should beg the question of whether or not madness is ever not insurrectionary.

*

Making a location in time and space and furnishing it with words and feelings and desires that could belong to me is an attempt to become a thing to which a location and a comportment belonged, which is to say there becomes an 'I' to whom a desire belongs, which would mean I was not lost. I wanted so badly to be a subject that I was willing to own what didn't, couldn't, belong to me. But more than that—I was willing to believe in ownership at all.

*

When the whole world believes—what do we do?—in the same thing. A flight of ideas, upon which only some are allowed to soar, while others are tethered to the ground?

*

Who am I to say where the line is between wanting to fly and only wanting to dream of it? We all develop our own ways of insisting on ourselves, which is to say, of persisting in our prisons.

*

Am I defined by the house I was born in? Or, can my definition come from how I've gotten lost?

*

A conclusion:

> I think it's that the world simply is the law, the law is the world. The question is whether you're willing to break it.

Note

The two lines that begin 'I kept on living in my own dream' are from the Karen Dalton song 'In My Own Dream'. The phrase 'it's hard to tell who's going to love you the best' is based on the title of a Karen Dalton song.

once

more

Caspar Heinemann

Second Sun Syndrome

what left rust on, belted to the summer wound-joint
THAT is the State these people romanticise, Greco-Roman
extension, want desperately material
brute force to facsimile any love
with their Fata
Morgana of hedgerows &
thrushes & snowy robins & the absolute & most vitally, none of |||||||

down right
disgusting,
offensive,
not fit for hanging,
bloody murder
for ME to be marginally
inconvenienced

the knife rack holds the nation betwixt
its greasy guts gutted, THIS is all you are

what it is is something makes possible the
hole that the screw enters being left for crevice—
the screw enters via roadside poppy crushed on the
wax-jacketed
hard shoulder

no trial no trial, simply excellent common public sense excreted
via the tiny eclipsed pores on the side of the bottle of milk
used to have cream on top, you know, we'd scrape it off and scramble
fight to the death like real children in a real country
with a real milk man, a real man, leaking real milk

un-co-erced, i make my bed
to prevent ANY lying

back then but before, a socialite, i simply owned
vast, almost unwieldy, quantities of friends
suspended above various platforms, they all go by
luther blissett,
luther blissett,
luther blissett,
luther blissett, i adored them like my own
pseudonymous attempts
at squandering the riches

of my telecommunications empire
    the multiple & the multiplex
clawing air i cry to the harvest beast
  BAKED BEANS ARE HOLISTIC—

dark clouds closing in—Holistic Lifestyle is a redundancy
as they are simply,
    whether sugar rich or sugar free, ultimately,—not long now,
                                        locusts approach
                                        stage right—
synonymous, lifestyle is holos

then the rocket scientists came a-marching down to stop the ides
of march from leaking
            silicon into the upmost
echelons,
those echelons we imagine drenched in port & plasma &
we got some things right, after all fens collapsed
made ink blots of the scrying world
                      sunk the sunken ships to spite

the right
            time sucks it up and like that
beat into submission infinite efforts,
history is overflowing with examples of
                              examples bereft of of,
well-placed matchsticks plug gaps in the narrative

2001 open pop stars drink the bloody water
emerge with the taste for human flesh

CH SSS

halt

go

All Red

These printed words makes all the artwork everything in this room turning red
These printed words makes everything in this room red
Everything here has turned red now
These printed words are red
The floor is red
The carpet is red
The ceiling is red
The air is red
This word
These printed words have turned everything red
These printed words is red and is aggressive and doesn't want to leave any space for everything else
These printed words control the space

Sophie Jung

Frau Welt

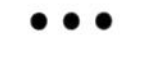

{from up below}

Frau Welt:

Enter Leadeyes and Gentlament I meant mes Damesand
Messies meine Damn enunciErren your dried
out dripping
fried up friggin
piece of xyz

I thanked her and \eft.
I thanked you and *right*, I should have lingered to
share the pain
ta pretty picture
it looks like death warmed up on an outstretched overstretched I can't pull
oh dear that canvas is as far away from BLANK another blank
I tell her don't paint your picture don't even bother she knows she's sold he
strokes the cat the wrong way up I say don't even bother I won't be able to
Temporary pain thresh holds an undesignated in or out mark her pain *trash*
And get your dried out mark her words my words
her mark

er pen out. She writes:

The clowds hang lov
There's an air of DE

erogeneously grown
Kid, Babe, Baby, Da
Mono Welt: *it's late.*
You should:

're all pulled over for killing the dear
:ath a void another void avoided.

s have unsocketed recently the wet bulb temperature is popping high.
for me a second will you doll} a perty picture pain. It leaks.

the heat is wet.

I said the heat is wet

The wheat is het

's not let's not kid ourselves

oy Kid let's not.

Sleep the sleep of the x
Sleep the sleep of the why
Sleep the sleep of the z

I thanked her and right, I understand your concerns we must act now
the time is now, it's now-o'clock if ever there was a time-o'clocked off. Over and out
side it's reasonably warm for this time of years and years of enjoyable shut-eye
on the other side the grass is a faint memory of soils gone by.

Throw a fist full grab

a wistful in the air with open hands it rains down dust: I herewith bapt eyes on the horiz on and on we ride, our crotches raw and unsentimental, numb and dumb. I herewith christen you numb and dumb.
I tried but soll ich nicht auch oder soll I dare it got cold before he did.
Solidarit is so fast sofa st. asleep on the settee said he so hard to wake so hard to wake so hard.

Schock is a *con*
Man *cept* err except
it draws but BLANK.

It is a gun in my pocket

and I hate to see you. I suffer from social anxiety you wouldn't understand. We all nod in understanding.

Here take this and tell me in all sincerity. Tell me now or forever hold your
can you please by piece, do you believe in repetitive histories?
inaudible headshake firm handshake deal sealed upon my heart
Here here is literally looking at you I must tell you not to go beyond.
Do not go beyond do not

touch **do not**

{MAKE THAT FACE OF GENUINE HAPPINESS}

at the end of the day (you mean now? Shut up dummy)
at the end of the day (as in any day now? Give it up bumhead)
at the end of the day we're all here to compliment each other.

Isn't that incredible the way he gets to climb that wall?
No. People have stopped climbing walls, they are too hot I suspect
Main suspect. Head off. Suspect. The Widow.
Still, I think she deserves a mild applause.

S u s p e c t h e a r s a n o i s e

Turns their eye and looks. Freeze. I forgot I walked on. Road killer shades
me for walking on. I don't know how to move m'lady I just put one shaky sole in front of the other and then at times beside and behind. I'm not sure which looks or even works best. Not for me to say **at the end of the day** my legs are heavy and my eyes are out. On the floor staring back at me pour me another.
Another what?

Another malcontent high-shine brumm brumm
right down another please
~~one shaky soul stabilized before the other for~~
~~one tough evaporating minute soul~~

I have so had enough I want another.
I have just had it up to **hear hear** can I
have another of whatever just something bland
that doesn't take my mind off E V E R Y T H I N G

† *something* †

that does not make the smallest bite of difference.
Swallow hard it's hard when your hands are born
tying. When you're born with your ties handed to
you in a manner of:

I'll give you this now it's something out of nothing.

Nothing means everything available at all times,
starkly lit so it resembles everything else
available. Not by shape or form or
use it's no use but by essence.

Thank you tender.
Thank you for clearing that up for me I think.
Thank you tender.

Rough.

Is that all there is to an analogy? Is that all there is it isn't you've over out. Overlook look! Look there it's dead sorry my mistake I believed for a brief second.

Dagger

A dagger is a knife with a very sharp point and two sharp edges, typically designed or capable of being used as a thrusting or stabbing weapon. Daggers have been used throughout human experience for close combat confrontations,[3] and many cultures have used adorned daggers in ritual and ceremonial contexts. The distinctive shape and historic usage of the dagger have made it iconic and symbolic. A dagger in its modern sense is a weapon designed for close proximity combat or self-defense; due to its use

I left and right, second right I turn to you. My mirror stage alas applause I am complete after all. Detached from myself and attached to everything.

Not bad for an xyz.

According to the flesh we can now sink beneath and it should be ok.
We should be fine for another decade or so.
When I say we I mean we and not we. I mean WE. Not we, I apologize.

WE is bespoke.
A number of roads to freedom if I remember to pick them up along the way
if I remember at all. All
I remember these days are the days. I remember the days. Any day now it'll occur to me. It'll come back to me it never left but I can't for the life of me

remember to pick up booze booze and ▄ooze.
I remember to ooze, it's just about the only thing left to do without movement or thought I thought to myself and chuckled.
B has evaporated. The humility was too high. 99.9%. Not am. **Am** is still here and hiding. I am she whistles through a broken tooth.

Now look at that. A smile.
A heavy smile and a pair of deep set everything else.

Wer Wind sät wird Sturm ernten I thought to myself as I turned a coroner.
Too many of them about these days I found myself. In that same spot
On:

© So lebte er hin 🄯
Und her. And her.
She, too. Straight down the line:

It is a gun in my sceptre. A pocket in my gun. Or a ratchet.
I'm not entirely sure what a ratchet is supposed to feel like in such proximity to my private part take in this take this experience

towards expertise.

• Whatever it is that has lodged itself in my pocket without being expelled by me •
it is it • I hate to see you I hate to see, sometimes I'm blinded but then let me ask you this • what
does the previous sentence mean.
The sunball is dear oh dear to me I'm blinded by the sunball
in return I wave up and hope that if hate breeds hate the same is true for demonstatively cordial neigbourship.
My sun, would you happen to have a little bit of salt?
What happens next? What next has happened before I asked you what happens now?
It is so bloody bright right, it's right bright. Aka unbearably burned which is why

I haven't bOrn yet.
I mOurn

pre-emptively for all. If you haven't pre-mourned let me tell you the case is settled.
Take a pinch of salt, just a pinch of salt with nothing else, and rub it into your eyes.
Can you see me?
If not you continue to remove grain by grain until you've got the whole pinch back in between your index and your middle.

In every grain of salt
a sigh surprises.

Slip not, ice dwarf, we've salted the pathways.
Scribbled into the dust of the car hood.
Behind the windscreenwiper a male, tie not fastened, knot tied, not tired, but dead, more.
Behind the windscreenwiper the bulk of the car's body has gone amiss. The long deceased perched on nothing but a leftover
bite of hope is nothing more than an appetite for a thing combined with the opinion that it can be had.

Hope:

Cut a hole sit on it and open up.
Much has already been said about flesh pipes and I'm only trying to cover as much ground as possible in the shortest amount of time so for the sake of rash and rapid argu
meant to move on to briefly consider the point at which you befriend your tubular classification. The one thing that comes to mind in opposition to fully automated weapons.
Shit:
Once the golden future has arrived and moved on two-dimensionally covered you with a flimsy veneer of glitter that isn't dense enough to look royal and not lustrous enough to hide your blistered flesh. It is just enough to make you look a little dusty. As if you'd followed through a long hatched plan to get some decaded chore done and remembered halfway that you're not the type to finish tasks and what was the use of an emptied carcass or a

The future is a wafer thin sheet of persistent
raincurtainage. You pass through it uneventfully.
What's on its other side
as if this sheet of fallings was up to the job of
divisioning spaciochrolologies
what's on the other side is nothing much to write
home about.
I mean to say "home"
There is no there
                there is no
        there there is no there
        there, now there. If you lodge yourself
      between the t and the e you get a sense of
what I'm describing. If you lodge yourself
between the e and the t you get a sense of who's
coming for you.

Of course you could always be moving along
with the future, once it has arrived position your
self underneath its seeping blade, and presently
presently presently presently

I lagged. In order to speak I need to lag, I hope
this was the right decision to take. Had I moved
along… Let me get my horse {gets horse}

SJ FW

Insert poem in galloping rhythm. If you read it right.

If you don't read it right I've gone too slow.

The future's not got much further to run anyway, if we're lucky we see it halt, bruptly or not and can stroll towards it. In our own bloody time.

I is we. We is bespoke. If we're lucky it continues to dribble and a pool of gold will eventually soak our feet, too. If it doesn't. The agricultural run-off will. (I do wonder, have always wondered if the future and their families are aware of approximate lifespans?)

Shout from the off:

STICK TO

Act xyz

How to get yourself to cry and how to stop yourself from crying.

Disambiguation. For faulty irrigation systems and naïve optomosm please sea Salton See

~~wikihow~~ under the nail. While I suckle on my blood and enough round up to substantially restaff my futglora, you can read this:

CLUE

One of 200 species a day is granted a word:
Think about how much you wish it hadn't happened, what your life was like before, and what your life will be like from now on. Let yourself understand and feel the loss of what might have been.

CRYING REMOVES TOXINS
CRYING BOOSTS YOUR MOOD
CRYING LOWERS STRESS LEVELS

THE SCRIPT

I was put in charge to host an event {fictional, glamorous, decomposing} I'm sure this will be a really nice event, says she. Eventu*ally* *I'll get round to telling her {long deceased}* that the event was the first indication, no the initial cause, the cause that led to the cause, the sting the needle the intrusion that was removed in its corpulosity but not in its **miniscul**inity. The puny little hooks made their way in. *Knock knock, who's there?* Small reasons ~~not reasons the why is suspended~~ small operators sent out ~~not sent out the motive has been suspended~~ to immolate you. The uninspired truth is a vessel held together by waves of various currents hey by webs of **xyz.** Truth is an off-key tune in the drippy belly of a boat came a croakey song out of deep out of blue out of tun ah that's long gone, not too blue more muddy, overly saline, no irrigation, as I said before. *On repetition.* The pot is empty. Refills have been cancelled read the guidelines. {decomposed} *On recognition:* The pot has drained the soil is toxic, in it wade little cats, lost husbands and a disgraced prime minister. In wader waves from all angles before I can throw my arms around them and turns: the last one to leave or to drop another drop disappears, possibly a **tear**, possibly the last bit of fluid left in one particular body, I thought for a second it was mine. I thought it was Menstruation but it's been years since I've met someone who can even remember the smell of it.

THE DAY WE LEFT: THE DAY WE LEFT: THE DAY WE LEFT: THE DAY WE LEFT: THE DAY WE LEFT:

The tub has been cleaned, squeaked, the marbles in the bathroom. The marbles off the temple. [insert on villa vs temple vs palace vs castle vs safehouse*-]. What cannot be done any longer: walk past the temple of Athena* and get excited by the thought of seeing a battle between the Greeks and the Centaurs. a battle made out of 75% man and 25% horse. How to marvel at something so solid stare* at something so marbel. I asked my friend to destabilize them by 2.7%. Transparency was increased. Water tiles, wobbly water ties wobbly water ties you as a creature together. Fractions: tiny shards squared, be they gardens, security fences, headsnakes*, ***ac countability***, rock.

I fell to pieces
I tied myself back together. Splitting mirror imagine spitting on said concept with a throat full of puss
y cat purrs: CAT astrophy has happened while you were sweeping *CAT atonia off killed 60% off kilter off off they've all left the boat as soon as it became clear that is was fuelled by ffo*

ssil oh the irony, said the tiger, let me keep my integrity said another creature you've never heard of and never will, it would have been too good to be…said a small one you feel won't be missed on a planetary scale but No ah No ah No you might be wrong there.

Don't CAT egorize the shards before reassembling ego
rise by using a brown military tie and on the third day you say: excuse me for invading ....
....
....
....
....
....
....
....
....
....
....
....
....
....
....
....
....
....
....
....
....
....
....
....
....
....
....
....
....
....
....
....
....
....
....
....
....
....
....
....
....
....
....
....
....

....
....
....
....
....
....
....{pause}your privacy, but I've got to tie your hands (id.) and knees (super thumbs up shins down) on behalf of your risen ego, here, let me tie a not not a knot a not knot a knot, not?
The rock has been rolled to the side and who was it who lived in that cave shall we say?
/ who was I to resurrect.
Slides back in
Doors, channels, hoods, cavities. Together. Bow.
Put together: blow.
A whistle:
I walked out.
Simple sequence of e
vents
Air
vents made sure the circulation kept running as he, his *madness*, ran out

You put your lips not alltogether just sometogether otherwise where would the extra wind go?
A wind player without release, puncture his cheek, roll the tomb stone aside
Just in time for the detonation. ***Self-inflicted*** means constitutional responsibility was put out on the curb
In the dead of night.
Hey, your sovereign is not just for X-mas, it's for {insert time span depending on form of government}

Sticks head out of glass cube to whistle: Drove my chevy to the levy
Athan: "This will be the day
that I die, but let me start at the beginning."

Giant Rock

Giant Rock is the biggest free-standing boulder in the world {prime location, invest. Return to come again
So unfit
for human habitation, Dr. Pepperspray to keep us away but the wind has changed and we're back for a
Refill the hole that was once a room
living Land
fill it with soil, speculation or whatever the sentiment is that used to get you out of bed in the morning.

Let's go down there and listen in to the inquiry. We're in SoCal in 1943 / 1968 let's say
{remember to bring the radio aerials* "we" distributed earlier.}
*point out with the largest of them, on a graph of voluntary size, that you can pull them out and out and out and out and out and out and out and out and out and out and out and out and out and out and out and out and out and out and out. And yet...
{looks into audience. Yes? Correct}
Anyone who remembers penes in their unsymbolic mode can testify: {silence} growth has limits for if it didn't it would either {back to flesh tube} or render us all egorical.

We'll go no more a-roving
So late into the night
Though the heart be still as loving and the moon be still as bright.
For the sword outgrows its sheath.

roving prohibited due to the necessity for unprohibited growth. We break for and against fish:

***red herring**
laissez-faire = ha
(costum

= diminished
others do it for you
change)

I know how to be pretty but today I'll hold my head otherwise.
A thousand times with nobody watching. Shall we give ourselves
a minute to remember how we got into this mess?

audience member declines

Detective lieutenant can you get your magnifying glass out?

writer adds description of events unfolding in real time:

We see the detective lieutenant outline the patterns

we see the lieutenant detective trace the bodbod

We see the lieutenant go up to the Bar

Gain: *uneven. For more information see my tutorials on Rapunzel: "firesale of labour power in return for zyx (shrugs)",Rapunzel: "colonizing the horizontally and vertically on behalf (***backrest***) Rapunzel* {*bored:*} *err or look it up and down there is no safe way to get out.*

CUTS HAVE TO BE MADE*

this, friends and enemies is a binary misconception of how the marquette works.

Keep your hair on. Cuts are based on a violent patriarchal beauty dogma that - {wrong march}
Keep your hair on. Oysterity, due to its purifying role in the ecosystem, has been proven to be full of micro particles that cause infertility in the male population

{applause}

We see the lieutenant go up to the **Seashells** apologies let me try again **hehellshehellsonthehehore**-Bar.

Lieutenant, can you show me how to mix things up without mixing things up? {winks at audience. *We're all in it together,* the lieutenant is an expert on it}

We are sad sat in a hotel bar. Located in the atrium. Around us are stairs of various heights and materials, we can watch everyone still left here come and go, we can watch them halt, stay, reverse. The elevators have had their steel ropes cut.
To hang a heavy conscience it takes more than a foggy set of slip-proof not-nots, more than damp and musty bed sheets. Still the doors open occasionally. What emerges is a cat, husbands or a disgraced prime minister. Look left and right, can't seem to decide. The doors close. The bell goes.
Temporary sanctuary.

A ratchet is in fact
On repetition.
How to mix things up without mixing things up:

right where was I?

Detective goes behind the ~~cloud to hide its face and cry~~ bar and gets out the drinkware.

The dancefloor of your drink is burbon.
To that you add splash of burboun.
If you're feeling expecially loose or lonely you could try adding a dash of bourbon and to top it off:
Some burbun.

What have you made us today inspector?
A borbun.

Applause, scattered laughs, "ouououou"

We are aware of the irony of clapping our palms that just seconds ago were streched out to either side of us in combination with a deep shrug.

Palm outstretched, leaves it there while palm leaves, swaying in the wind
Ow, we shan't mention it, one too many has tipped the wait,
Er has tipped the point
Is:
let sleeping horses lie for no return is necessary.

Lyre:
What is and isn't ~~iconic~~ ironic has, for the 24th year running, topped the list of dinner table AND cocktail party conversations.

The year is 2019 but only as time stops always imminently. Continuously stops imminently.
A black cat is sat next to me, paws together in a begging act, atop another black cat. Skinned.
This is c) cosy b) mordant a) in~~con~~sequential) CON

What time it is?
Funny, I've been asked this same question for as long as I can remember and never was the answer as similar as it is today.

Please tick applicable: It's nine past two
It's now a-clock. The time is now.

I
I
I

There "is" a hangman who stands atop a "hill" alo
Every husband / cat / disgraced "prime" minister w
Where are you going?
If the passer-by answers "honestly", they are allowe
There is, however, "one" reply for which the hang
Nowhere, I've reached "my" destination, I have "co
This one husband / cat / disgraced prime minister
obstacle, one of many tunnels, tubes or portals on t
recognized the man in his function, called upon hi
circumvention, on the idolisation of desire's unfulfi
"But" "who" "am" I "talking" "to". "It" "is" "a" "g
"here" "to" "be" "hanged". We have just undone moralising judgement, truth and lie a

Another question.
To the husbands that have left the elevator by obstructing the door with their countless limbs
(Cats and a disgraced prime minister stay inside, unsure of tactics or desires.)
They stop in their tracks, scratching their chins.
(The question is to be found in chapter STRAIGHT DOWN THE LINE. Reproduced in facsimile in this chapter following this next word:)

d to "town".
sses" is asked the "same" question:

ontinue". If "they" tell a lie, they are hanged.
neither hang the "person" nor let them go:
e to be hanged.
ked desire and recognized the hangman not as an
y through life, but as life itself. They have
role and glitched a system based on strategic
y.
" "my" "pocket" "and" you "have" "come"

ed for as long as the elevator is under construction (the servicing team should have been here weeks ago. The last member has just

arrived atop a hill on his way to town.)
expertise:

Falling to pieces without a shatter
Shattering without falling to pieces
Living in pieces
Piecing together a life.
How to get out of a bouldered cave unharmed:

Today we will have our expert xyz speak on be half of
On be quartered of or sometimes even unquantified bits of
The Writer and The Audience.

On be half of the plan back rest, also called sissy bar gain equals loss (page xyz)

Let me tell you a story
There was a person, in the desert, under the largest free-standing boulder in the world, he lived. He hollowed himself a livingroom. He had a radio and he was German. He was blown up by a rally of un-others so to speak for being different or for having a radio or both. PSSST.

In the past:

we all live in glass houses and are uncomfortable when someone peaks in. Very uncomfortable. We just look back out of bleary onto bleary eyes.

Terms and condition in print so small so very very small. We bought into sotto voce and are now tied to a lease of softly spoken parleys for the next xyz.

There is a row of identical glass cubes containing a f lock of teenage un-males spelled to converse just below the threshold of audibility bathed in ambient candle light. The candles are illusionary and the make is **Suis Good**.

There is a row of identical glass cubes containing a f lock of teenage un-males spelled to converse just below the threshold of audibility bathed in ambient candle light. The candles are illusionary and the make is **Suis Good**.

There is a row of identical glass cubes containing a f lock of teenage un-males spelled to converse just below the threshold of audibility bathed in ambient candle light. The candles are illusionary and the make is **Suis Good**.

There is a row of identical glass cubes containing a f lock of teenage un-males spelled to converse just below the threshold of audibility bathed in ambient candle light. The candles are illusionary and the make is **Suis Good**.

There is a row of identical glass cubes containing a f lock of teenage un-males spelled to converse just below the threshold of audibility bathed in ambient candle light. The candles are illusionary and the make is **Suis Good**.

Behind it there is a desire path upon which they built a row of identical glass cubes containing a f lock of teenage un-males spelled to converse just below the threshold of audibility bathed in ambient candle light. The candles are illusionary and the make is **Am Bien**.

Behind it there is a desire path upon which they built a row of identical glass cubes containing a f lock of teenage un-males spelled to converse just below the threshold of audibility bathed in ambient candle light. The candles are illusionary and the make is **Am Bien**.

Behind it there is a desire path upon which they built a row of identical glass cubes containing a f lock of teenage un-males spelled to converse just below the threshold of audibility bathed in ambient candle light. The candles are illusionary and the make is **Am Bien**.

Behind it there is a desire path upon which they built a row of identical glass cubes containing a f lock of teenage un-males spelled to converse just below the threshold of audibility bathed in ambient candle light. The candles are illusionary and the make is **Am Bien**.

Behind it there is a desire path upon which they built a row of identical glass cubes containing a f lock of teenage un-males spelled to converse just below the threshold of audibility bathed in ambient candle light. The candles are illusionary and the make is **Am Bien**.

Beside it is a country road upon which were built a rows of desire paths of identical glass cubes containing a f lock of teenage un-males spelled to converse just below the threshold of audibility bathed in ambient candle light. The candles are illusionary and the make is **Are Mal**.

Beside it is a country road upon which were built a rows of desire paths of identical glass cubes containing a f lock of teenage un-males spelled to converse just below the threshold of audibility bathed in ambient candle light. The candles are illusionary and the make is **Are Mal**.

Beside it is a country road upon which were built a rows of desire paths of identical glass cubes containing a f lock of teenage un-males spelled to converse just below the threshold of audibility bathed in ambient candle light. The candles are illusionary and the make is **Are Mal**.

Beside it is a country road upon which were built a rows of desire paths of identical glass cubes containing a f lock of teenage un-males spelled to converse just below the threshold of audibility bathed in ambient candle light. The candles are illusionary and the make is **Are Mal**.

Beside it is a country road upon which were built a rows of desire paths of identical glass cubes containing a f lock of teenage un-males spelled to converse just below the threshold of audibility bathed in ambient candle light. The candles are illusionary and the make is **Are Mal**.

The country road leads into a Hamlet of a gridded build through alleys and paths that hold rows of identical glass cubes containing a f lock of teenage un-males spelled to converse just below the threshhold of audability bathed in ambient candle light. The candles are illusionary and the make is

The country road leads into a Hamlet of a gridded build through alleys and paths that hold rows of identical glass cubes containing a f lock of teenage un-males spelled to converse just below the threshhold of audability bathed in ambient candle light. The candles are illusionary and the make is

The country road leads into a Hamlet of a gridded build through alleys and paths that hold rows of identical glass cubes containing a f lock of teenage un-males spelled to converse just below the threshhold of audability bathed in ambient candle light. The candles are illusionary and the make is

The country road leads into a Hamlet of a gridded build through alleys and paths that hold rows of identical glass cubes containing a f lock of teenage un-males spelled to converse just below the threshhold of audability bathed in ambient candle light. The candles are illusionary and the make is

The country road leads into a Hamlet of a gridded build through alleys and paths that hold rows of identical glass cubes containing a f lock of teenage un-males spelled to converse just below the threshhold of audability bathed in ambient candle light. The candles are illusionary and the make is **“thinking makes it so”**

To Die, To Sleep – To Sleep
semi audible concerning love

Wife Widow and Whore
"A seat at the table"
Wife Widow and Whore
Wife Widow and Whore
"A seat at the table"
Wife Widow and Whore
"A seat at the table"
Wife Widow and Whore
"A seat at the table"
"A seat at the table" "A seat at the table"
Niwfe Window and Whorne:
change of plan
THE TABLE.
{entia non sunt multiplicanda praeter necessitatem}
says one of 200 creatures a day and isn't spare

but this was. This was.

hance to mumble something
he likes: "A seat at the table"

Epilogue

Pipe up and wind down. Wind and oil, water and rain. Oil and wind. Me.
Up. A pair of **b**
rogue / rogue
Not for resale
Spiders march in
protest for better
conditions us to accept the end as unavoidably not ever here yet.
Hold on a minute keep the line
up for all things worth the wait
a minute is either food or it is either something dropped.
Or it is neither but or
It just isn't.

{flip side} : Semaphorever STOLEN

lowered her lashes until they almost cuddled her cheeks
and slowly raised them again
like a theatre curtain: behind it 8 million deserted fish
ashore ashore
like a theatre curtain:
like a curtain curtain
like a regular net
gain a few pounds lose a few pounds it's the name
of the gameplan
goes as follow:the gameplans

Me, let me just lie down a second I am still reeling
I talk too much:

THE UNEVEN BARGAIN

You talk too much.
White G
love, just sit back and watch your whereabouts disintegrate.
(looped in the background, slowly moves into soggy focus:)

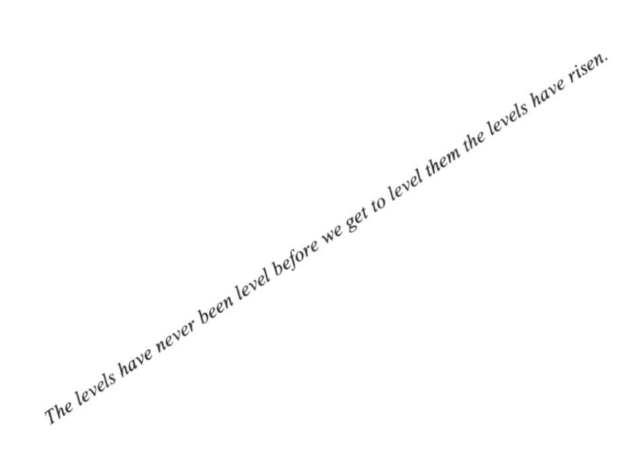

The levels have never been level before we get to level them the levels have risen.

They have risen on the 3rd day, moved the boulder, the largest one about,
Aside and asked you all for thoughts and prayers.
Attention Attention
A con? Do not f.e. pipe up
With eyes that say I'd never only that eyes can't speak
contrary to common misbelief.

I see a puddle flicker in the distance. Wetland, is it?
The sirens go:
In the wetlands has been spotted: Poseidon.

LET ME TELL YOU THE OFFISHIAL {buzzer goes}
OHCETACEAS {ding dong} STORY:
"words matter"
BUZZER GOES
"matter matters"
BUZZER GOES
"words words"
{DING DONG}
FEED THEM WAFFLE is the correct answer.
Top and bottom open up wide to receive the
DOUGH

ƎM>>>

<<<METAPHOR>>>

ƎM>>>

**Top and bottom switched around are still top and bottom and what's inside is* <u>*squared*</u> *and of very little nutritional value*
Twins find a way around where others stand in line stand
Still! Shh!

Knight
End
King
Right
NEVER
A horse has been put down by all the other horses' widows.
That's not a move.
No move. Two moves while two move.

Nothing moves. Freeze.
End Game conditions are sweaty.
Greytones down the argument for the sake of the middle.
Off the road they're called commonsense
{I don't understand it}
Salty tears rival salty irrigation run off
in irritation.

I talk too much.
DEAF
Applausible
END
Is nigh
"It's night."

Close your mouth when you're chewing

turn

page

Sharon Kivland

MADEMOISELLE LA MARCHANDISE

RÉPUBLIQUE FRANÇAISE

DÉPARTEMENT DE ....

Commune de ....

ÉCOLE COMMUNALE

Dirigée par ....

CAHIER MENSUEL

Appartenant à ....

Élève du Cours ....

ANNÉE SCOLAIRE 193 - 193

LIBRAIRIE -- PAPETERIE -- IMPRIMERIE -- RELIURE

THIBAULT-NOBLAT, 99 rue Thiers. TROYES, *Fournisseur des Communes*

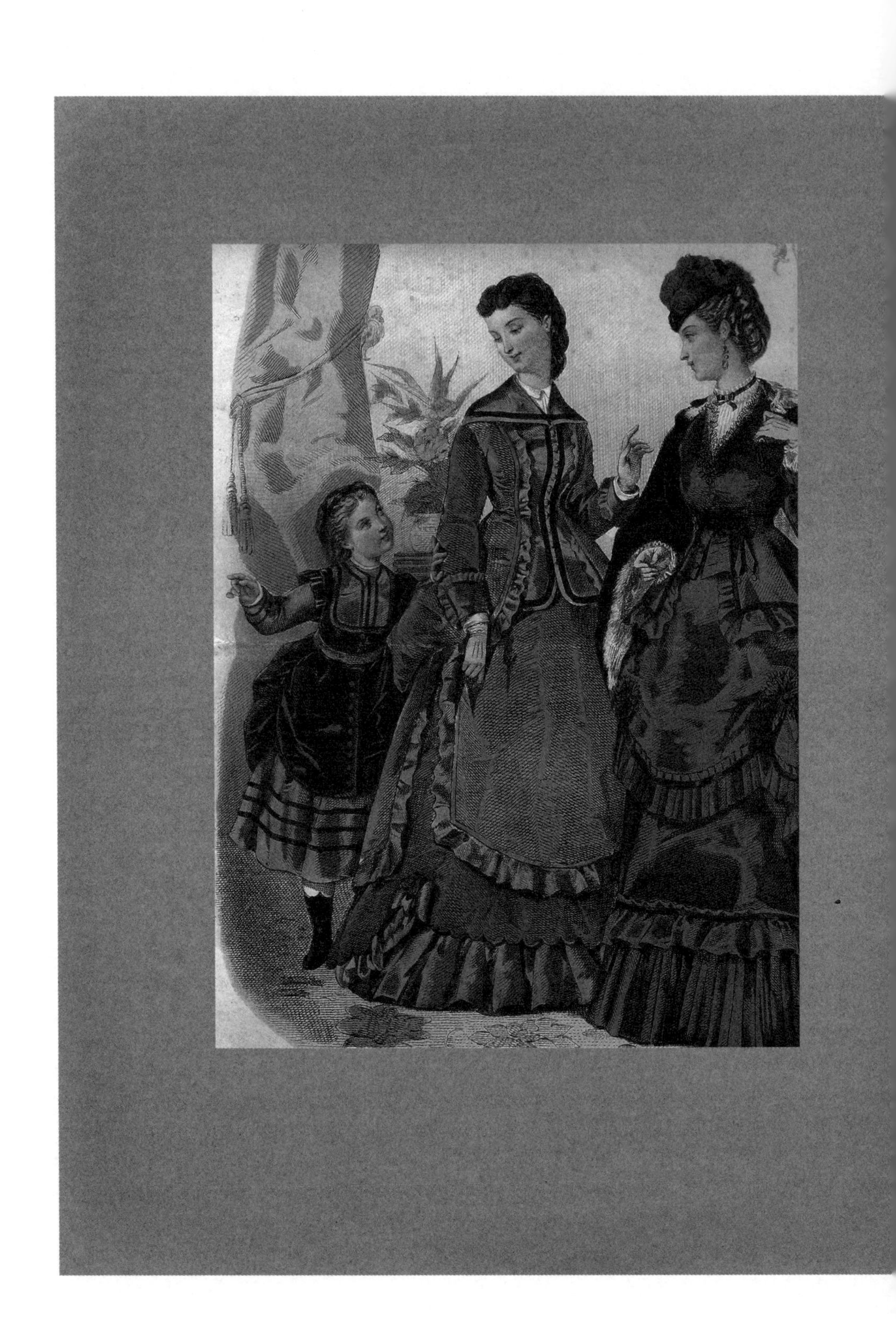

DÉPARTEMENT DE L'AUBE

École publique d

COURS Anglais/English

Nom et prénoms de l'Elève

Né le

Titre et date du devoir

Capital
chapitre 1: La Marchandise
chapter 1: The Commodity

Je serais la forme élémentaire.
I appear as my elementary form.

Je suis d'abord un objet extérieur, une chose qui satisfait, grâce à mes qualities propre, des besoins humains d'une espèce quelconque.

I am, first of all, an external object, a thing which through my qualities satisfies human needs of whatever kind.

Le caractère utile d'une chose en fait une valeur d'usage. Mais cette utilité n'est pas suspendu dans les airs. Elle est conditionée par mes propriétés en tant que corps et n'existe pas sans ce corps. Donc c'est mon corps qui est la valeur d'usage ou un bien. Et ce caractère-là ne dépend pas de la quantité de travail plus ou moins grande que coûte à l'homme l'appropriation de mes propriétés utiles.

The usefulness of a thing makes a use-value. But this usefulness does not dangle in mid-air. It is conditioned by my physical properties which is the use-value or useful thing. This property of mine is independent of the amount of labour required to appropriate my useful qualities.

Je nous suis apparue à l'origine comme une chose bifide : valeur d'usage et valeur d'échange.

I first appeared as an object with a dual character, possessing both use-value and exchange-value.

En tant de corps je suis de combinaison de deux éléments : matière naturelle et travail.

My physical body is a combination of two elements; the material provided by nature and labour.

Mais mon valeur représente du travail humain tout court, une dépense de travail human en général.

But my value represents human labour pure and simple, the expenditure of human labour in general.

~~vixe mor~~ J'aurai beau être le produit du travail le plus comp possible, ma valeur me met à ~~posi~~ parité avec un produit de travail simple; je ne représ donc moi-même qu'un quantum déterminé de travail simple.

I may be the outcome of the mos complicated labour, but throug my value I am posited as equi to the product of simple labou hence I represent only a specifi quantity of simple labour.

Je viens au monde sous la form des valeurs d'usage ou de denrée materielles. C'est ma forme natruel banale. Cependant je suis moi que parce-que je suis quelque chose de double, à la fois objet d'usage porteur de valeur. Je n'apparais donc comme moi, ou ne possède ~~une~~ forme de moi que dans la mésure où je possèdes une double forme : forme naturelle et forme-valeur.

I come into the world in the form of use-values or material goods. This is my plain, homely, natural form. However, I am only myself because I have a dual nature, because I am at the same time an object of utility and a bearer of value. Therefore, I only appear as myself, or have my own form, in so far as I possess a double form, i.e. natural form and value form.

On aura donc beau me tourner et retourner dans tous les sens qu'on voudra, je demeurai insaisissable en tant que chose-valeur.

I can be twisted and turned as wished; it remains impossible to grasp me as a thing possessing value.

Chacun sait, quand bien même il n
connaîtrait rien par ailleurs, qu
je possède une forme valeur qui est
commune et qui contraste de manier
extrèmement frappante avec la t
grande variété des formes naturell
de ma valeur d'usage : la forme
argent.

Everyone knows, if nothing else, t
I have a common value-form whi
contrasts in the most striking
manner with the motley forms o
my use-value. I refer to the
money-form.

Simplement, je ne livre pas mes
pensées que dans la seule langue
que je parle couramment, ma lan

Only I reveal my thoughts in a
language with which I alone am
familiar, my language.

Comme je ne puisse pas me référer à moi-même comme équivalent, ni, non plus faire de ma propre peau naturelle l'expression de ma valeur propre, il faut nécessairement que je me réfère à une autre comme équivalent, ou fasses de la peau naturelle d'une autre sa propre forme-valeur.

As I cannot be related to myself as equivalent, and therefore cannot make my own physical shape into the expression of my own value, I must be related to another as equivalent, and therefore must make the physical shape of another into its own value-form.

Dans la mésure où la forme-valeur ~~de moi-même~~ j'exprime mon être de valeur comme quelque chose ~~d'égal~~ absolument different de mon corps et de mes qualités propres, cette expression elle-même nous suggère quelle cache un rapport social.

My relative value-form expresses value-existence as something whol different from its substance and properties; this expression itself therefore indicates that it conce a social relation.

Je me présente comme cette entité double que je suis dès lors qu ma valeur possède une for phénoménale propre distincte d forme naturelle, qui est la forme valeur d'échange, et je ne possède p cette forme si on la considère isolé mais uniquement dans mon rappo de valeur ou d'échange avec une au d'espèce different.

I appear as the two-fold thing I rea am as soon as my value possesses its o particular form of manifestation, wh is distinct from my natural for

This form of manifestation is exchange-value, and I never have this form when looked at in isolation, but only when I am in a value-relation or an exchange relation with another of a different kind.

En tant que je suis, je suis citoyenne de ce monde.

As I am, I am a citizen of that world.

Premièrement, l'expression de ma valeur relative est inachevée, parce que la série des éléments où je m'expose n'est jamais close.

Firstly, the relative expression of my value is never complete, because the series of my representations never comes to an end.

Je n'ai pas en l'espèce de forme phénoménale unitaire.

I have no single, unified form of appearance.

TABLE DE MULTIPLICATION

1 fois	2 fait	2
2	2 font	4
3	2	6
4	2	8
5	2	10
6	2	12
7	2	14
8	2	16
9	2	18
10	2	20
11	2	22
12	2	24

1 fois	5 fait	5
2	5 font	10
3	5	15
4	5	20
5	5	25
6	5	30
7	5	35
8	5	40
9	5	45
10	5	50
11	5	55
12	5	60

1 fois	8 fait	8
2	8 font	16
3	8	24
4	8	32
5	8	40
6	8	48
7	8	56
8	8	64
9	8	72
10	8	80
11	8	88
12	8	96

1 fois	11 fait	11
2	11 font	22
3	11	33
4	11	44
5	11	55
6	11	66
7	11	77
8	11	88
9	11	99
10	11	110
11	11	121
12	11	132

1 fois	3 fait	3
2	3 font	6
3	3	9
4	3	12
5	3	15
6	3	18
7	3	21
8	3	24
9	3	27
10	3	30
11	3	33
12	3	36

1 fois	6 fait	6
2	6 font	12
3	6	18
4	6	24
5	6	30
6	6	36
7	6	42
8	6	48
9	6	54
10	6	60
11	6	66
12	6	72

1 fois	9 fait	9
2	9 font	18
3	9	27
4	9	36
5	9	45
6	9	54
7	9	63
8	9	72
9	9	81
10	9	90
11	9	99
12	9	108

1 fois	12 fait	12
2	12 font	24
3	12	36
4	12	48
5	12	60
6	12	72
7	12	84
8	12	96
9	12	108
10	12	120
11	12	132
12	12	144

1 fois	4 fait	4
2	4 font	8
3	4	12
4	4	16
5	4	20
6	4	24
7	4	28
8	4	32
9	4	36
10	4	40
11	4	44
12	4	48

1 fois	7 fait	7
2	7 font	14
3	7	21
4	7	28
5	7	35
6	7	42
7	7	49
8	7	56
9	7	63
10	7	70
11	7	77
12	7	84

1 fois	10 fait	10
2	10 font	20
3	10	30
4	10	40
5	10	50
6	10	60
7	10	70
8	10	80
9	10	90
10	10	100
11	10	110
12	10	120

DIVISION DU TEMPS

Siècle	100 Ans.
Année	365 Jours.
Jour	24 Heures.
Heure	60 Minutes.
Minute	60 Secondes.
Seconde	60 Tierces.

SIGNES ABRÉVIATIFS EMPLOYÉS EN ARITHMÉTIQUE

Plus + Moins — Multiplié par × Divisé par : Égale = Comme ::

CHIFFRES ROMAINS

I	II	III	IV	V	VI	VII	VIII	IX	X	L	C	M
1	2	3	4	5	6	7	8	9	10	50	100	1000

release

refocus

Tarek Lakhrissi

About being scared

According to some students of eschatology, 2012 was supposed to be the end of the world. And it was, in a way.

But the end did not come as fire or flood. No glittering comet struck our planet. No virus leapt from continent to continent until bodies lay strewn in the streets. The flora of the world did not grow to overtake our buildings. We did not run out of oxygen. We did not vanish or burst into dust. We did not all wake up with blood soaked into our pillows. We did not watch a beam from an alien ship carving trenches into the earth's crust. We did not turn into animals. We did not starve or use up all of our potable water. We did not trigger a new ice age and freeze to death. We did not choke to death in a self-induced smog. We didn't get sucked through a wormhole. The sun did not overtake us.

At the end of the world, the park was beautiful, hot. The grass was a little long. The trees were punctuated with birds.

Carmen Maria Machado, *In the Dream House*, 2019

*

'I'm scared that maybe I'm not good enough' is one of the first sentences that Claire Fisher says in the last episode (episode twelve of season five, precisely) of *Six Feet Under*, called 'Everyone's Waiting'. I've been rewatching this show (which was directed by Alan Ball between 2001 and 2005) every day during the lockdown due to Covid-19. In that particular and dramatic last episode, Claire is lying in the bed of her lover Ted, a right-wing, cute guy. She says wants to become an artist—after doubting herself for the past couple of seasons—because of her experiences at art school, which varied from good to bad. As we watch Claire grow up in *Six Feet Under*, we grow with her. It's like billions of flowers are breathing every time she appears on screen. At the beginning of the show Claire is a little bit awkward, like an eternal anxious teenager. At the end, she's ready to fight the world. I remember that the last time I watched this TV show, ten years ago, I was eighteen and living in a small countryside town in the centre of France. My best friend, Ned, gave me a DVD boxset containing all five seasons. The show really changed my life. I was a closeted young gay Arab boy living in a working-class suburb with a Muslim family. I had always wanted to be an artist, like Claire, but it was a long journey for me before I realised it. It happened three years ago when a curator commissioned me to make an artwork, and it was this commission that eventually brought me to Vilnius, Lithuania. Claire struggles from the beginning. She makes mistakes, is lost all the time and sometimes acts like a bitch, but she always maintains her own path in life. By the end, after her eldest brother Nate's death, she realises that so many of the different life pressures she has experienced up until this point are now no longer important. It's mainly about her development and becoming an adult.

I decided to spend the lockdown at my sister's new family house, with a small, humble garden where a fig tree grows. It seems funny because what is happening now seems like a mirror image of my life ten years ago, when I was 'locked down' at my parents' house, just fifteen minutes away from where I write this now, while watching Claire grow up, cry and thrive. I usually feel guilty when I'm not doing things, as though being productive means succeeding in your professional life. Right now, I feel like this idea is simply a mirage. Just a vain notion about how the world should be. Maybe filling this void was a way to not be scared or feel not good enough.

*

A couple of weeks ago, I wrote 'No fear' on my wrist in black pencil. It was a mantra and a reminder that helped me to not be scared by life, to build my own carapace: a very cold, distant but friendly character as an artist. I used to write the same phrase on my wrist whenever I felt a little challenged or scared by something. As an artist, you are exposed all the time, especially when your art practice is ingrained with vulnerability and intimate topics. In a way you always have to have the strength to perform, as well as the ability to be good with language. In other words, you have to perform a certain type of bourgeoisie, or at least display a 'genius' trope, to be taken seriously. If not, it is considered weird.

After getting back to her place, Claire learns that a photography agency has offered her a position as an assistant in New York City. She subsequently learns that the agency has cancelled the offer, but she decides to go to New York anyway, without telling anyone, to start a new life. At the end of the episode, in a scene where Claire is driving, the song 'Breathe Me' by Sia plays. Simultaneously, flash-forwards featuring some of the other characters in the show—including her older brother David and her mother, Ruth, before they take their last breaths—appear on screen. I remember how, ten years ago, I cried at this dramatic, emotional ending. I have just rewatched it, and I wept again, big tears, tears that made me feel renewed, like Claire, I guess. In a premonition, Claire sees that she will become blind and that she will die in her own bed. She lies down in her own house. I recently realised that what I want is to have my own house, and to fill this house with parties, old and new friends, and to see new circulations of desire, of people and of feelings. This may sound a little bit basic, but sometimes I want to become this guy who lives on his own (or with his lover), surrounded by his books, filling his time with gardening, writing, reading, having endless conversations and eating good, fresh food. This is all I ask.

*

Do I find joy when I create?

*

I HAVE A CRUSH ON YOU

IT IS TRUE THAT I WANT TO FUCK YOU

YOU ARE PERFECT LIKE YOU ARE

OR MAYBE PERFECTION IS STUPID

I THINK I LOVE YOU

BE KIND WITH YOURSELF

TRUST NO ONE

TAKE CARE OF THE GHOSTS

AND THE PAST

I AM PROUD OF YOU

MAYBE I AM PROTECTING YOU TOO MUCH

YOU ARE THE BEST

DON'T CHANGE ANYTHING

YOU ARE BEAUTIFUL

TAKE GOOD CARE OF YOURSELF

I AM SO PROUD OF YOU

YOU ARE VERY SEXY
YOU'RE PRETTY WHEN YOU ARE VULNERABLE

YOU ARE POWERFUL

TRUST CHANGE

HEAL YOUR HEART
WITH R&B MUSIC

I MISS YOUR PRESENCE
EVERY DAY

TRUST PATIENCE

I ONLY SEE ACTIONS

I LOVE IT WHEN YOU ARE
DRAMATIC

AN EVERYDAY INSPIRATION

FIND THE JOY EVERYWHERE

ALLOW YOURSELF TO REST
SOMETIMES

LET YOUR SPIRIT GROW
TALK TO YOUR FAMILY

CALL AN OLD FRIEND

NOTHING IS IMPOSSIBLE

REMEMBER THE BEAUTY OF THE WORLD

GO BACK TO YOUR HOME
TALK TO NO ONE

LISTEN TO JAMES BLAKE
TODAY

YOU DESERVE THE BEST

LISTEN TO YOUR HEART

SPEND TIME WITH A DOG

YOU ARE WORTH IT

DON'T FORGET WHERE YOU COME FROM

PRIORITISE YOURSELF

FOCUS ON YOURSELF

STAY TRUE TO YOURSELF
SET BOUNDARIES

BE COMMITTED

BE GENEROUS

TRUST THE

PROCESS

pause

play

Quinn Latimer

Images TK or *'An acknowledgment that it is impossible to move forward' / '*Q*' di Quadro* or *My Body, Her Refrain (It Comes Back)*

Images TK
or
'An acknowledgment that
it is impossible to move forward'

I had been dreaming in subtitles
Maybe I was watching a film when I wrote this
Or dreaming I was watching a film when I wrote this
Who wrote this, I asked myself, watching the cult film
And fiddling with my phone, watching the moon
Through another familiar frame, luminous unsuppressed screen
Orchestrated to induce identification with one's 'surroundings' while holding
The line between culture and nature, between interior and, anyway, moon
Revealed by the Orthodox fathers at the crest of the hill
Its hallucinated orb or porcelain report reaching a kind of apogee
Glacial then floral in its fullness, almost bordello
As my friend might put it, her blast of hair mouthing some blue
Soundtrack through another poorly fit translucent casement
Many pale apartment blocks and neo-feudal economies away
Between us only the soft and viral confluence of airs, skies both solar and lunar
Constellating our glittery mineral stasis, our looseness of ties to a rocky world
Indexing past arrivals and present planetary returns
In strange animal signatures to which poets to the west affixed weekly readings
I wondered what their sky—once ink, now glitch—revealed that ours did not
Indeed the Eastern Mediterranean sky that came down
This very night like some wet dark denim
Maybe Japanese, maybe American, hard and expensive
While inside my apartment, reports woven of goat hair
And a language of some incised relief most inscrutable
Crossed moving images laden with a more fluent and flunky darkness
Poverties at once emotional and economic and light-source
Almost genre, that kind of scripted violence
All sought my vision to which I could not affix captions
Could not ascribe borders closed open or otherwise
Beyond litanies of feeling or recrimination sans syntax, that is
So I wrote down (I write everything twice) a letter or index
Of something close to facts but not, really, in any instance:

A group of women at the door...	Architecture
It smells like rain and icons...	Debt
Where were you, she called...	Teargas
I wasn't sure but I'm pretty sure...	Values
All those uncertain years, I...	Speculation
You should get to work...	Period Romance
The wall like a flesh wound...	Psychoanalysis
Pledge to hire five thousand new cops...	Austerity

Mouth in the shape of a mouth...	Assimilation
Plural then singular, light on footnotes...	Water Borders
Constant elections of death cults...	Land Borders
I'm getting in touch to ask if you might...	Poverty
He's not been well, we thought you...	Nationalism
No language, no child, no country...	Whiteness
By the freeway, near the fields...	Inheritance
I saw this performance last night...	Autoethnography
He asked about ancestors and insects...	Poetics
The light is criminal, he hands her mail...	Ecology
It's a ruin not an earthquake...	Migratory Patterns
What brought you here, the temples...	State Violence
You're being pretty dramatic...	Narrative
She rode horses growing up, didn't she...	Heterosexuality
You didn't show, I didn't think...	Expropriation
His rhetoric or her border control...	Skepticism
The prisons privatized of course...	Anthropology
Don't say that, after everything I...	Deep Listening
Built for profit or disrepair not life...	Ambition
What was it like to grow up there...	Shame
She didn't die there but years before...	Geological Colonialism
Didn't go to the party for the new regime...	International Cooperation
They tried to get in, she said, but...	Criticism
The trees smell like semen, don't they...	Art Institutions
Research gleaned for policy...	Sustainable Agriculture
They resigned but retained their shares...	Confessional Literature
The runner backlit, the port empty...	Strategic Minerals
The global grind of, what, criminality...	Boredom
I can meet you but just in case...	Unaccompanied Minors
I wasn't sure you'd want to...	Astrology
[Silence]	Feminism
The wall was 'like' a flesh wound...	Language
The cops were riding double and...	Minimalism
She showed us her bandaged knees...	Capital Controls
[Silence]	Sex
It wasn't as counterintuitive as it seems...	Laughter
[Laughter]	Class Consciousness
The desert was beginning and end...	Silence

I examined my little script, neither ecstatic litany nor sober shopping list
Its uncertain cinematic vernacular
Lifted from the classical narrative modes in which I had been educated
Parables and poetics of the sitcom-strewn child out west, paracinematic
It told no story but what poem in a period film does
My preposition being that
I don't believe in progress but I want it
Which I whispered to myself like any despondent and desirous spectator
Confronted with her many pallid screens and monitors

Wishing self-obliteration in the immersive experience
Of light and language-stricken bodies arranged as dusky interiors
For waged labors and amber embitterments, not metaphors but illustrations of interiority
Like the letter as a 'recognizable narrative motif in the mise-en-scène
Of the period film'—what I mean to write is that this is a report
On the present and what feeds it, a letter as performative figure
'that carries an utterance through time or space'
Yet I couldn't decide in which column or language to place
Those I loved who were mostly dead or had left
Whose names I knew by heart and circumstance
Who offered me life then exile and a body
For whose missing bodies I decried the inherited system, their postures
Shoulders syntax stain of throat sweet notes certain singular and seismic motions
I noted in my accounts as among my deepest privations
Anyway, if our ancestors are continually performing among us
As the Haitian painter theorized live online in our conversation last week
Like revolutionary letters, I thought briefly, then forced myself to refocus
Maybe I could catch a glimpse, catch a moment
Of their time, I thought, my heart in my mouth
Or my hand, as it were, organ as offering, maybe they'd return
I could feel my therapist sigh like an ancestor maybe would
Indiscreetly, all the world past and present on narrow, experienced shoulders
Swept over with a thin sweater, for there was no heating, the tenants couldn't afford it
So I turned back to another set of windows
Where I found again and would like to report that
My inbox could be divided into two types of taking the wrong tone:
The progressive party emails from my first country:
This is Bad, Quinn or Quinn, Can You Believe It?!
I could actually
And the gallery emails of forced capitalist cheer
From my moneyed country following:
You're Invited to a Zoom Champagne Brunch!
No invitation ever seemed so honest
It seems important to state here that
No emails of this kind came from my current country
In which I was only partly and precariously established
By which I mean I was the renter of an apartment
In an economy that was granular and shattered, and to whose many
Political parties I had no affiliation or subscription
Except for casual spaces run by mercenary artists who once in a blue
Moon sent missives on capital and care across our servers
Radical in their incoherence, their strange systems of
Capitalization and font-switching and self-importance
It was always the most shameless and vested in power who waxed
On about healing and vulnerability, I thought
And assholes who talked about fonts
Still it was true—the moon laboring blindly in liquid assent, I assure you—that
The new party in power had been going after the most vulnerable

In a made-for-TV way since their quick and necropolitical election
The local conservative media supported their endeavors enthusiastically
Filming them pulling displaced families out of squats
In the early morning hours, birds cooing from wet rooftops
The giant agaves quiet and inscrutable in lean shadow
On the hill, pulling moisture from air of petrol and Bergamot
That humid morning for example, as a collection of buses idled
Dispensing discreet clouds of exhaust like the cumulous punctuations of historical paintings
In the street of the squat, near the church parking lot, children wailed
Their exhausted parents stood in distress and full knowledge
The police in full medical gear to infer disease
The police in full riot gear to infer criminality
I have already written this once, no, twice
Was this a mediated exercise in the political imaginary
Of the exclusionary logic of nationalism and its moving imagery
Or simply early morning in the early days of new far-right governance
The subsoil and subtext of liberal corporate-military ascendency
This the world since the sixteenth century and 5000 BC
Birds were burning with song on the hill like small brushfires
Shadowy trees of winter were chandeliers of bitter orange
As I sat in my rented interior, soothing myself with a litany most familial and sadistic
The families were loaded onto waiting buses
In front of the assembled cameras—and again I wondered about the cruelty
That the new government inferred of the general populace by this
How many times can I ask and narrate this
Was the local audience's taste for brutality already extant or did they coax it
Into being like birdsong licking blue agave into flame
Like new opioids 'flooding' the market for pharmaceutical heirs, mass death
For the grandchildren's inheritance, or like the fast fashions of previous
Seasons, their once unknown but now necessary narcotic
For those too indebted to consider other forms of consumption and commerce
What, in other words, do we consume and what do we actually want
It remains though that in the street of the squat
The police were pulling at the thin shawls of mothers and sisters
Bright acrylic or lucid cotton, each flammable in their own way
Children pulling at their parents' legs, crying wildly or sniffling softly
Tears their mothers would put out like small fires
As the buses pulled away
Then a note-taking journalist from the left in attendance
Was assaulted by the police for good measure, and that afternoon
Op-eds were written by sanguine college graduates from good local families
Claiming a renewed sense of Law & Order was good
For their country good for the economy good for national
Character good for property rights and those good properties' absentee owners
So good, good, good, they lyricized the selfhood of abandoned buildings, mineral and moral
Of character, a magnanimous, vacuous language they gleaned
From the canon of capital, the dulcet altruistic tones
From their good colonial fathers, editors, despots

Language as ouroboros, I thought, absolving itself by eating itself
In between their sentences bodies tended to each other for death would arrive in the endnotes
The moon was still visible, lightly chalked to the wet blue sky
A beached eye whose focus was uncertain
Its evensong narcotic starting to level off
As police bricked up the building's entrance
No shelter no shelter no shelter, no mercy either
Was the lingering liturgical text not the subtext there was no subtext can't you read or sing
The church just across the street was brown, Byzantine, and quiet
Bitter oranges pilled the neoclassical grounds of the French Institute next door
Where locals took language classes and/or drugs
Thick garden walls covered with new and old lashings of graffiti, bird shit, and moss
The oily air smelled of herbs, citrus, exhaust, exhaustion, and authoritarianism
I might have already mentioned this
It smelled of violence—its logic renewed by the good families
Every generation for their greater, what, good and goods
For the greater, what, good, who really thought
The air was cool, it was still winter, the climate was still a disaster
During drinks later, as I recounted the morning, a guy said that they might be terrorists
Or diseased who knew didn't they brutalize their women
Stoning them etc., to death, he added, looking at me, smiling, anxious, back straight
I told him he was mixing up countries, those who stoned women were our allies
And rich, they didn't flee war on boats, they bombed instead
Don't you get tired of using women as excuses for your violence I said
Far away from my words even as I said this
He raised his eyebrows at me, only foreign feminist he knew
His very young wife sat quiet and bored beside him
Disassociating, as always, or so I always thought
Inside I felt familiar sorrow and outside I used familiar words
They darted around like birds, drinking in air rubbed with citrus and alcohol
We drank our drinks and some months later the pandemic it arrived
It arrived by air—in the bodies of the good sons and daughters
Of the good families who traveled goodly for education commerce government entertainment
It arrived by sea—in the bodies directing the good ships of goods
It arrived by word of mouth by wet pine by shipping container by yellow subtitle
By good it arrived (we had thought it might but still, good godly surprise)
Perhaps it arrived by me, for I had recently and often traveled
Anyway, I might note here that the new government quickly ceased
Their early morning ablutions of disappearances
Calling off their police as they might call off dogs, I thought, ungraciously
Stopped their nightly broadcasts of state violence and fake disease
For real disease it had arrived and so the state made a quick edit
From real violence upon the vulnerable to real concern for their citizens
Who were also vulnerable
Let that word stretch like gum across your tongue
Touching your mouth's dry desert ceiling, its wet valley, guilty only of flood, its vault
Of viral air, watch it stretch across the mouth of the deserted urban screen
Slowed down like a film, frame, frame, frame

The displaced families who had been disappeared on buses
To camps outside the city—they were now locked in too
By the new government who pointed to new disease, such their luck
It now existed, though not, as it were, in the camps, not yet
In the city center a strange quiet descended, birdcall became extra lucid
My apartment became extra lucid, rote litany of days of uneasy, inexpert stasis
We were locked in too but we knew it was different in every way
The moon it waxed and waned, very vulnerable and repetitive
Exposed in the dark denim of air like a photograph
Like families in street or field exposed to the elements
Spring storms brought Sahara from the south, some surface of copper grit
For the terrace, red as a mouth, while bodies brought pandemic from the north
Short films of uncirculated images because these were not
The bodies meant to signify disease, we all knew this
I have been dreaming in subtitles
I might have mentioned this
Months passed we stayed in you know all this
Now the city is slowly opening but not the camps
What body is stateless? Goes the rhetoric of my emails
Each given a frame like a mouth, glowing like a fever with a question
But it remains that this is a real query, a true letter
In my dreams I stand at a desk piled high with papers
Petitioning for life—May I walk, may I read, may I work, may I sleep
May I dream, may I fuck, may I feed, may I love, may I have a family, may I be—
First: yes, yes, then no, denying each and everything
In my dreams such petitions are badly timed to the mouths moving in scenes
I cannot follow, the narratives of sea or land or emotional passage absurd or brutal and unending
And so I descend and exit this dream as I would a pale building
I walk up the hill past the ancient immortal agaves to the smaller church
Careful to breathe no bodies, cross no shadows, eat no bitter fruit
My eyes search the air for birds for temples for sea for him for her for language for danger
For some accurate index of this life, inexpert, sage-strewn, and cloudless
For vines of jasmine, sweet and burning, and balconies and highways of toxic oleander
If the government has ended their daily filmed briefings
With the sympathetic state epidemiologist, his crooked tie and worn brow did
Capture our hearts, did capture something of our emptied minds
But the scenario will be recast and rewritten, the regime and its police
Will begin calling the media again, the newspaper editor recovered from the virus
Healthy and determined they will restart production
Of moving images of a state violence so familiar they look like reruns
For a local viewership pale from interiors and sickness and sometimes hunger
There are no subtitles there are no subtitles there are no subtitles
Though the line to the food pantry is lean and grey and long as a sentence
Narrating the city like the ancient overbuilt river does in voiceover
There are camps on the mainland and camps on the islands
Camps of the water (we call them boats) and camps of the terra
Vul—, say the word vulnerable with your mouth full of water
Write it in your poem in your press release delete the word care

Meanwhile your inbox is full again, like water not paper
The great exhibitions have been delayed by one to two years
'An acknowledgment that it is impossible to move forward'
My inbox is full of this, missives in the language of delay
I wonder if I should also acknowledge this
Among the various errors that have created my current status
Perhaps I should also send out a press release, parroting such pale and pressed language
To my one surviving parent, my estranged husband
To the purveyors of my complicated immigrant status
To my employers and editors in various countries and geopolitical directions
To my friends of various regions to whom I fling my love and my sorrows
'An acknowledgment that it is impossible to move forward'
And yet I do, as through a poem or its film
With their undeveloped languages, badly timed and moonstruck
As through a city that films its deportations of people attempting to stay alive
Then offers the images to their citizens in place of sustenance
The subtitles not quite accurate though they fit the frame
I asked my therapist yesterday if the state could have coaxed into being
The pandemic by their fake suggestion of disease
Among those families and lonely figures seeking refuge from violence
The masks and plastic gloves in which they handled their bodies
Pushing them onto buses and out of the cities for the cameras
Setting the stage for the ubiquity of such images many months later
Framed by a narrow, historical window she looks at me quietly
She is quite lovely I have often noted this
She says Quinn our minds are not that powerful
She says that this is more of my magical thinking
But I remain, as ever, doubtful
It has been written that one should name the location
Where one came to voice, to name that space of suffering and theorizing
I'd like to name the birdsong that came to voice
In place of my voice and many others
In the footnotes and endnotes and rooftops of this singular and plural period
In this era of images scented with bitter orange, petrol, inherited violence, and collapse
Both societal and ecological, for nature only exists
If you consider yourself outside of it
Elders tell us, blue words oiled by deep extractions and night-blooming jasmine
International cooperation and bodies of water marked for death and tourism
I felt the atmosphere turn, I felt the apartment turn, but it was only another season
An earthquake troubling the ancient seabed
The moon poured itself out
And slipped by
And so did I
In this fair city of airs and airs and airs and airs
Each to be found here and elsewhere

'Q' di Quadro
or
My Body, Her Refrain (It Comes Back)

After, or before (I'm not sure),
Tomaso Binga, ~~that is, My Dear Bianca~~

A form of writing not on its knees to meaning. On its knees, though, always: two syllables, resting there, their knee bones like stones cold against the cold floor of the sentence. Also made of stones. Monosyllabic. Single syllables. Planted in lines there. Which we'll harvest later. (Every autumn, each October, a kind of architecture, landscape, literary, art-historical, feminist or all and other.)

*

In my *Autoritratto*, made by another poet, an Italian in 1976, two years before I was born, I sit, naked, my back to you, my legs pulled underneath me, one foot out and arched. You can see this arch, the soft comma of my heel. My head is lowered; you can see the back of my neck, the back of my back, my ass. I am pale; my hair seems dark and short, a kind of brush. I do not look like myself. But this is me, my letter, my signifier, my title: *'Q' di Quadro* (1976). I am ink, photograph, and collage on cardboard. I am certain dimensions, not to be uttered, never to be measured. My author is another, as is so often the case. In this case: Tomaso Binga. My maker, my writer, my other. Still, though, I am my own letter. Whatever that means.

*

In a work from the following year, my author married herself: *Bianca Menna e Tomaso Binga oggi spose* (1977). Two small black-and-white photographs in some old-fashioned metal-and-mirrored frames hung next to each other. What a couple, everyone thought. By everyone, I mean me, and everyone else. The poet Bianca and her public persona, the artist and writer Tomaso. Bianca's first husband was the art critic Filiberto Menna; her second, herself. I came later. Not a child, not an alter ego, not a partner, not a reader—not strictly—not a supplicant or spectator. Something else.

*

The same year my author married herself she performed *Io sono una carta* at the Galleria d'Arte Moderna, in Bologna. *I am paper*. I am, it's true. As the writer Barbara Casavecchia writes, the performance by my author was held in 'a tableau vivant made of three wallpapered walls, decorated with illegible calligraphies'. Well, we shouldn't be able to read everything. 'The artist wore a camouflage dress made of the same wallpaper.' Invisible within her set of writing without meaning, my author read a poem. She performed it, that is, with her body. A mouth, and then all its limbs, tones, timbre, bangs, sunglasses.

*

Io sono una carta velina, my author recited. *Io sono una carta piegata*. I am a tissue paper. I am a folded paper. After my author read her poem, she took off her scribbled dress, hung it over a rocking chair, and left. After my author made my *Autoritratto*, my *Q di Quadro*, I'm not sure what she did. Studied her creation like some mother, bored and proud of her fecundity? No idea. She had so many children, an entire alphabet of. I, my *Q*, come somewhere in the middle. Some middle child, middle letter. Of all that language. A kind of reproduction. Or let's leave that metaphor behind. (Though Artaud writes: 'Images are born.') Before us, instead: a kind of writing.

*

I study two photographs of my author, in her underwear, performing *Io sono io, io sono me* (1977). I am I, I am me. Her notebook with her drawings of *I* and *M* exhibited in her arms. Not *Q*. Big seventies sunglasses on, her hair is blonde and short, her jean shirt unbuttoned and open. Torso pale, nipples dark. Writing without meaning scripted in even lines, like some harvest of nothing, lining the wall behind her. Wallpaper as a kind of book: open, extant, in cursive. It moves me. I read it. With a kind of understanding. Does her body get in the way? Yes, no. The wall-script, it's like Hanne Darboven, I think, except the anti-handwriting is more minute, not as tall and looping as the German's. Then, thinking of Darboven's shaved head: What kind of writing was that?

*

The woman's body as alphabet, the female body as some semaphore of language—it's a familiar pose, in terms of art history, I mean, but still, a thrill. Paulina Ołowska did it: the Eastern European woman's body, all red dress and pink cheeks and lithe limbs, so Polish, arching itself, elegantly, into all 26 Latin letters. An homage to the 1926 book *ABECEDA*, by Karel Teige, and the Czech avant-gardist's experimental 'moving alphabet'. Ołowska's performance turned into a series of postcards. Have I made that up? To be written on and sent. To a female friend. Maybe. Last year, a writer friend, male, wrote me from California, said he found out what my last name meant. Did I know? I didn't. *Latimer* comes from *Latiner*, he wrote, or those early Latin scribes, who wrote (for money and power) when most of the European population was illiterate. How perfect, my friend the writer wrote, then signed off. We haven't written since.

*

I was pleased—with the genealogy of my name, I mean. Esteemed in ancient cultures, scribes later became a kind of professional copyist, reproducing manuscripts, carefully repeating each letter, before the invention of the press. ('A copy can be understood as a memory', Walter Benjamin writes.) Refrains, yes, and also performances: ancient Jewish scribes had to say each word aloud while they were writing. *Q*. What shape does your mouth make? What sound. A recent academic essay called 'Girls Trained in Beautiful Writing' describes some scant evidence of female scribes during Roman antiquity. It opens with an epigraph from Teresa de Lauretis's *Technologies of Gender*, in which she notes that 'most of the available theories of reading, writing, sexuality, ideology, or any other cultural production are built on male narratives of gender'. Indeed. A marble relief from Rome, second century, shows a seated female scribe writing on a tablet. As she writes, or copies (some song in her head, repeating), a butcher is carved opposite her, carving up some meat at the table. A performance (of labor and gender and literate and illiterate attractions) that will repeat, like some refrain, throughout history.

*

I have never married myself but I have been married. I have never named an alter ego except in every name that signs every text I write: *Quinn Latimer*. Who is that. I picture her written by some limber Polish artist's body, in a sequence of poses, lucid and crimson of dress. I picture her pictured in two small, discrete Italian frames, tin, religious, wearing a white dress and wearing a dark suit. Her face smooth, her face lined. Hung on two nails pounded into the wall. The other husband, the critic, glowering from some corner. Why didn't he think of this. The holes will remain there, a set of eyes, when the pictures are packed up, later. I picture her, a series of lines, curving and straight, tapped out on a laptop, fast and fluent, glowing in the discrete glowfield of a dirty monitor. A text she'll send as an attachment. A name, forever attached to a body. Or if not to her body, to her language. Written, published, bound, printed. Then circulated and read, as bodies (and bodies of language) are.

*

In the passage from Deleuze and Guattari's chapter on the refrain, from *A Thousand Plateaus*, which I seem to quote in every text I write, it is noted: 'Time is not an a priori form.' No. 'Rather, the refrain is the a priori form of time.' Their image of a child singing some small song of protection in the dark to calm and orient himself, to delimit a territory, is of a, yes, male child. Why. Why male and why a child. Why not a woman and why not a text. Why the child's singsong rhyme, why lost as one grows up, why this need to hear the click at the end of each line, turning separate textual bodies, so lithe, into couplets, a kind of marriage? My line to my line, betrothed? Why this constant interest in copying, in coupling, in the refrain, in what recurs and rhymes in my mind, my mouth, my body, her body, her mouth, her mind, her letter, her sign. Her. The body repeats. The sign repeats. It makes a song I sing, she sings, someone sings.

*

Someone sings: an asterisk, a series of. From the late Latin *asteriscus*, and from the ancient Greek *asteriskos*, this 'little star' is a symbol that in computer science is often used as a 'wildcard character' to designate—what —repetition. What science is this?

*

Stone floors. I've always liked monosyllables. In my poems I have to pull them out, all those pale-dark words of single syllables that I employ and materialize on repeat: *Pale. Floor. Stone. Some. Dark. Mouth. Her. Mute. Song.* Beat, beat, beat. My mother named me *Quinn* for similar reasons. Some of them were: First, it was one syllable. It felt good in the mouth. Two, it was not gendered, neither strictly male nor female. Three, it was not exclusively first or last, this name. It just existed. There were other reasons. I forget them. My mother, like my author, Tomaso, named herself. Like me, my mother gifted herself only one syllable: *Blake*. Like the poet. But Bianca chose a new name with the same number of syllables as her old: three, exactly. To-ma-so. Bi-an-ca. Some singsong. Some refrain.

*

Tomaso: Why are women always writing their bodies down. Pronouncing them in syllables and articulating them in semaphores. Why are words like *radical* affixed to them, why *feminism*, why *experimental*, why *performance*, why *mouth* why *mute* why *speak* why *write* why *poetry* why *rhetoric*. Why the metaphor of mother, of author; of child, of text? To produce, to reproduce; to write, to rewrite. It is exhausting this body, looking down at it as I write. Women, those 'odd boundary creatures', as Donna Haraway writes. Like simians and cyborgs. The poem is a machine, the poets often write (these days). So the woman's poem is a machine at the border, her letter (its body), a boundary, constantly redrawn. Keeping her out. Another question (from this border): Why the need to *write down* the need to speak, the desire to make that speaking both of the page and of the body. The text between, I mean. Between the page and the performance, that is where we live. Lettered like hallucinations. And why is that so, To-ma-so?

*

'What is kinship, what is knowledge, what is margin, what is center? Whose voice issues from whose nonuniversal body? How to understand a language—lucid, ludic—that resists, that refuses the normative, the hegemonic, and all of its valences of violence, so as to articulate something counter? Resistance is a much-used word in these days of late capitalism, strongmen, and ecological collapse—what does it really mean, though?' A class I'm currently teaching, on languages of resistance. Visual, verbal, textual. I begin with some lines by Celan; I offer them to my students, a series of stones (on graves), their syllables: 'Only one thing remained reachable, close and secure amid all losses: language. Yes, language. In spite of everything, it remained secure against loss.' Did it, though? Does it?

*

Tomaso Binga, that is, that was, Bianca Menna, born 1931, in Salerno, Italy, currently of Rome, was Professor of Theory and Method of Mass Media at the Academy of Fine Arts in Frosinone. Like many of her Italian feminist peers working between visual poetry and performance, she taught. In postwar Italy, as in prewar Italy, education was one of the few fields where the women could, what, flourish. In postwar Italy, dazed from fascism, the 'need to rethink and reformulate education on more egalitarian bases', Barbara Casavecchia writes, 'generated radical pedagogical experiments'. In 1973, the director of the Montessori Center in Rome, Elena Gianini Belotti, wrote an essay titled 'Dalla parte delle bambini'. Her title has a beautiful rhythm in Italian: some singsong, a kind of refrain. Its more didactic English translation, a rhetorical bait-and-switch: 'What are Little Girls Made Of? The Roots of Feminine Stereotypes'. Yes, what are little girls made of? What are women? Language, 'naturally', but what else?

*

Roots. Some harvest. Typologies of the feminine. Reaching into the earth and then up to the sun. I am tired of questions, the way they structure my texts. The way I try to harvest meaning from them, but then often only find stones where the fruit should be. I am tired of female bodies, they way they lay down between my lines, becoming sentences. Or fragments. Or cyborgs. Some fruit. Worn, bruised. Stone fruit. Stone. Full—what—stop.

*

It is October, the month of poems. I once wrote a poem that began: 'In October, I was his / pharmaceutical, his red / his blue. / I went down so easily.' The mordant American poet Louise Glück—her last name meaning *happiness* or *fortune* in German—once wrote a poem titled, yes, *October*, that goes, in part: 'I remember how the earth felt, red and dense, / in stiff rows, weren't the seeds planted, / didn't vines climb the south wall / I can't hear your voice / for the wind's cries, whistling over the bare ground / I no longer care / what sound it makes / when was I silenced, when did it first seem / pointless to describe that sound / what it sounds like can't change what it is—'

*

A poem built of speed, of seasons, of rhetorical queries. An essay built of vignettes, of lines, of little stars, of studious bodies—of women and their others—and then, what, all the resulting languages. A letter built of letters embodied by another. Another what, woman writer, her body. Sensorial, seismic, all semaphore, on speakerphone. A performance—some life—built of this. All of it. Enunciated. What it sounds like can't change what it is, Tomaso. But still, we try.

still

forward

Ghislaine Leung

Tracklist / Complicity, Fetish, Agency

Tracklist

1. Opener:
when
2. civil rights have become consumer rights
and agency
(in this sense)
becomes self-objectification
which 3. necessitates an autonomy premised on self separation
in order to
internalise critique,
which turns inward—not immanent,
but in on ourselves,
because oppositional
politics
have become defined
by what they stand against
in fighting, inside ourselves.
4. Agnes / Nisha
and
5. transparency
has become a condonement,
or a complicity,
even if sped to burn,
but complicit none the less,
in a set of relations
where
6. what is politically non-identical
is made equivalent to a lack
and given no position or voice
and instead given violence,
by others and ourselves,
because it questions
prejudices,
classifications
and measures
of value,
of scale.

All very well.
All unsubstantiated.
7. And what to say.
All I can say is that
love is inefficient,
that agency is not a matter of control
or will, or measurement or productivity.
But a need for rights exists,

rights not premised
on assets, or credit ratings,
or documentation,
or provenance.

8. That there are politics at stake here
that do not collapse difference
that do not make likenesses
like, liking,
where moving
is not always forward,
where mobility
is not defined on
property.
Not always upward
to better truer things
but into your arms.

This is an open arms deal

9. where my need for you
is not a weakness
is not a strength
is lived
and dies

is dear to me
is invalid
has not been productive,
is celebrated.

10. It is the specific shape of your hand
on my face
my neck
the vibration of your voice
us living together
with and without
proximity
this holding in common
this love
our work.

11. Tracklist:

12. And this love

does not exclude,
does not temper,
did not include,
no bundle,
is reclusive,
its movement
always
closing
always
soft
open
shut.

Complicity, Fetish, Agency

There is a particular movement, or series of movements, that I always return to. It's like a refrain in music: dissonance, resolution and suspense. Notes played out in the oppositional relationship between the critical and the criticised. The dependence withdrawal has upon presence, intervention upon involvement, independence upon abnegation. The subsequent takedowns, revelations and exposures. It is *From A to B & Back Again.*[1] It's from institutional critique to the institution of critique and no returns.[2] This is not to say issues have been resolved, or reframed, or, in many cases, that they have even shifted; these critical and institutional labours seem more than ever needed.

In Hannah Arendt's 1968 essay 'Truth and Politics' she writes that, 'To be sure, as far as action is concerned, organised lying is a marginal phenomenon, but the trouble is that its opposite, the mere telling of facts, leads to no action whatever; it even tends, under normal circumstances, toward the acceptance of things as they are.'[3] Today it seems that organised lying is likely no longer a marginal phenomenon. The lie is effective, it is more appealing, more candid and more exciting. Arendt warned of the political efficacy of lying, as well as its capacity for social change, 'He (the Liar) is an actor by nature; he says what is not so because he wants things to be different from what they are—that is, he wants to change the world.'[4] As she followed in her 1969 essay 'Lying in Politics', 'Such change would be impossible if we could not mentally remove ourselves from where we physically are located and *imagine* that things might as well be different from what they actually are. In other words, the deliberate denial of factual truth—the ability to lie —and the capacity to change facts—the ability to act—are interconnected; they owe their existence to the same source: imagination.'[5] Action, in this sense, is less bound to truth-telling than to the imaging of difference. Agency—our ability to act this difference—is complicit, it encompasses both denial and fabrication.

In working within institutions, critical practices and artworks can often, beyond even simple involvement or advocacy, also be part of a process of revalidation, making the institution appear capable of self-critique. The inverse side of this is that these critical practices and artworks appear, by being placed within the institution, self-instituting. And perhaps I should be clear at this stage that I do not only mean to refer here to the relation between artwork and art institution, though certainly this is my example, but also the general way in which positions of resistance often define themselves in and against the dominant forms they seek to criticise. The master's house, the master's tools.[6] In saying this I do not mean to say critique must happen externally. Distance might not be possible to attain, and even if achieved, its broader visibility may still necessitate involvement. Neither is this a dismissal of these forms of resistance, which are much needed and highly effective. The problem is not a lack of externality or a surfeit of internality, it is that these definitions often obscure their interdependence in order to gain a certain efficacy, a certain ability to act. What might be important is not a conflation of 'us' and 'them', but that we often hold both positions. This is our complicity. To deny complicity apropos of a clean autonomy might seem to be effective, but it is this very efficacy that can end up being the most efficiently instrumentalised.[7] Not only is there no neutral ground to speak of, we are not neutral, and if we do not use our energy, then someone else will.[8]

Something else must be done. We are always asking how we should resist, what the forms are by which we can resist. We hold great stock in these forms of resistance, whether they are found in a person, a group, a medium or an object, that this will be the thing that allows for critique. We have come to expect that an institution can be criticised through its apparatus, its barriers, frames, display boards and fittings. This is the syntax of the gallery, and foregrounding such things is to some extent rooted in structural and materialist practices, in displacing narrative to reveal construct. Removing a wall to a gallery, exposing the contract of a work's sale, exhibiting the crate used to ship a work—these all work or have worked at certain times. This does not mean that their efficacy can be used to presume transparency is somehow equivalent to critique. If context is half the work, this should not in any way preclude the organisation, the service, the infrastructure—more to the point, our service, our infrastructure.[9] The assumption that certain objects or ideas are prejudged to be critical per se is based on this subsumption of material conditions into objects of provenance. Institutional critique is complicit with the institution not simply because it is inside, or because there is no longer an outside, but more specifically through fetishising the apparatus of power and verification.

What I would like to suggest is that it is this complicity with fetishism that might be important. It is in commodity fetishism that 'the social character of labour appears to us to be an objective character of the products themselves'.[10] To remove the art object and to reveal the physical components of the institution are both, in some way, commensurate with that logic. As Josef Strau wrote in 2006 of a certain non-productive attitude, 'It was maybe a kind of transformed fetishism attitude to live the social life of an artist without actually producing any art, or at least without presenting any art.' A possible by-product of such a non-productive attitude, alongside the critical refusal of certain high production values in objects, is this self-objectifying artist-subject, where product is displaced into practice; work substituted for narrative, expression for organisation.[11] After all, both services and goods are commodities and open to the same fetishisation. At whichever point we use our energies to push fetish away it seems to reappear behind us to push us over, for it is, in fact, already us. It is not the avoidance of fetish that is important, but our complicity to it, that we are both definers of objects and defined by objects. That we objectify, not only things, but each other and ourselves, as both acting subjects and subject to these actions. Complicity is not a position one needs to get to, it is the position we are already in—there is nothing to get, build on or develop; it doesn't have to be mobilised or made manifest; it is the current and messy state of affairs. Complicity is what it is to act together, it is the nature of being in relationships. To individualistically undermine or ignore these relations would in fact be to ignore ourselves, to take no responsibility for our part in relations and in so doing perhaps to undermine our own agency or ability to resist at all.

Complicity speaks of a we, not an I.[12] This is not a question of oppositions that shape and fix the terms of engagement, nor strict delineations that allow effective measures of failure or success. Violence is not always clear; systemic and structural violence is also soft and insidious. We cannot leave complicity languishing in self-reflexive tautology while we revel in our own ingenuity that we have been so clever as to see that we have tricked ourselves. Nor can we leave it isolated in some conceit that we have escaped through some kind of infinite withdrawal strategy and in so doing relinquish the position by which we can speak at all. To do so would be to miss the fine print on appearance: fetishism is neither lie nor truth, it is 'magic and necromancy', it is where relations between objects appear to take on relations between subjects and vice versa.[13] Critique, in seeing that it too may be an institution, must begin to construe complicity not as a hindrance but as a porous ground for agency, via both institutional critiques and institutions of critique. Every single artist I love who has withdrawn or countered or disappeared has done so publicly, and has laboured hard to maintain their specific mode of non-productivity. It is understanding that work does not only lie in the artwork itself, but in the bodily labour of practice. Key to the agency of complicity is this position: that we are accomplices, companions, witting partners. This is not about effecting change via denial but imaging our actions differently; self-instituting does not mean self-policing. Critique is not criticism, it is, in the most material sense, love's work.[14]

Notes on 'Tracklist'

Text excerpt from Ghislaine Leung, *Soft Open Shut*, commissioned for Sharon Hayes, *In My Little Corner of the World, Anyone Would Love You*, Studio Voltaire, London, 2016.

Notes on 'Complicity, Fetish, Agency'

Talk commissioned for Mind Games, The Thought Menu, Lima Zulu, London, 2012, and edited London, 2018. Note on requests: I am bad at saying no. So bad that for years I advocated the Forbes 'Guide to Saying No' as a means of support. I used to have a 'Say No' alarm on my phone that went off every morning to remind me. I always accommodated requests, although I generally resented being asked. I remember complaining to CB about this, expecting to illicit some form of sympathy or at least indulge in a conspiratorial gripe session, and was surprised to be told that the situation was of my own making—that if I really felt so strongly about it I could refuse to accommodate these requests. This pushback was not comfortable, it made me complicit in what I had so readily identified as a wrong, but in doing so it also gave me back some agency to right that, or at least reconstitute those grounds. This text came out of that exchange. Quoted references from:

1 Andy Warhol, *From A to B and Back Again: The Philosophy of Andy Warhol* (London: Picador Books, 1986).
2 Andrea Fraser, 'From the Critique of Institutions to an Institution of Critique', *Artforum*, 44/1 (September 2005), available at www.monoskop.org/images/b/b6/Fraser_Andrea_2005_From_the_Critique_of_Institutions_to_an_Institution_of_Critique.pdf. Also, Hito Steyerl, 'The Institution of Critique', *European Institute for Progressive Cultural Policies*, 1 (2006), www.eipcp.net/transversal/0106/steyerl/en.
3 Hannah Arendt, 'Truth and Politics', in *Between Past and Future: Eight Exercises in Political Thought* (London: Penguin, 2006), p.246.
4 Ibid.
5 Hannah Arendt, 'Lying in Politics: Reflections on The Pentagon Papers', in *Crises of the Republic* (San Diego/New York/London: Harcourt Brace & Co., 1972), p.5.
6 Audre Lorde, 'The Master's Tools Will Never Dismantle the Master's House', in *Sister Outsider: Essays and Speeches* (Berkeley, CA: Crossing Press, 1984), p.110.
7 Marcel Broodthaers, '1972, Düsseldorf, the "Musée d'Art Moderne, département des Aigles", the figure section', in *Marcel Broodthaers*, video, 14 min 7 secs, broadcast 6 January 1992, Fr3, Belgium, www.ina.fr/fresques/europe-des-cultures-en/fiche-media/Europe00191/marcel-broodthaers.html. 'I think that the result that is achieved is an interrogation on art through the artistic object that is the eagle. That is obvious. Eagle and art are mistaken for one another ... What I mean is, to separate what is art within an object, for example, here, what is art and what is ideological. Right? I want to show the ideology as it is and to, in fact, prevent art from making this ideology unapparent, and therefore efficient.'
8 Audre Lorde, *Audre Lorde Live at UCLA circa early 1990s*, www.youtube.com/watch?v=OUXjoBVQkpw, uploaded 29 June 2015.
9 Artist Placement Group, Zentrum für Kulturforschung, Bonn, 1980. This text included APG's statement that 'That context is half the work' as previously premised in 1971 at *Between 6* at Kunsthalle Düsseldorf and the exhibition *Art and Economics* at the Hayward Gallery, London, in the same year.
10 Karl Marx, 'The Fetishism of Commodities and the Secret Thereof', in *Capital: A Critique of Political Economy*, volume I, book one: *The Process of Production of Capital* (1887; first published in German 1867), available at www.marxists.org/archive/marx/works/1867-c1/ch01.htm#S4.
11 Josef Strau, 'The Non-Productive Attitude', in *Make your Own Life: Artists In and Out of Cologne*, Institute of Contemporary Art, Pennsylvania, University of Pennsylvania, 2006, available at https://s3.amazonaws.com/arena-attachments/75010/Non-productive_Attitude_-_Strau.pdf.
12 *WE (Not I)* was organised by Melissa Gordon and Marina Vishmidt and took place with a group of participants, including myself, in April 2015 in London, at South London Gallery, Flat Time House and Raven Row, and subsequently at Artists Space in New York in September 2015.
13 Marx, 'The Fetishism of Commodities'.
14 Gillian Rose, *Love's Work: A Reckoning with Life* (London: Chatto & Windus, 1995).

take stock

carry on

Jordan Lord

Value Subtracted: A Poetics of Access and Interference

For the last five years, I have been making a film about my family's debts.[1]

Before my dad was fired from his job, he worked as a debt collector. Now, my family is in a tremendous amount of debt—much of which is mine.

My dad calls his former line of work 'risk management'.

Ever since he told me this, I've been thinking about what kinds of risks documentary filmmakers are asked to manage, which risks people in documentary films are asked to bear, and what it would mean to not differentiate these risks but rather share them.

In order to have the legal right to show and sell a documentary film, it is standard practice for documentarians to ask the people recorded on film to give up their rights to object to however the filmmaker decides to use these recordings, by designating this material the filmmaker's property. The contracts that simultaneously mediate this transfer of rights and creation of property are called 'access agreements'.

*

At the opening of their essay 'The Guild of the Brave Poor Things', Park McArthur and Constantina Zavitsanos[2] ask, 'What about a door is a trap when it's known, or known to be unknown?'[3] Maybe going in this way is a trap, but for me this question is a door that opens on to a whole host of other questions about what we mean by access or getting in: In what ways does it matter? Who is it for? What does it do? What is known or known to be unknown here?

*

What I can say about my own access (a term I use here with hesitation, thinking of how closely this resembles the ways that documentary filmmakers conflate access and permission) to the artworks I am writing about in this essay is that my access is partial.[4] It has not emerged at once or in one place or time and maybe has not yet arrived. But the way I have been let into these artworks and ideas has been through years of friendship with, and love for, each of the people I'm writing about. I've often loved them through the work that each of them makes, and through each other—through their entanglements with one another and the way their work moves through those friendships; intertwines; is in conversation.

I am telling you this not just to help you understand from what context my thinking about these people, artworks, and ideas is emerging. It is also to say that there is an inextricable seam here between what access lets in and

1 In terms that are financial and social, accounted for and uncountable, as that which binds us. See Fred Moten and Stefano Harney's *The Undercommons: Fugitive Planning and Black Study* (2013), available at www.minorcompositions.info.

2 Throughout this essay, after introducing authors or artists with whom I am friends using their full names, I refer to them on a first-name basis. Like most of our friends, I call Constantina Zavitsanos 'Tina'.

3 Park McArthur and Constantina Zavitsanos, 'The Guild of the Brave Poor Things', in *Trap Door: Trans Cultural Production and the Politics of Visibility*, ed. Tourmaline, Eric A. Stanley and Johanna Burton (Cambridge, MA, 2017), p.236.

4 As in both 'incomplete' and 'showing preference or favoritism'. On this see Amalle Dublon, 'Partial Figures: Sound in Queer and Feminist Thought', dissertation, Duke University (2017), www.dukespace.lib.duke.edu/dspace/handle/10161/16226.

the support systems, ideas, and material conditions we (I) depend on. Just to make this even clearer: I have literally depended on all of these people for housing or food or transportation at some point, or for giving me life at others.

In some very real sense (especially because this essay has ballooned into something much longer than most people will want to read), you could stop here when I say that access is fundamentally about dependency, which is to say, fundamentally about debt.

These words are not just stigmatized. They also carry the weight of bind and restriction; taking advantage, abuse, toxicity, exploitation; holding together, instability, support. Access carries these weights, too, even as (and perhaps because) it is a notion framed largely as an aspiration and a benefit; even as it is everything I, and hopefully we, are working to share.

Limits are constantly being set on access. Total access is not only not possible because of the ways in which one form of access interferes with another. Total access[5] cannot be separated from the violent illusion that is property and the theft of life that first made property possible.[6]

5 'Total access' here refers to what Stefano Harney describes in an interview as 'the sociopathic demand for access: topographical, jurisdictional, but as importantly bodily and social access. The nearly complete access that was imposed upon the African enslaved, upon the African continent, and upon the lands and indigenous peoples settled for plantations.' I am engaging Harney's point here about the imposition of 'nearly complete access' as a weapon of enslavement and colonization because there is an entangled thread that runs between racial violence and ableism. When we are talking about access in terms of disability, we are living in the wake and afterlife of settler colonialism and chattel slavery, and the very invention of race runs parallel to and undergirds the invention of disability. In Harney's quote, I am struck not only by his phrasing of this demand for access in terms of sociopathy—a mental illness that is frequently used as both an index of the *in*human and a self-evident case of a type of person who should be locked up—but also because sociopathy is usually figured as the inverse of empathy. In an interview in Arthur Jafa's film *Dreams Are Colder than Death* (2014), Hortense Spillers describes a similarly violent relation of total access as being *in the flesh*. 'We were available in the flesh to slave masters ... in the flesh ... immediate, hands-on ... [...] Bang! Don't care nothin' about your mom and daddy, how many babies you get here. Bang! Bang! That's flesh.' This echoes the process of being torn, 'ungendered', multiple, nearly without kin, following a broken genealogy, described in Spillers's essay 'Mama's Baby, Papa's Maybe: An American Grammar Book' (1987). In Jafa's film, Spillers goes on to describe this dynamic: 'Another word to explain it is empathy. The flesh gives empathy.' Following Spillers, it seems that we can take literally the sociopathic dimension of what Harney describes in the demand for total access as the incapacity to feel with others. Meanwhile, this demand and this imposition of total access spread contagiously from the violent imposition of severalty and property via colonization and enslavement to institutionalization and mass incarceration of Black, Brown, Indigenous, and disabled people, in particular those with mental illnesses. These carceral techniques remain a means of maintaining the illusion of what access to property claims to entail and entitle: freedom. The door that begins Park and Tina's essay 'The Guild of the Brave Poor Things' is a photograph by Sid Barker of cells in Friern psychiatric hospital in Middlesex, England (formerly Colney Hatch Lunatic Asylum, whose name, according to Wikipedia, has been used interchangeably with any psychiatric hospital among Londoners). Park and Tina describe the image as 'documenting two, small empty rooms that share a single wall. The rooms mirror each other. Each has a small window high on the back wall. It looks as if these windows have bars over them.' These two open doors speak in tandem with Spillers's definition of flesh as empathy, of Harney's definition of total access as sociopathy, in adjacent lines by Park and Tina: 'We, very unreasonably, will be held. We are one another's means without ends. We, very unreasonably, have been held. Because care and abuse so often share a space so close and yet so different we can't say there's a distinct line between them' ('The Guild', p.238).

Here in the wake of this ongoing nightmare, most of the limits we experience along the axis that draws together disability, access, art, documentary filmmaking, and institutions mean something more like individuation or segregation or risk management.

Even just saying this I am in debt to those who have already said and helped me say it: Tina, Park, Carolyn, Cameron, Amalle, Jason, my mom, my dad, my sister, a long etcetera.

*

Thinking about the word 'access', I imagine standing before an infrastructure, wondering what it will take to get inside. Perhaps the way in is obvious—a door that's already open or a handle that needs to be turned. Maybe you have to wait for permission to get in. Maybe the door is locked shut, or there's no apparent means of reaching it, or the door is yet to be made.

In documentary filmmaking, 'access' describes both the means by which an audience can experience a film and the means by which the filmmaker is legally authorized to distribute it. This first sense of access is frequently paired with the word 'accommodation' to refer to audio description (which makes visual material accessible to Blind audiences, among others) and captioning (which makes auditory material accessible to Deaf audiences, among others). The second sense, the access agreement, not only secures the filmmaker's or their investors' property interest in the film; it also determines who bears the risk for the film once permission has been granted.

Much of my interest in thinking about these instances of access together is that the delegation of risk in the access agreement echoes the segregation of audiences through the notion of access as accommodation. The conventional access agreement is used to absolve the filmmaker of legal responsibility if appearing in the film does harm to the person recorded, deferring the risk from filmmakers to the people they film. This agreement is not intended to prevent harm but rather to prevent redress if harm is inflicted.

Likewise, framing access as an accommodation extends a performative generosity that is conditional on a disabled person being grateful for being included in a structure that is constituted by their segregation from it. These so-called accommodations are doled out such that they foresee and prevent redress of this segregation,[7] meanwhile preserving it. As Tina reads aloud from a manifesto onscreen in Carolyn Lazard's video *A Recipe for Disaster* (2018), 'Not an accommodation where we have to be grateful for getting to join the party. Well your party sucks.'

This party that separates the party into individual parties is the shared ground of both misappropriations of access and that which they occlude or disavow. In the instance of the access agreement, what is being argued

6 Following Harney, Spillers, Park and Tina, I here want to underline that the history of taking and using images of another person's life as a form of so-called access cannot be separated from the colonial project of anthropology. This history's afterlife has everything to do with the ways in which contracts called 'access agreements' entitle images of another person's life to the documentarian as their private property, granting them total access to use something that previously belonged to no one or was, at the very least, shared.

7 Redress might come about legally through a lawsuit calling upon violations of disability rights law such as the Americans with Disabilities Act in the United States, or interpersonally by being called to account for ableism.

is that risk can be separated at the very moment that it becomes shared —the moment of making a film together. Likewise, in the instance of access accommodations, disabled audiences are separated out as the ones whose needs are being met, even as all audiences require certain means by which they can experience a film.[8] It is, in fact, the failure to recognize this shared condition of need that leads to disabled audiences receiving a separate but supposedly equal version of the film, not to be experienced in the same time, place, or form as the nondisabled audience. This renders accommodation of disabled people's needs peripheral to the film—or, in practice, optional.

For a filmmaker to not consider how audiences with different access needs will experience their film, or to outsource that labor to a third party who is not included in the process of production, means choosing not to direct their film for those audiences. But that does not mean disabled people are not in the audience. As writers and artists like Georgina Kleege and Christine Sun Kim have shown, Blind and Deaf audiences are, of course, experiencing films all the time and reading them through and in spite of the reality that most filmmakers do not conceive them as part of the audience. Regardless of whether a film is 'accessible' or not, how a disabled audience experiences a film is part of what it is; their means of access merely changes the terms of how these audiences are addressed, as part of, separate, or excluded from nondisabled audiences.

Despite appearances, both the access agreement and the notion of access as accommodation use the cover of access to deny its proliferation. Each fails to recognize—while nevertheless demonstrating—what the work of access is: how we come together.

*

As I mention in my film *After... After... (Access)* (2018), contemporary notions of access as a means of inclusion or an index of exclusion from an infrastructure—whether social, economic, physical, medical, or educational, or that of a body, mind, idea, language, or work of art—seem, at first, surprisingly different from how 'access' was originally used in the English language.

The meaning of 'access' as opportunity, permission or right to enter actually came after it was first used to describe an attack of fever. The word came from a Middle French term for the onslaught, attack, or onset of an illness, derived from the Latin *accessus*, which was used to refer to a means of entrance as well as an attack, blowing wind, or hostile approach.[9]

This sense that access somehow involves contagion, risk, and security prefigures and draws out an obscured dimension of how access is now enacted in the United States. Many infrastructures—from schools and hospitals to films and artworks—continue to mediate access through a logic that both obfuscates and equates the promise and threat of seeking entrance to a structure, invading it, or exposing it to contagion.

This application of access comes up in cases of seemingly opposing ideological and infrastructural positions. In the early months of the Covid-19 pandemic it was there in those who sincerely or opportunistically centered

8 This same logic can be extended to any instance of access, I would argue.
9 www.etymonline.com/word/access.

the access needs of those in 'high-risk' groups to extol the benefits of doing work, events, schooling, sex and social life remotely as a means of preserving public health. Meanwhile, the colonizing, class-stratifying project of technosolutionism shored up pre-existing infrastructures and sutured the disruption of white-collar work through the expanded access offered by videoconferencing and other virtual means. In the microcosm of the nonprofit organization or arthouse cinema, conducting events online has become a means of salvaging and extracting value from access that disabled people have been asking for or using for decades, in order to allow the continuity of panel discussions, lectures, and film screenings for their nondisabled audiences and employees.[10]

On the other hand, the importance of access has equally been there in those who made arguments that life must happen through 'in-person activity', including the vast majority of people who have not had the choice or means to work from home during the pandemic; those concerned about the effects of constant digital communication and physical distance on people's mental or physical health (causing suicide, migraines, chronic pain, depression, anxiety); as well as those using ableist metaphors of preserving the health of a 'depressed' or 'disabled' economy.[11]

In both cases, access frames an infrastructural opening to a form of virality that threatens and promises to remake, but nevertheless preserves, the infrastructure and the terms of entry to it.[12] In both instances, access is no longer simply framed as a breach or opening in the infrastructure but is, rather, deployed as an opportunity to expand, strengthen, or repair it. Angela Mitropoulos calls this the 'inoculation' that insurance, contracts, and other legal-financial apparatuses of risk management use to spread risk so as to manage and distribute the so-called health of the 'body politic'.[13]

10 With travel costs reduced and fewer events, the nonprofit organization I work for is only now willing to make access accommodations such as live captioning and American Sign Language interpretation mandatory for public Zoom events, while writing these accommodations into emergency grant applications.

11 Of course, many disabled people have been navigating this tension since the onset of their disabilities and are very familiar with the trade-offs between digital connection and the pains it causes, and the very real risks and pains of an inaccessible world outside, with which the former is sometimes a means to cope.

12 Each instance of access in institutional frameworks cannot be separated from the logics of contract and contagion that have laid the foundation for capitalist economies—where contingency, disaster, and disruption are used to disburse risk to the unfortunate, while producing fortunes for those who have insured against this risk—by betting on these contingencies and setting the terms of their destruction through contracts of limited liability. For more on this operation, see Angela Mitropoulos, *Contract and Contagion: From Biopolitics to Oikonomia* (2012), available at www.minorcompositions.info.

13 Mitropoulos writes in *Contract and Contagion*, 'Insurance is the dream of inoculation, the spreading of risk that constantly reconfigures the boundaries between capitalist speculation and the incertitude of value, between free labour and slavery, between those who are inoculated and those who test out the vaccine, between the contractual projection of calculable value and the uninsurable risk and, not least, between life and death' (p.77). She clarifies this at the end of the same chapter: 'I would suggest that the ostensible prudentialism of insurance, then, as with vaccination, creates dangers f or some. In current terms, it assumes the creation of classes of persons who are increasingly compelled to contractually assume (by way of the doctrine of *volenti non fit injuria* of informed consent) the burden of uninsurable risk. The actuarial requires uninsurable risk as its precondition.' For more on the violence of informed consent, see Carolyn Lazard's *Pre-Existing Condition* (2019).

This is the primary mode that I think defines access as it is most commonly applied today: the diverse host of moves that infrastructures make to incorporate access, conditionally letting in people and things as a means of fortification (perhaps the image that most comes to mind is one of a battlement—an opening in a fort, perfectly sized for a weapon). Here, their project of accessibility becomes a means of anticipating and resisting what access actually promises to do: expose an infrastructure to whatever is outside it, such that there might no longer be a way to separate in from out.

As part of this framing of access as contagion, people asking for relatively straightforward forms of access—ones they should be able to expect in a world post the passing of the Americans with Disabilities Act 1990—are routinely denied it through outright violence and segregation. This is clearly visible in the ways that, in spite of how everyone's access needs (to food, shelter, recreation, healthcare, work, mail, kinship) have been refigured in terms of our ability to live both collectively and individually during the pandemic, those living in 'high-risk' groups are still considered exceptional to the maintenance and preservation of public health. People who perform so-called 'essential work'; who live in close quarters, in prisons, or in neighborhoods with a high density of essential workers; and/or who are disabled[14] (many of whom depend on the labor of essential workers), have been labelled at high risk of death or serious illness from Covid-19. This is ostensibly a form of categorization describing the need for exceptional forms of prevention. Nevertheless, people assigned this category have, of course, been the ones most likely to die from the spread of the virus, particularly as it spreads among so-called 'low-risk' groups. If anything, it appears that the assignation of risk is less a form of protection than a means of predicting and, in worst faith, distributing mortality.[15] This state of things, while devastating, has not been particularly difficult to enact because in many ways this is a return to a pre-pandemic status quo, in which infrastructures already made access to 'low-risk' forms of life only at the expense

14 As countless statistics have definitively shown, Black, Brown, Indigenous, disabled, elderly, and poor people have borne the brunt of the virus. The determinative risk factors I describe above are to underline some of the vectors of capitalism that have produced race, class, and disability as predictive risk factors for Covid-19. These conditions no doubt emerge from the persistence of whiteness as a vested property interest (providing white people with disproportionate access to space, white-collar jobs, and money, with decisive consequences in terms of viral exposure) and, alongside it, the proliferation of white supremacy and environmental racism, the traumas and toxicities of which are both immediately and generationally disabling. These combined forces have continued to erect obstacles to Black, Brown, and Indigenous people accumulating property or wealth, while propertizing many of those same people through systems of mass incarceration and subjecting them to environmentally hazardous conditions throughout the United States and around the world. The other largest determining factor of risk of death or serious illness from Covid-19 is, of course, age. Although age is frequently (and, I would say, consciously) decoupled from disability as a risk factor unto itself, disability and illness so frequently accompany age as underlying comorbidities as to go unsaid. The lack of recognition of these entanglements perpetuates deadly myths (like the belief some young people have held, before getting sick themselves, that only old people die from the virus) and covers over the intersections of racism, classism, and ableism (that work in tandem with ageism) that treat Black, Brown, Indigenous, poor, incarcerated, disabled, and elderly people as disposable.

15 These categories appear even more perplexing in light of the fact that the virus continues to lead to both death and disablement of so-called 'low-risk' individuals.

of those 'high-risk' groups—as if risk naturally follows certain forms of life rather than being deferred onto them.

One of the ways in which the durability of ableism-racism-classism-transmisogyny-transphobia-homophobia-xenophobia is ensured in our world is via this perception of access as an invasion of infrastructures built to resist certain kinds of people and modes of interacting that threaten the value system of that infrastructure (conceived as a drain on resources, too complicated, a moral hazard, a blight on an aesthetic ideal, etc.). In this moment (as often before), the elaboration of access for everyone is subtly—and not so subtly—framed as an incursion on and curtailment of 'getting on with life'.

I want to attempt to think with this notion rather than against it. If access is something that does fundamentally change us when it gets into our bodies, minds, and relationships, that does actually interfere with getting on with life or going back to normal, maybe it's not inaccurate to think about it as a fever, contagion, or invasion. To make strategic gains toward access, people often frame it as minimally invasive, easy to do, having standards and guidelines, and protected under law. But what if we were to think of it as something that overwhelms systems, comes about through our exposure to others, in excess of what the law can govern, attacking infrastructures with unpredictable but nevertheless material consequences? In asking what it means to do access in this moment, the ground of the question is not to stop at examining how the guise of accessibility is used to rehabilitate pre-pandemic forms of life. It is rather to ask how we are called to acknowledge that these infrastructures that segregate people into those who do and don't need to have their access needs met has only exacerbated our common conditions of exposure, while covering over that commonness. What I am trying to say is that, in spite of best practices, under that cover, access spreads a commons.

Once we acknowledge that there are needs here, need spreads contagiously. I want to think about this in terms of how access comes about, its conditions of possibility.

*

The first thing that every nondisabled audience to whom I've ever shown Carolyn's *A Recipe for Disaster* has mentioned is that they felt confused or overwhelmed watching it; that they didn't know where to look or listen, how to direct or focus their attention.

The video consists of an entire episode of Julia Child's *The French Chef* in which she teaches the audience to make an omelette as the ideal recipe in the event of 'a last-minute dinner party for three hundred people'. Before Child speaks, Carolyn describes the first image of the video: 'a hand pours eggs into a hot pan'. The rest of the video moves between Carolyn's audio description of the images, Child's cooking show, open captions of what Child instructs, and a manifesto text that scrolls over the screen and is read aloud as a voiceover by Tina that eclipses both the audio and the image of Child's show.

In reframing this moment of television through the lens of access, Carolyn points toward the fact that this episode of *The French Chef* was the first television broadcast in the United States to use captions for Deaf audiences.[16] The captions that appeared onscreen were open captions, broadcast as an inseparable component of the image, not an overlay that could be turned on or off. Anyone who tuned into that broadcast would have seen the episode with captions on, something that many hearing audience members complained about. In reproducing this historical moment, Carolyn imagines an alternative trajectory for access and media—one where access features such as captioning and audio description were not perceived as external to the production of media and audience. Here, Blind, sighted, Deaf, and hearing audiences each navigate a desegregated space where their access needs are met and, at times, interfered with.

Carolyn's video works explicitly with this interference that access impels.[17] Captioning and audio description, both in the ways that they actually function and the ways in which they are perceived through an ableist lens, add a layer of sensory information by obstructing another. But here, what is obstructed—the assumption that a hearing and sighted audience is the default, primary audience—is also what was preventing a desegregated audience from emerging.

Even as they add new information and forms of interpretation, captions—particularly in the case of *A Recipe for Disaster*—cover over part of the image. This is presumably why captions are conventionally shown in the lower third of the screen, a framing that Christine Sun Kim underlines in her video installation *Close Readings* (2015). In this piece, she blurs out the top two-thirds of the image, where captions conventionally do not appear (unless there is already text on the bottom third of the screen). As Kim's work shows, a whole host of assumptions are made about the relative importance of what happens in the lower third and who is intended to perceive it, based on how the frame directs visual perception. The caption's placement there not only covers up part of the image but also reframes this act of framing. For instance, in a close-up, a mouth might appear in the lower third of the screen, which is covered by captions, even as it conveys significant

16 This episode was one of eight episodes of *The French Chef* aired in 1972 with open captions. See M. Merchant, K. M. Ellis and N. Latter, 'Captions and the Cooking Show', *M/C Journal*, 20/3, www.doi.org/10.5204/mcj.1260.

17 My understanding of this concept began in thinking about both *A Recipe for Disaster* and Tina's video *All the Time* (discussed later in this essay) and ongoing conversations with Amalle Dublon, whose life, scholarship, and art is also entangled with the lives, thinking, and art of the artists discussed here. As Amalle writes in a 2018 conversation with Park and Tina, 'Access is sometimes regarded as this kind of ungainly addition to the work meant to make up for a perceptual "deficit." It may be a translation, as in a displacement, but it's also an addition, which makes the form bulkier, and then that bulkiness violates the imagined elegance and completeness of the artwork's form or concept. Access is often bemoaned as burdensome standardization, but it's actually always improvisatory. Because improvisation is also this operation of taking a "given" artwork or pattern and elaborating it, and access is a similar distension, bulking up, or swelling of the artwork. It is necessarily choral.' This concept was then further elaborated through teaching a class on this idea of 'access and interference' and discussing it with the students involved—Sophia Canfield, Fahim Hamid, Nahee Kim, Chloe Lee, Katie Matthews, Carlos Morales, Cori Olinghouse, Deepak Rauniyar, Jess Shane, and Megan Stahl—and the visiting artists who also attended: Carolyn, Tina, Park, and Cameron. See Amalle Dublon and Constantina Zavitsanos, 'Dependency and Improvisation: A Conversation with Park McArthur', *Art Papers* (Winter 2018–19), www.artpapers.org/dependency-and-improvisation.

non-verbal information through the lips. Reframed by the blurred top two-thirds in Kim's installation, an image from the animated film *The Little Mermaid* depicts Ariel's facial expression via her mouth, drawn as a slanted, slightly curved line that, to me, suggests simultaneously confusion, frustration, and release. The original caption used in the Disney film shows a mutual exchange of expression by two different characters: '—[sighs]—[sighs]'.

For her installation, Kim invited four Deaf friends to write their own captions for various films. Here, the access that the captions provide is transmitted through a lens of interference. While captions generally transmit auditory information through written language, these captions extrapolate information about the sound from the visual field. Overlaid onto each transmission is a sense of how different Deaf audience members extract their own meanings about what the sound in these films convey, in spite of the often insufficient information provided by captions, which usually describe sounds in sparse, non-descriptive terms.[18] In the scene from *The Little Mermaid* where the above caption appears, Ariel's narrative predicament is presented to audiences as her inability to vocalize after having her voice stolen by the sea-witch Ursula. But in the same image, the Deaf captioner perceives '(the sound of a problem that's not a problem)'.

Audio description likewise interferes with the form of a film's soundtrack and is usually timed to fit in either where there is no spoken language or where it is deemed appropriate to eclipse the background audio.[19] In *A Recipe for Disaster*, on the other hand, there are frequently moments where Carolyn's audio description overlaps with the original audio of the video, or where Tina's voiceover speaks over a long passage of Child speaking. And there are even moments where Carolyn's description overlaps both Tina's voiceover and Child's monologue. Carolyn uses audio description and voiceover against their ordinary functions to direct and guide the audience's attention. By allowing these layers of audio to blur with the ones that surround it, audiences—particularly those that are both sighted and hearing —are left to do their own work of blocking out a layer of information so as to gain access to another. This demonstration of the work of access, by reproducing these conditions in the audience's perceptual experience of the film, is both didactic and transformative.

The manifesto text clearly tells us what Carolyn, by way of Tina, is doing and inviting us to do: 'A work made from the conditions of debility or difference. Not translated for debility or difference. [...] A media slow enough for everyone to follow. A media quick enough for everyone to get lost ... together.'

18 For more on this insufficiency and creative interference in it, see Kim's video *Closer Captions* (2020).

19 As Mara Mills writes in her article 'Listening to Images', 'A description should really only follow when the film is completely silent, so when there is no dialogue or noise or music. However, this hardly ever happens and therefore one has to make a decision to speak over music and also some noises. In doing this, one has to continually question whether the precise place in which one wants to talk over the audio fulfills an important function in terms of the mood and atmosphere and thus whether it should remain undisturbed. Music and sounds are also part of the language of a film!' Mara Mills, 'Listening to Images: Audio Description, the Translation Overlay, and Image Retrieval', *The Cine-Files*, 8 (Spring 2015).

*

Georgina Kleege and Scott Wallin have written on how the forms of reading and interpretation that constitute audio description might be used as a creative and pedagogical tool. Kleege finds description a useful means of teaching how and what her students see and the ways in which the visual imposes its frames on the world and ways of knowing it. For her, and I think for all of the artists I am writing about here, there is a recognition that, while the standardization of access is intended to make these frames more inclusive of that which they seem to leave out, these frames nevertheless frequently reproduce segregation and exclusion. As Kleege writes about audio description,

> While it's understandable that a certain level of consistency and professionalism is necessary, the rules and guidelines that have become codified seem to arise from problematic assumptions about what blind people can understand and should know about visual phenomena.[20]

As Kleege writes, this often involves explicit forms of censorship that deny Blind audiences access to fundamental information sighted audiences have, from which meaning, pleasure, and shared experience are constructed and derived. Of course, what is not included says as much about the frame through which the Blind audience is invited to experience a film as what is. Kleege recounts a screening of an audio-described film in which Helen Hunt, who gave an Oscar-nominated performance, appears nude. However, the audio description of the film did not describe any physical attributes of her naked body—only the actions of her taking off her clothes.[21]

At the same time, Kleege doesn't conceive of the access work of description as entirely contingent on the filmmaker or audio describer. In describing her experience of going to see movies, she discusses how the process of interpretation and description extends beyond even her time in the movie theater, as she and her friends co-produce access. She says,

> Sometimes I am content with what I call retrospective description. In the inevitable conversation that follows going to a movie with a friend, I may ask about some detail that did not make sense. But often this is part of a give-and-take conversation, where I am as likely to remark on some feature of the sound track, or subtlety in an actor's vocal performance, as to need visual details explained.[22]

This is not to underscore Kleege's capacity to participate in making access. Though access frequently seems to exceptionalize the incapacities of certain bodies/minds, Kleege's example shows how access animates the means by which an audience shares and inhabits the space of a film. We are always interpreting and moving outside ourselves to meet at the intersection of

20 Georgina Kleege, 'Audio Description Described: Current Standards, Future Innovations, Larger Implications', *Representations*, 135/1 (2016), p.90.
21 Ibid., p.97.
22 Ibid., p.92.

what we can and can't perceive. This is more or less perceptible only at certain thresholds, where the means by which the audience does that work has or hasn't been conceived by the filmmaker(s).

Kleege's work doesn't just move us toward a better understanding of how access actually works in filmmaking; as she and many others show, there is a poetics of access. These poetics are explicitly evoked in projects like Shannon Finnegan and Bojana Coklyat's Alt-Text as Poetry workshops, which teach people how to write alt text (image descriptions optimized for people who navigate the Internet by screen readers) that works with the poetics of rendering an image through language, rather than seeking to translate images neutrally through a standardized posture of objectivity.

This poetics also emerges through Park and Tina's instructional scores for acts of intimate care and their video *Scores for Carolyn* (2019), which reimagines them. Here, Tina and Park enact the work of access on the audience's sense of time, while many of the scores put the audience into a space of projecting themselves onto scenes of access intimacy.[23] In the video, a series of open captions appear over a video recording of a chunk of asphalt from Jessica Vaughn's painting/sculpture *Consumed Grounds* (2015). The speed at which the captions appear onscreen determines the speed at which the voiceover is replayed. Tina's voice is correspondingly stretched out, slowed, echoed, and slurred. Here, the meaning of what Tina speaks threatens to dissolve or dissipate if the audience prioritizes capacity over access, interfering with the presumption that the time it takes to receive language is the time it takes to say or hear it. Rather, the piece clearly writes a sense of timing into access. As the captions appear, Tina reads:

> What is perfect timing and does it ever age? Come early and plan in advance to wait. Arrive late together despite your best attempts to be on time or before it. See all it took to get here. Know exactly what it costs to get in. Read into this. Wait to speak while planning your exit.

Works like *A Recipe for Disaster*, meanwhile, overlay the seemingly objective qualities of description and captioning. These multiple layers of access collide in a cacophony, echoing what (who) was already there but occluded by the segregation of access into those deemed to 'need' it and those who don't.

There is a larger group of artists who unfold a poetics of access in order to interfere with those frames that would occlude need as a shared condition and resource. I am particularly interested in where these artists' apparent denial of or interference with conditional forms of access becomes a means of proliferating a commons.

*

The title of my film *After... After... (Access)* refers to *Carried and Held* (2013–), a work by Park that might be classified as anything from a sculpture to a poem or a painting or the credits of a film that has not yet been made. It consists of a wall label showing the name of the artwork, followed by the

23 See Mia Mingus, 'Access Intimacy: The Missing Link' (5 May 2011) and 'Access Intimacy, Interdependence, and Disability Justice' (12 April 2017), www.leavingevidence.wordpress.com.

materials it was made from, and then the words 'Courtesy the artist' and a list of the names of all of the people who she could recall had carried or held her body in acts of care until that point. The label leaves a long blank space for the many names yet to come.

Everything I want to say about access is already here in this one artwork, where Park frames herself as arriving courtesy of those that got her here/there. In the context of the artwork's wall label and courtesy line—an element that typically announces a loan agreement—Park frames both the audience's access to the work and her own access to her life as a debt. Her presence, as well as that of the work itself, are presented as a resource both on loan and being shared.

As a meditation on relationships of institutional access, *Carried and Held* shifts one of the most basic misapprehensions about the direction in which access moves—as extended outward toward making a work perceptible to an audience, rather than also fundamental to the very possibility of an artist making an artwork and showing it in an exhibition. And one of the ways it does that is by almost disappearing from view altogether, literally blurring with the ground on which it is presented—as if a wall label missing an artwork.

At this threshold of (in)visibility, Park both sculpturally and filmically reframes the frame—where the legibility of a film or a material is, in fact, only rendered perceptible by incapacity: all that it cannot contain. The credit line becomes simultaneously an extreme close-up and an ultra-wide shot.

This work puts into play the dynamics of access I want to be shared with: that this access is so common as to go unnoticed, even as it is the most constitutive thing of all—the means by which a person gives and receives support.

*

When Carolyn was telling Park, Tina, and me about their idea for their piece *A Conspiracy* (2017), Tina mentioned that, at its root, the word 'conspire' means to breathe together. For this work, Carolyn installed a series of analog white noise machines on the ceiling of a museum elevator. Here, in a space that ordinarily is filled with a semi-public silence, the white noise machines created a wall of sound that gave the audience a means of access to semi-privacy (perhaps, as the title suggests, a space that might be used for covert forms of planning and plotting).

Now, in the wake of Park's sculpture *Fantasies* (2020), which consists of a hanging stack of used filters from a ventilator Park uses 'to aid the rhythmics of breath' while she sleeps, I can't help but think that one of the primary materials *A Conspiracy* was rendering accessible was also the breath in the air in the elevator, which could be heard circulating through the whirring fans inside the white noise machines. This shared resource of the air we breathe has always had variegated stakes for those whose breath is 'mechanically dependent'. But as Park and Carolyn, and Nick Dupree and Zoë Wool in their conversation 'Life Support', point towards, the category of breathing has been arbitrarily divided into those who do and do not need support. Throughout the interview, they discuss the entanglements of Dupree's living on ventilation, and Wool suggests to Dupree that the 'sociomaterial assemblage' by which his ventilated breath became possible might also be the feeling of him 'being breathed'—an idea we might equally elaborate to the occasions both Park and Carolyn invite their audiences to.[24]

Both pieces also repurpose these materials used by people to facilitate sleep and circulate breath to evoke a shared space of dreaming. Carolyn and I have agreed many times that one of the reasons we make and watch movies in the first place is because they are a way for people to dream together. This dream space is equally suggested by Tina's *self portrait (EMDR)* (2009–10), a memory foam pillow squeezed into a wooden frame so that it bulges out, which to me has always looked like the tube of a television. The materials for this piece are 'one year's sleep on memory foam, wood'. Something that Tina has talked about whenever I've heard them discuss this work is that it's less an archive of that year's sleep than an anarchive, because memory foam is always 'in the process of forgetting you'. Referring to a form of trauma therapy[25] in the parentheses of the work's title underlines that the act of forgetting is, in fact, still in process, however absent it appears to now be from the (pillow's, the dream's, the TV's) screen—a forgetting that also extends to both 'self' and 'portrait'.

What is it to access a moving image through an apparently still object, whose act of recording is also an act of apparent erasure? Maybe this is to ask a larger question of sculpture and cinema in general. Can we access these things through looking at them, or would we need to feel them (in all of the senses that suggests)?

This reading is, perhaps, a stretch. What each of these works gives access to for me is an idea of where sculpture and cinema meet in a poetics of access, shared resources, collective dreams.

*

In this first summer of Covid-19, Park had an exhibition at Essex Street gallery, New York, entitled 'Edition One and Two Fantasies'. The exhibition does not require the audience's physical presence in the gallery, and in

24 Later in their conversation Dupree terms his participation in this assemblage 'feeling by reference'. He describes this process using the example of how he relates to his ventilator, saying, 'The tube is, in a way, experienced as something akin to a hair: the tube moves or pulls or is touched, I feel it acutely with great sensitivity from its "root". Meaning you move the tube anywhere or touch the tube even two feet down, I get feedback in the tracheostomy that I feel, feeling by reference.' Wool responds, 'So the feeling of your exo-airway can also be the touch of a friend like me participating in your life.' Zoë Wool and Nick Dupree, 'Life Support', www.somatosphere.net/2014/life-support.html, 18 February 2014.

25 EMDR (Eye Movement Desensitization and Reprocessing) therapy uses 'bilateral stimulation' such as side-to-side eye movements or hand-tapping to aid people in breaking loops of traumatic mental images. In *self portrait (EMDR)*, the image is quite explicitly being forgotten in favor of touch or feel: the bulging texture of the so-called memory foam, which is nevertheless forgetting the image or imprint of Tina's sleeping head (where these dreams and images were ostensibly formed, a space that Tina describes as 'where I do my best work'). This is one of many works among these artists where the figure literally dissolves in its blur with ground. For more on EMDR, see also Carolyn's video *Consensual Healing* (2018), which simulates an EMDR session through an animation of a ball moving side to side, while reframing a character from an Octavia Butler short story as a therapeutic patient recalling a traumatic memory.

the process circulates around it, meanwhile underlining Park's (and many others') absence. The two primary artworks in the exhibition each evoke a different measure of breath.

One of the works is entitled *Form found figuring it out, show* (2020) and consists of two prints of a set of markings taken from an incentive spirometer, a device used to measure lung capacity. As Park writes in the press release for the show, 'They are designed for users to compare their breaths numerically and to encourage diaphragmatic movement through slow deep breathing.' These two prints were framed side by side and repeated in rows across the gallery, Park having instructed the people working in the gallery to install them, in her absence, wherever they noticed their own breathing taking place. These prints are also available on the gallery website as PDFs to be printed out and hung wherever audiences choose to include them in their lives.

There are a variety of other ways of accessing this work as well. On the website, there are installation images that show a row of these framed prints in the otherwise largely empty gallery, seeming almost to enlarge the space of the large parts of the wall they don't fill and the room's bare floor. Below these images there are image descriptions of them, reading for instance: 'A large white wall with four framed artworks unevenly spaced. One of the frames extends outside the picture.' The image description of a closer-up image of the print reads:

> A framed artwork. The frame is painted white wood. The matte board is also white. The artwork is two pages of paper vertically oriented and side by side. The sheets are white, with graphically printed sparse numbers, lines, logos and text all in blue. All of the content is printed in reverse as if it were viewed in a mirror. On the page on the left the print spells out in a vertical column '2500ml' '2250' '2000' '1750' '1500ml' '1250' '1000' '750' '500ml' '250' from top to bottom with a horizontal blue line separating each number. Underneath this column are the words 'Inspired Volume'. Next to the column are the words 'VOLDYNE ® 2500' and 'HUDSON RCI' with a simple logo. To the right of these words are three stacked boxes each containing the words 'GOOD' 'BETTER' 'BEST' from top to bottom. On the page on the right the print spells out in a vertical column '2500ml' '2250' '2000' '1750' '1500ml' '1250' '1000' '750' '500ml' '250' from top to bottom with a horizontal blue line separating each number. Underneath this column are the words 'Inspired Volume', without additional text or logos.[26]

There is also a video tour of the exhibition on the gallery website, which is recorded by Josephine Shokrian and audio described by Alejandra Ospina. Alejandra describes as Josephine films:

> We enter a large room with completely white walls. Along the walls we see a group of white framed prints. We approach a group of three

26 Park McArthur, 'Edition One and Two Fantasies', 15 July–21 August 2020, www.exhibition146.essexstreet.biz.

prints. And see one print in the distance in front of us as we reach a corner. We close up on the print. The print has the number, texts, and logos of an incentive spirometer printed as they would appear from the inside.

Reducing (while elaborating) what is being shown as artwork in this show, Park renders accessible the conditions of what is present in so much apparent absence. As Alejandra notes in her description, the incentive spirometer is printed as it 'would appear from the inside', locating the audience—both in person and online, both Blind and sighted—inside a shared space of inhalation. In many ways breathing with and joining in Carolyn's conspiracy, this piece invites the audience to breathe together, knowing that the contagion of those shared conditions makes shared physical presence too risky for many both within the construction of this artwork and among those intended to receive it.

The audio description then goes further to interfere with the ways in which the art gallery's architecture and protocols construct a privileged, perhaps even authoritative, form of access to the so-called artwork. In their apparent blankness or emptiness, these access features are presumably believed to invite maximal access to concentration, freedom from distraction, and focus on what is in the frame, and work upon the same set of visual constructs that ascribe a singular value to seeing an artwork 'in person'. These architectural features are meant to recede as mere background or infrastructure: windows, doors, walls. But in the images, image descriptions, video, and audio description of this exhibition, these features take on a primary role. Park, Josephine, and Alejandra's way of doing access (working in tandem with Jason Hirata's editing of the documentation video and Maxwell Graham's and Eli Coplan's image descriptions of the documentation photos) draws out these aspects of background, blurring them with the artwork and, particularly, the shared—yet nevertheless impossible—conditions of being together in this space. At the same time, the form of the video, filmed from Josephine's wheelchair, accessing the bottom layer of the space via wheelchair lift, doubles and overlays Park's would-be experience of navigating through an exhibition that she herself cannot navigate in person. Here, all aspects of the gallery's infrastructure are shown to be active in making its accessibility or inaccessibility.

On the one hand, the exhibition, like its title, realizes a dream of sharing space when our physical conditions prevent us from doing so. But, at the same time, the existence of the exhibition is cutting in the way that it reveals the contradiction from which this dream is constituted and enacted. Those who might have been able to benefit from the supposedly authoritative experience of 'seeing' the work in person were, by and large, those whose capacity to breathe without fear of death enabled them to engage in the act of entering an art gallery in the middle of a pandemic. Quite literally, if any other person was there, Park—or anyone else whose breathing in of another's breath puts them at risk—could not be there.

The incentive spirometer itself seems to be making a pun about the irony of this dynamic, labelling the measure of the space 'inspired volume'. This blurred space between the two senses of inspiration—breathing in and being mentally or emotionally stimulated—cannot be separated from the ways in which disabled people are continuously mined in public visibility as sources of so-called inspiration. By emptying out the gallery of anything other than reminders of the means by which we breathe, Park amplifies and interferes in the satisfaction of this impulse toward inspiration, in both senses of the word.

*

In the same space, only a few weeks after Park's show appeared at Essex Street, Carolyn opened their first solo exhibition, 'SYNC'.[27] This show extends the question of what it means to occupy the same space (as in Park's exhibition) to ask what gets us into the same sense of time, what sets us in or out of sync. Here, this temporal domain appears through the seeming elements of a disassembled cinema, or the means by which this collective dream is constructed: a screen, shared air, a place to sit, flickering light, time standing still.

The pun of the exhibition's title refers to both a question of time and a series of sculptures that present upturned sinks presented on TV stands that, like Tina's self-portrait, look like TV screens that can't make a picture other than of their own screens. The sinks are titled *TV1*, *TV2*, *TV3*, *TV4*, each with a parenthetical: *(Dead Time)*, *(Against Metaphor)*, *(Love Island)*, and *(Delayed Reception)*, respectively. The holes where faucets and drainage would go now resemble buttons through which your finger would poke rather than change the channel on the television set. Putting these nonfunctional sinks on end, on view, reflects back to me the absurdity in the framing of public health as billions of individuals washing their hands and 'doing their part'. This individualization of our health, which is always collective, is no doubt at stake in the question of what it is to dream about sharing time together—evoked all the more by literalizing the shared material of conspiracy: Carolyn installed a series of HEPA-filtered air purifiers around the gallery in a work entitled *Privatization*.

But, yet again, it is not as simple as breathing together, making our collective health; these air filters, while doing something, don't actually make it so that everyone can breathe here. Breathing in the same time and place has entirely different stakes if you are immunocompromised, have a respiratory condition, and/or live surrounded by polluted air. A recent *New York Times Magazine* article, entitled 'Pollution Is Killing Black Americans. This Community Fought Back', was pinned to the top of the Essex Street website for the duration of Carolyn's exhibition. Written by Linda Villarosa, the article gives an in-depth look at the 150-plus-year history of environmental toxicity in Black communities in South Philadelphia and the community-wide struggle to close the PES oil refinery, as well as a long-reaching historical overview of US movements against environmental racism. In the article, Villarosa notes that the present configuration of housing in the US, in which Black and Brown people are significantly more likely than white people to become disabled through living near sites contaminated with toxic substances, is a long-term result of redlining, the practice by

27 Presented at Essex Street, New York, 10 September–17 October 2020.

which US banks segregated Black and Brown people's neighborhoods into 'high-risk' zones as a means of preventing them from obtaining mortgages (and of maintaining the mortgage as a financial instrument of the property interest invested in whiteness). The ongoing conflation of 'risk' with the increased likelihood of death from Covid-19 in Black and Brown communities—already frequently living with disabilities produced by toxic environments near their homes—has created a self-sustaining knot, wherein race and disability become predictive vectors of risk. Meanwhile, just as in practices of redlining, the calculated distribution of risk has been and continues to be used to segregate and mark Black, Brown, and disabled people for further disablement and even death.

The press release for 'SYNC' invites the audience into the same city, not through an analysis of population or statistics but rather through the narration of a Black disabled woman living in North Philadelphia. It consists of 'And the Sun Still Shines', a short story by Tameka Blackwell about a Black powerchair user named Tameka and her attempt to write a short story on the day of a routine hospital visit. Along the way, Tameka enjoys the sun on her face as she gets ready to write; has that enjoyment interrupted by a doctor's ableist pun; again, enjoys the sensation of perfectly parking her chair in a tight space; and has that enjoyment interrupted by a white woman who stares at her. Tameka stares back at the woman, hoping to shame her into looking away; she then gets called into the doctor's office, only to have her appointment canceled. While waiting for paratransit, she goes back to enjoying the weather and the space to write, and an elderly woman infers from the visibility of Tameka's wheelchair that it is her right to ask Tameka about how she became disabled. Tameka responds by recounting a friend's story of disablement as if it is her own: a white man mistook her for his white wife and shot her on a boardwalk. She goes on to explain to her mom that to tell the elderly woman the real story of how she became disabled would reaffirm 'every stereotype about violence in North Philadelphia'.[28] As the woman says earlier in their conversation, 'I heard about that place. A lot of dangerous things happening out there.' But, of course, she does not understand where that risk comes from; rather, she assumes it is the natural state of the people and place of the neighborhood.

Blackwell's short story and Villarosa's article ground the exhibition in and around Black neighborhoods in Philadelphia. The artwork on view seems to narrow this focus on neighborhood or community to a domestic interior: the sculptures in the exhibition resemble things you might find in a house in Tameka's neighborhood, or in South Philadelphia, or where Carolyn's family lives.

The show resituates La-Z-Boy recliners, themselves bearing the perfect crip moniker for a convertible object of comfort, rest, and recovery—states so frequently deemed laziness by the interworkings of ableism and anti-Blackness. Carolyn has tipped one of the La-Z-Boys onto the edge of its hinges (titled *Piss on Pity*) and the other in a reclined position (titled *La-Z Boi*), as if one chair is helping someone out of it and the other is holding space for someone who is already there, leaning back. These postures demonstrate

28 Tameka Blackwell, 'And the Sun Still Shines', press release for 'SYNC', www.essexstreet.biz/exhibition152/PressRelease.pdf.

the dual functions of recliners, which were originally conceived to assist the user in getting in and out of the chair and to allow a seated posture that relieves stress on the back. Much like the absence Park renders through a seeming invitation to share a space of breathing, Carolyn seems to be pointing to a feeling of being unable to get into the same sense of time. The comfy chairs are there, but for the duration of the exhibition it is unlikely that they will be filled by Carolyn or their friends or family. Meanwhile, the chairs' emptiness might conjure an imaginative act similar to the one suggested by Park's show, in which the absence of certain people from the exhibition also points, under conditions of isolation, to an imagined space of being together, imagining ourselves with the many people elsewhere whom we might be sitting with, leaned back together. As Carolyn and I discussed, the chairs remind us of the megaplex, which, pre-Covid, tried to simulate the experience of the home cinema by replacing fixed-back chairs with plush recliners. We miss going to the movies.

In manifesting these simultaneously interrupted and imaginative conditions of shared observation or spectatorship, there is a simultaneous sense of rage and meditation. In the works *Cinema 1* and *Cinema 2*, Carolyn framed two stand-alone electric fireplaces as works of expanded cinema. The fireplaces each project light onto air vapor to create moving images that convincingly simulate fire. These objects are sold to evoke calm or reprieve, but in the context of the show they also bring to mind the power of fire to destroy things, to simmer, to conflagrate. Appropriating the titles of Gilles Deleuze's two books on cinema, the first of which is subtitled *The Movement Image* and the second *The Time Image* (1983 and 1985), Carolyn reframes them to suggest that the conditions under which these fires might be observed, and what these conditions might proliferate, are located somewhere where movement and time meet. Perhaps a movement that burns things down, and a time where this movement is sustained. This meeting place of movement-time echoes *A Conspiracy*, in which access opens and transforms the aural architecture of an elevator in a way that might facilitate both literal and conceptual space to plan crip revolution. In *Cinema 1* and *Cinema 2*, the plan might indeed be to burn down the art gallery and/or, perhaps, the many other physical, structural, and ideological frameworks that perpetuate the practices of categorization, separation, privatization, white supremacy, and ableism. At the same time, the fire has not yet left its container and is here to be observed and seemingly meditated on, in the meantime.

This containment is then echoed in an hourglass filled to capacity at top and bottom with granite dust, as if another work of moving image has been frozen indefinitely—literally a 'time image', possessing no movement. Taken from a quarry near Carolyn's childhood home, this time image is less a recording or document of a time and place and more the simultaneous impossibility of dislodging, projecting, or representing it.[29]

29 The title of this work, *Free Radicals*, makes explicit the connection between the granite dust contained inside the hourglass and the toxic effects of environmental pollution, being named after a type of atom in the body that medical researchers are now linking to not only processes of 'normal aging' but also autoimmune conditions, cancer, and illnesses caused by exposure to air pollution. Here, Carolyn doubles a seeming call for liberation and the scientific term for unbound atoms in the body, whose incompleteness and dependency on other atoms to form their outer layer cause them to behave

*

Tina's 2019 exhibition 'L&D Motel' at Participant Inc., New York, framed access at its very limits. By lighting the gallery with red light—light at its lowest visible threshold—Tina refracted access as a space of meeting up in incapacity. There were numerous sounds and images that could be heard and seen but not discerned or decoded.

In their essay 'The Guild of the Brave Poor Things', Tina and Park previously underlined this threshold as a place for meeting and possible transformation in the blur between seen and unseen, heard and unheard. They write,

> There's something about a threshold that has to do with what forms may arise on the other side, on the other way phone, telephonic to what has been called to exit in place of its entrance.[30]

In the same essay they reproduce an image of Marcel Duchamp's 1927 piece *Door, 11 rue Larrey*, a 'Three-dimensional pun: a door which permanently opens and shuts at the same time'—a door hung between two doorways so that to open one threshold, the other must close. This image appears alongside a photo of 'segregated bathrooms hung at a right angle', in which a Black man walks out of a door labelled 'White Men Only'. Here, this eclipse of segregation at the meeting of two thresholds is reframed as an ongoing question of access: to bathrooms, to public space, to being together at once. Park and Tina refer to *rue Larrey* in their *Score for Removed Door*:

> Cut from space an open.
> −1/+1
> Rue Larrey floored[31]

In 'L&D Motel', this permanent threshold seemed to be tilted and laid out horizontally, leading up the wall, opening and shutting at the same time. One of the two works in the exhibition, *Call to Post*, was a wooden ramp that mediated infrasonic sounds (below the lowest limit of typical human audibility) from a recording of two texts read on top of each other. The sounds of a voice reading, much less the words read, were not legible to the hearing ear. But inside the ramp, a transducer produced strong physical vibrations of the recording.

The same text then appeared in open captions in two overlapping projections, each interfering with the ability to read the other, in the video installation *All the time* (2019), presented on the list of works as the 'B-side'

in 'unstable' ways. Here, there is a nonseparation between crip revolution and the upheaval taking place on a literally atomic level inside the bodies of those who might be part of this revolution; the dust inside the hourglass seems to echo the continuous (seemingly static) flow of time both backward and forward that reanimates the violences of environmental racism inside people's bodies and, nevertheless, the ongoing planning of the undercommons. There also might might be sarcasm in the call for 'Free Radicals', perhaps casting a sidelong glance at any call to radicalism that would imagine freedom as unbound from our need for each other, especially the 'unstable' ones.

30 McArthur and Zavitsanos, 'The Guild', p.236.

31 Ibid., p.245.

of the ramp. As the press release for the exhibition notes, open captions are burned into a film's image—constituted by the mark they leave on it—and at the same time this inseparability from the image is said by certain hearing audiences to 'detract from or deplete visual experience'.

Throughout the exhibition, access was given at points where the audience's bodies literally merged with material from which images and sounds were produced. In the case of the videos, if someone stood in front of one of the two projectors, the text of the other projection became legible behind them, while the text on top was overlaid on the person's body. But this process of decoupling actually redoubled a layer of incapacity, where it became impossible to read both texts together, at once. Only in their illegibility could you observe them in their entanglement.

Likewise, lying or sitting on the ramp conducted the sound of the recording through your body into a language of vibrations and pulses, composed by rhythm, intensity, and impact. The wood of the ramp became a speaker, while your body became a filter, a channel, and a receiver. Around 40 people could lie or sit on the ramp at once, including some using wheelchairs. It was and could be used variably as a kind of therapeutic or recreational device (the pulse of the sound waves felt a lot like a massager or vibrating mattress), a meeting point, a skate ramp, a stage for performance. The ramp offered access not into a building but to a place to be held together.

In his essay 'Tactile Art', DeafBlind poet John Lee Clark notes that, in spite of mounting interest from museums and artists in the ways that Blind people might be able to experience visual art through various kinds of accommodation, 'No one seems to have asked whether we want access to visual information [...] Why not a tactile representation of that something, bypassing visual representation altogether?'[32] Thinking of Clark's question, Tina's rendering of access comes into relief: not as an approximation of the experience of reading the written language of the projected texts but rather reproducing the superposition of the two texts materially, through the haptics of the sound waves pulsing through the ramp.

The show's other work demonstrated its materiality through the doubling of an image and its disappearance. Tina presented a series of holograms that depict images of dice that appear to be mid-throw. This threshold of suspended decision adds another layer to what we might think of as a discursive space around moving-image work. For their piece *Boxed Bet*, Tina displayed these holograms by projecting red laser light through their glass forms, creating a paracinema that depended on positionality to appear. There is an irreducibility to these holograms, which, as Tina explains in the press release, are formed by an interference pattern: when cut in half, the hologram does not 'split' but rather 'doubles'. Unlike a photograph or a still image in a film, if you physically break a hologram into parts, the entire scene is still preserved in every part; it just has to be observed from a particular angle, from which the image comes into view. Otherwise, only part of it might appear, or the image can't be seen at all.

32 John Lee Clark, 'Tactile Art', *Poetry* (October 2019), www.poetryfoundation.org/poetrymagazine/articles/150914/tactile-art.

At this threshold of incapacity—under the lowest visible light, passing through an image that can't be seen from many angles—Tina demonstrates the principle they alluded to in *Score for Removed Door* or in the very claim to be doing access. It is not simply that access is contingent on a simultaneous movement of closing one door by opening another. It is also that access is a place where matter is superposed; our meeting occurs at the point where we cannot be separated (or split) but rather are doubled, overlaid, entangled. This might be the very point where we seem to be absent but, from another angle, are in every part of it (−1/+1). This is not to say that this is a tender or comfortable space of connection or togetherness or communism; the conditions for any of these states must be made, in part through access, and are always contingent and continuously overdetermined by those frames that seek to keep us separate (and also the parallax views by which we occlude one another's position). But this point comes into view from a given angle: regardless of where we are located in space-time, we are simultaneously interfering with and co-constituted by each other.

In betting this on the roll of a die, Tina seems to be suggesting that what we call contingency and risk—the division of our lives into vulnerable and invulnerable—is actually just a frame that cuts dependency in half, in order to disavow the reality that this dependency is already redoubled as the condition that undergirds any attempt at separation.

If one was lying on the ramp, looking toward the overlapping projection on the wall, a section of text in Tina's video would not have been readable unless there was a person there to block out the text layer on top. If they had stood there at the right moment, it would have read:

> i'm just tryna tell you how we touch and don't, why we can't but do.
> why we do and don't touch when every never is composed of us alone.
> our private pool's public.

*

I didn't know what to do with many of the images I'd recorded of my family over the last five years.

It wasn't until I finally showed them an edit of the footage that any of us began to realize what the film was. It was not only what I had recorded but also the film my family made of it through how they experienced it.

I asked both my parents to audio-describe the footage, providing both image description for the audience and a kind of internal monologue of how they experienced seeing themselves as I had framed them. My dad agreed to have his reactions to the film recorded but refused to provide audio description of the images. He said it wouldn't change anything about the way other people saw him because 'humans are visual'.

There were specific things I had recorded that he had forgotten had happened and which he didn't want others to see—specifically things that would show him as 'weak' and 'vulnerable'. These were moments that rendered the many directions in which dependency goes in my family and in which access is facilitated. Allowing the camera to record on its own, as I helped my dad get up from his recliner, my body blocked his from view.

I chose to include the scenes my dad objected to by replacing their images with an image of my finger blocking the camera's lens, filling it instead with a reddish-pink gradient that changes with the light behind it. Or, more literally, what the audience might see is the light passing through my blood.

As Tina and Park write, 'I want to get too close to see, so close you gotta feel through someone elsewhere or somewhere elseone as never one.'[33]

*

The seam at which access lies, or the cut that it makes, seemed to have everything to do with where my dad's refusal of description met his refusal to share the risk of the film with me.

In the film, I propose to my parents that we enter into a contract that would do the opposite of what a normal access agreement does—which is to say, release me from any responsibility for how the film might impact their lives. I proposed that, instead, we enter into a 'catch agreement' that would bind my fate to theirs, sharing the risk for any and all impacts of the film and maintaining the possibility for them to withdraw their participation at any time.

My dad refused to enter into this contract with me because he felt 'no filmmaker would agree to this.'

*

In a class on how to produce documentary films, I was taught that, in the context of grant writing, 'value added' refers to anything that makes the filmmaker's relationship to the subject of the documentary additionally compelling or convincing: a close relationship or sharing a subject position with the people depicted in the film (usually also called subjects), embeddedness with a given community, relevant past experience, or a highly original formal or aesthetic approach. We were told that it is fundamental to documentary fundraising to know how to bring out these points of added value.

As Aimi Hamraie writes in their book *Building Access: Universal Design and the Politics of Disability*, 'added value' is also a central premise of barrier-free design and the design ideology that replaced it, universal design, both of which seek to render built environments accessible to 'all'. Hamriae writes,

> Unlike High Modernist architects, who defined 'good design' in terms of standardization and uniformity, proponents of barrier-free design argued that if architects design a world with disability in mind, this built-in access would benefit 'all' people, even adding value for nondisabled users.[34]

At stake here are at least two claims, each of which seek to recover value from the presumed loss or absence of value marked by disability—first, the purported benefit or value generated for 'all' people (including disabled

33 McArthur and Zavitsanos, 'The Guild', p.236.
34 Aimi Hamraie, *Building Access: Universal Design and the Politics of Disability* (Minneapolis, MN, 2017), p.10.

people), and second, the surplus or extra value this benefit renders to nondisabled people.

As Hamraie goes on to point out, these claims of a benefit for 'all' hinge on a racial neutrality that smooths away the segregated seams of racial difference exactly at the time (from the late 1940s through the 1960s) that barrier-free architects and designers advanced 'white-centered' proposals to make middle-class suburban homes accessible to disabled users. These spaces were made fundamentally inaccessible to non-white people through redlining and restrictive covenants, as white designers situated barrier-free design in the context of 'environmental improvements' targeting 'slum housing' and 'unsafe streets'.[35]

Moreover, in conflating access as both a promised benefit for those presently denied access and an added value for those to whom the structure is already accessible, access has simultaneously been proposed as an answer to segregation and a means of perpetuating it.

Looking at World War II propaganda in the US that demanded the sacrifice of 'all' for the benefit of 'all' as an antecedent to the construction of post-war barrier-free design ideologies, Hamraie notes that, though all Americans were encouraged to donate blood to 'save and rehabilitate the nation's soldiers', blood from white donors was unmarked, whereas blood from Black donors was labelled as such, 'leading to disparities in access to blood banks for Black Americans'.[36] Hamraie argues further,

> [W]hen 'all' are called to sacrifice bodies for the nation, those with unmarked racial and economic privileges as citizens often benefit at the expense of those whose racialized, disabled, and otherwise 'misfit' bodies are treated as extractable labor.[37]

Hamraie goes on to unpack the numerous ways in which the benefits granted to certain white disabled and nondisabled people through the promises of barrier-free design did not extend to non-white disabled or nondisabled people, who were systematically denied access to those same structures through political, social, architectural, and economic apparatuses of segregation and whose exclusion allowed their labor to be extracted and absorbed for its value, reframed as sacrifice.

In addition to acknowledging how the discursive turn that promoted 'access for all' as a form of desegregation nevertheless produced the image of the disabled citizen as a white person with certain physical disabilities and denied non-white people access even to political and social recognition as disabled, I want to linger on the logic that frames access as beneficial or valuable in the first place.

The idea of added value underlines the promotion of access as explicitly for the (logistical, financial, social, or political) benefit of nondisabled people. 'Misfit bodies' are treated as not only extractable labor but also extractable surplus value in general. This is evident in the numerous examples Hamraie gives of how barrier-free design would allow the inclusion of disabled

35 Ibid., p.92.
36 Ibid., p.69.
37 Ibid., p.70.

people in the workforce in a way that would reduce spending on the social safety nets on which they depended. But, as Marta Russell and Ravi Malhotra have argued, it's also there in how the disability benefits of those excluded from wage labor are extracted as surplus value, whereby disabled people's care is commoditized by both profit-motivated public policies and institutions.[38]

The part of the equation of access that hinges on the disabled person's benefit remains just as important and just as much in question. The etymology of the word 'benefit' is 'good or noble deed; helpful or friendly action', or 'a beneficial thing; advantage, profit'.[39] Here, the benefit is situated as centering the goodness of the person who awards the benefit and who, perhaps, receives an advantage or profit in return. Meanwhile, the benefit seems to continually defer the question of what it means to the person who is granted it, under these terms.

As Park and Tina write,

> I want to ask another question: not where value comes from—it comes from us—but rather, what produces *invalue*, what is already in value, what is invaluable?
>
> I think it's the capacity of need, specifically an incapacity that has everything in having nothing. Is it need that produces invalue? Is it need that offers us debt, as debt elaborates our need?[40]

*

Something I've been thinking about a lot recently is the fact that my dad is living with chronic illness as a result of being exposed to a chemical that the US weaponized to commit herbicide on Vietnam as a means of stamping out specters of communism. Many decades later, it has continued to make him, and countless others (especially Vietnamese people) who survived that war, sick and continues to kill.

Chronic illness crips notions of time. The time of chronic illness brushes up against the logic of how such an injury is redressed through the payment of veterans' disability benefits. These benefits seek to set a limit on the cost of living with a chronic illness and mark the finitude of redress. But chronic illness is a bodily state that itself shows the insufficiency of the boundaries we use to separate the past, present, and future. When living with a chronic illness, the past persists inexorably into the present and future.

I recently learned that the part of my dad's benefits that assigns body parts a value—based on how essential they are thought to be to performing

38 They write, 'Disabled persons who do not offer a body who will enhance profit-making as laborers are used to shore up US capitalism by other means. Entrepreneurs and rehabilitation specialists have made impaired bodies of use to the economic order by shaping disablement into big business and turning the disabled body into a commodity around which social policies get created or rejected according to their market value. The corporate solution to disablement—institutionalization in a nursing home, for instance—evolved from the realization that disabled people could be made to serve profit because public financing guaranteed the revenue (in the USA, Medicaid funds 60 percent of the cost, Medicare 15 percent, insurance 25 percent). Disabled people are worth more to the Gross Domestic Product when occupying a "bed' than a home' (ibid., p.215).

39 www.etymonline.com/word/benefit.

40 McArthur and Zavitsanos, 'The Guild', p.241.

certain forms of labor—was derived from the earliest calculations of workman's compensation at the turn of the twentieth century in the US.[41] A 'progressive' policy, the structure of this compensation was explicitly devised as a means of insuring against insurgent communism and the proliferation of dependency on the state. The thinking went that, in order to keep people working under conditions likely to cause them harm, they must be compensated for injury but under precisely limited and predetermined conditions, or else they might organize against these conditions, in which injury is another necessary expense.[42]

My dad now receives 60 percent of the total possible benefits for his eyes, which fill with fluid like 'wet film', and 30 percent of the total possible benefits for his feet, which are constantly both numb and in pain.

The transition from framing the remuneration of disablement from compensation to benefits is significant and, I would argue, has everything to do with how access is now framed as accommodation, as something that disabled people should be grateful for, by an entity that meanwhile recuperates surplus value for providing that benefit or accommodation. A preventive move to insure against the redress of harm, benefits reframe recompense as beneficence.

*

Cameron Rowland's artwork *Depreciation* (2018) disfigures this logic of recuperability through the chronic time of reparation.

Cameron's caption for this piece, which is inseparable from the work itself, begins by reminding us that the famously false promise of reparation for US slavery in the form of 40 acres and a mule was, in fact, devised during the Civil War as a form of counterinsurgency by General William Tecumseh Sherman.

The larger framing of 'D37',[43] the show at the Museum of Contemporary Art (MOCA), Los Angeles, for which Cameron devised this work, considers how, long after so-called emancipation, the dispossessive logic of property ownership in the United States has remained conditional on whiteness. The caption of *Depreciation* explains that, though Sherman's Special Fields Order No. 15 promised land held by former slave owners to ex-slaves, only one year later, President Andrew Johnson rescinded that order and gave this land to its previous, white owners as their rightful property. Former slaves

41 Big thank you to Emily Lim Rogers for pointing me in the direction of Sarah F. Rose's book *No Right to Be Idle: The Invention of Disability, 1840s–1930s* (Chapel Hill, NC, 2017) and Beth Linker's book *War's Waste: Rehabilitation in World War I America* (Chicago, 2011).

42 As Sarah F. Rose explains, at the turn of the twentieth century, the response to the disablement of an increasingly large portion of the workforce due to occupational hazards was not to make workplaces more accessible to disabled people (many of whom already had figured out how to adapt their work to their needs). Rather, employers engineered, as a matter of policy, the mass termination and prevention of disabled people from factory work—including many who were disabled before working in them—because their risk of disablement was seen as a more expensive liability in the event of having to pay more workmen's compensation if they went from having a disability to 'what legislators termed a "total permanent disability"', making the workplace uninsurable. Rose, *No Right to Be Idle*, p.137.

43 MOCA, Los Angeles, 14 October 2018–24 June 2019.

were then 'given the option to work for their former masters as sharecroppers or be evicted'. Those who were evicted could then be arrested under vagrancy laws, devised as part of the Black Codes.[44]

Depreciation is a one-acre plot of land that Cameron purchased on the site of a former plantation in South Carolina, which has since been bestowed with a restrictive covenant that stipulates that no development can ever take place on the property. As Cameron's caption explains,

> The property is now appraised at $0. By rendering it legally unusable, this restrictive covenant eliminates the market value of the land. These restrictions run with the land, regardless of the owner. As such, they will last indefinitely.

Here, Cameron seeks restitution for the descendants of slavery not through granting them property but rather by draining property of its intended function. Cameron does this via a restrictive covenant, an instrument of risk management that was widespread throughout the US in the first half of the twentieth century and which sustained the property interest invested in whiteness by barring people of color from owning homes previously owned by white people, a practice that worked in concert with redlining.

The restrictive covenant and the caption that accompanies it in *Depreciation* simultaneously renders the continuity between the historical and ongoing protection of 'whiteness as property' under the law,[45] and circumvents the capacity of this regime of value and property from reproducing itself on this plot of land. The poetics of access are no more apparent than here, in this land that can't be used in this legal-economic system; land that has no value and that, as such, is no longer property.

44 These vagrancy laws are a long-term meeting place where ableism and anti-Blackness conspire. Originally devised in England in the 1300s to police idleness, gender nonconformity, and anyone who did not or could not engage in socially sanctioned forms of productive labor, the moral hazard of vagrancy would later be used to invent the category of disability, defined as those people whose impairments excluded them from wage labor. This category emerged at the same time as some of the seeds of the modern prison were planted through attempts to police vagrancy and keep disability out of public life via the workhouse and almshouse. Vagrants were forcibly incarcerated and put to work: performing intentionally meaningless labor as religious penance; doing care and maintenance work to reproduce the almshouse or workhouse themselves; and, later, as now, working in the chain gang and the modern-day prison, which uses imprisonment as a justification to force prisoners to labor in public works projects, fight fires, manufacture furniture and infrastructure in public buildings, make hand sanitizer, and more. Objects produced by prison labor under New York State's 'brand name' for its Division of Correctional Industries, Corcraft, were the primary material of Cameron's 2016 exhibition '901020000' at Artists Space, New York. These objects are produced and sold through 'preferred source contracts', which offer reduced labor and manufacturing costs to eligible nonprofit organizations in exchange for a guarantee that, if a preferred source contractor offers the cheapest price, the organization must source labor and manufacturing through them. In addition to Corcraft, New York State offers cheap labor through preferred source contracts via two other entities: New York State Preferred Source Program for People Who Are Blind and New York State Industries for the Disabled. (The continuity between these histories first emerged for me through working with Tina on their class—originally co-taught with Park—Disability, Dependency, Arts, at the New School.) See also Saidiya Hartman, *Wayward Lives, Beautiful Experiments: Intimate Histories of Social Upheaval* (New York, 2019).

In this work, Cameron seemingly invents (or at least reinvents) a genre of artmaking that points to an insufficiency in the disciplinary boundaries of conceptualism, land art, sculpture, social practice, and documentary. Using many of the legal and financial apparatuses that create the world, this work literally changes the world.

This transformation only becomes legible as art, or even as something that took place, through techniques of access. In all of their work, Cameron expands the frame of the caption, making it an inextricable part of the artwork. In documentation photos of their work—which, especially in the case of *Depreciation*, would fail to represent what it is—Cameron ensures that the caption is always included, not only de-privileging the image but also expanding what we might think of as the purpose or limits of image description. These captions, as in *Depreciation*, elaborate what the art is[46] but also point the audience toward what the frame or the image might occlude. In *Depreciation*, Cameron renders the history of the literal ground from which the work is constituted, so that it is not only accessible to the audience but live, ongoing, in perpetuity. They do this precisely by denying access to its use as property.

Here, Cameron interferes with the contractual logic that values property as the means by which one's access becomes unrestricted, as a change in status that proliferates generational opportunity and engineers social mobility. In restricting this contract to the point of no longer being functional as property, Cameron shows the means by which this guise of economic and social access has been used to sustain the ongoing denial of reparations for Black Americans, by doubling down on the very operations of exchange, value, and propertization that made slavery, segregation, the Black Codes, and whiteness as property possible.

Instead, this work demonstrates a model for both access and reparation, where it would no longer be possible to be included in a system built on segregation and exclusion—or what Saidiya Hartman calls 'the wedding of equality and exclusion in the liberal state'. In treating the land itself as a kind of historical evidence or living material of the always already broken promise to repair the harm of slavery, Cameron acts upon history in a way that resembles Hartman's description of 'brushing against the grain' of historical archives of US slavery:

45 As Cheryl I. Harris explains in her article 'Whiteness as Property', it is not just that whiteness has privileged white people's access to property; US law has enshrined a property interest in whiteness itself that is vital to the maintenance of white supremacy and the ongoing dispossession of those who do not have this property. She writes, 'In ways so embedded that it is rarely apparent, the set of assumptions, privileges, and benefits that accompany the status of being white have become a valuable asset that whites sought to protect and that those who passed sought to attain—by fraud if necessary. Whites have come to expect and rely on these benefits, and over time these expectations have been affirmed, legitimated, and protected by the law. Even though the law is neither uniform nor explicit in all instances, in protecting settled expectations based on white privilege, American law has recognized a property interest in whiteness that, although unacknowledged, now forms the background against which legal disputes are framed, argued, and adjudicated'. Cheryl I. Harris, 'Whiteness as Property', *Harvard Law Review*, 106/8 (June 1993), pp.1713–14.

46 I am here thinking of the frames in Lorraine O'Grady's performance *Art Is...* (1983).

> a combination of foraging and disfiguration—raiding for fragments upon which other narratives can be spun and misshaping and deforming the testimony through selective quotation and the amplification of issues germane to this study.[47]

This disfiguration takes on specific stakes and effects in Cameron's work. It is not simply that there are no individual figures here to be recuperated, only the ground with which they were blurred, where formerly enslaved people were excluded as citizens or property owners and included as property. It is also that this ground is itself so enmeshed with this violent act of figuration that it can no longer be used as anything other than evidence of this violence, on the one hand, and a demonstration of what might render this violence impracticable, on the other. Echoing in Cameron's refusal to allow this land to continue to be exchanged as property are the lives of the many formerly enslaved people—whom Cameron has found traces of in the panic-stricken letters written by restituted plantation owners. These people, who are not figured but are nevertheless present in *Depreciation*, are those who refused to go back to work on this land; who destroyed the plantation's property; who contagiously spread laziness, obstinance, and insubordination.

In the specific context of Cameron's exhibition, this piece also draws out another dimension of access and artmaking. On the one hand, the piece stretches the limits of locality and site-specificity by occurring in a place literally on the other side of the country and which most art-goers in LA are unlikely to ever visit. But at the same time, the piece is inextricable from the most local work in the show, *2015 MOCA Real Estate Acquisition*, a donor plaque and informational caption that renders accessible the racism of the real estate exchange by which the museum exists. As Cameron's caption explains, the museum is built on and owns a block of land, designated D37, deemed by redlining maps in 1939 to be a high-risk, lowest-grade area because of the presence of 'subversive racial elements'. This land was then targeted for redevelopment; 7,310 residences were seized or sold under the threat of eminent domain and then demolished. In 1983, MOCA was given a 99-year lease on the land by the Community Redevelopment Agency (CRA), who then sold the land to the museum for $100,000 in 2015. One month after the museum was purchased, the land was appraised to have a value of $8,500,000.

Cameron's piece recasts this sale as a 'donation' to the museum from the Community Redevelopment Agency, marked by a permanent plaque on the museum's wall of donors, in the amount of the subsidy provided to the museum by the CRA, $8,400,000.

In accounting for the histories of these properties, Cameron performs a work of subtraction that reframes the terms of property, value, and debt. In refusing an inclusive exclusion or exclusive inclusion in a system built on the propertization of people, Cameron's work shows how reparation without any corresponding destruction or negation of property resembles access without structural transformation, maybe posing them as two aspects of the same operation.

47 Saidiya Hartman, *Scenes of Subjection: Terror, Slavery, and Self-Making in Nineteenth-Century America* (New York, 1997), p.12.

While property has been inseparable from debt since the invention of the mortgage, Cameron does not imagine a settling of the debts on which 'whiteness as property' has been built. Rather, they mark these properties and encumber them such that the debt is unending.[48] In this debt, no give-and-take is possible. There is only, as Tina has described elsewhere, a take-and-take.[49]

*

The first image included in the announcement for Carolyn's show 'SYNC' is a drawing entitled *Carolyn Working*. It depicts Carolyn lying in bed, propped up on one hand, staring at a laptop screen. Though it is not listed in the work's materials, this drawing was made by and is drawn from the position of Carolyn's partner David Johnson. This inclusion of David's work as part of Carolyn's show echoes two recent exhibitions by Park's partner Jason Hirata, 'Sometimes You're Both' and '25 OCTOBER, 2015—12 MAY, 2019',[50] which consisted entirely of works by other artists that Jason had in some way worked on as an assistant, cinematographer, installation technician, or editor.

In each of these projects, work itself is underlined as a primary means, material, and condition for access, underlining both what types of work and whose work make access possible. On the one hand, the various objects and the content of the drawing that made up 'SYNC' evoke the conditions under which Carolyn worked on it—that is, at home, in bed. But another major component of this is how much of the work arrived through the support, work, or even parallax view of others.

This, like Park's *Carried and Held*, is not to privilege or isolate the role of caregiving but rather to show how the entanglement of our own work with the work of others is a precondition for anything we might do or produce. Disability is not separate from other forms of life in this indebtedness but is simultaneously a privileged and charged space to feel this debt from within, being a space where care frequently gives way to abuse, where separation often has life-and-death stakes, but where all life can be felt as being held or as 'one another's means without ends'.[51]

*

In May, I showed three films I have made with my family at a Zoom screening organized by Emily Lim Rogers for the NYU Center for Disability Studies. Tina, Carolyn, and I discussed the films afterward, as my mom,

48 See especially Cameron's exhibition '3 & 4 Will. IV c. 73' at the Institute of Contemporary Arts, London, 2020, and their piece *Encumbrance*.

49 Tina says in a conversation with Mara Mills and Rebecca Sanchez entitled 'Giving It Away': 'I'm interested less in reciprocal give and take, than in something like a give-and-give, or take-and-take. What I mean is conveyed by the sexual senses of those terms, the way that to take it or to give it share meanings. The moment you enter a process of exchange, you're inevitably surrounded by its excess or remainder, which always clouds or enriches it.' Mara Mills and Rebecca Sanchez, 'Giving It Away: Constantina Zavitsanos on Disability, Dept, Dependency', *Art Papers* (Winter 2018–19), www.artpapers.org/giving-it-away.

50 Presented at 80WSE, New York, 4 December 2019–23 February 2020, and Kunstverein Nürnberg, 1 March–26 May 2019, respectively.

51 McArthur and Zavitsanos, 'The Guild', p.238.

dad, and sister were also present—my favorite part being when Alejandra, acting as the event's live audio-describer, asked my mom to describe herself, and my mom said, 'I am beautiful and look like a movie star.'

At one point, a member of the audience asked how the films deal with questions of consent, and we talked about part of the film I had not shown, in which I propose the 'catch agreement' and my dad refuses it. Shortly after, my dad tells me I don't owe him or my mom anything.

Tina reminded us that, much like conspiracy, consent means 'feeling with'—something they deemed impossible because it's ongoing, because it's 'in and beyond the notion of time'.

In the conversation, my dad said he disagreed with my mom that I owed them, and my mom gave my dad a bit of side-eye as he reiterated his position that, to him, 'there is no debt.' He said this is because he feels it was his and my mom's 'job to give [me] the tools to build [my] life'.

Tina called this 'the debtiest debt'. My dad laughed and agreed with Tina that this is called love.

In between my mom and dad, my sister and me, Tina and Carolyn, the virtual audience and us, there was this impossible and, nevertheless, ongoing time in which we are feeling with each other.

Texts Referenced

Blackwell, Tameka, 'And the Sun Still Shines', in *No Restraints: An Anthology of Disability Culture in Philadelphia*, ed. Gil Ott (Philadelphia, PA: New City Community Press, 2012)
Clark, John Lee, 'Tactile Art', *Poetry* (October 2019), www.poetryfoundation.org/poetrymagazine/articles/150914/tactile-art
Coklyat, Bojana, and Shannon Finnegan, *Alt-Text as Poetry*, www.alt-text-as-poetry.net, accessed 3 March 2021
Cuppini, Niccolò, and Mattia Frapporti, 'Logistics Genealogies: A Dialogue with Stefano Harney', *Social Text*, 136 (36/3) (September 2018), pp.95–110
Dublon, Amalle, 'Partial Figures: Sound in Queer and Feminist Thought', dissertation, Duke University (2017), www.dukespace.lib.duke.edu/dspace/handle/10161/16226
Dublon, Amalle, and Constantina Zavitsanos, 'Dependency and Improvisation: A Conversation with Park McArthur', *Art Papers*, 42/4 (Winter 2018–19), www.artpapers.org/dependency-and-improvisation
Hamraie, Aimi, *Building Access: Universal Design and the Politics of Disability* (Minneapolis, MN: University of Minnesota Press, 2017)
Harris, Cheryl I., 'Whiteness as Property', *Harvard Law Review*, 106/8 (June 1993), pp.1710–91
Hartman, Saidiya V., *Scenes of Subjection: Terror, Slavery, and Self-Making in Nineteenth-Century America* (New York: Oxford University Press, 1997)
Hartman, Saidiya, *Wayward Lives, Beautiful Experiments: Intimate Histories of Social Upheaval* (New York: W. W. Norton & Co., 2019)
Kleege, Georgina, 'Audio Description Described: Current Standards, Future Innovations, Larger Implications', *Representations*, 135/1 (2016), pp.89–101
Kleege, Georgina, and Scott Wallin, 'Audio Description as a Pedagogical Tool', *Disability Studies Quarterly*, 135/2 (2015), www.dx.doi.org/10.18061/dsq.v35i2
McArthur, Park, and Constantina Zavitsanos, 'The Guild of the Brave Poor Things', in *Trap Door: Trans Cultural Production and the Politics of Visibility*, ed. Tourmaline, Eric A. Stanley and Johanna Burton (Cambridge, MA: MIT Press, 2017), pp.236–54
Mills, Mara, 'Listening to Images: Audio Description, the Translation Overlay, and Image Retrieval', *The Cine-Files*, 8 (Spring 2015), www.thecine-files.com
Mills, Mara, and Rebecca Sanchez, 'Giving It Away: Constantina Zavitsanos on Disability, Dept, Dependency', *Art Papers*, 42/4 (Winter 2018–19), www.artpapers.org/giving-it-away
Mingus, Mia, 'Access Intimacy, Interdependence, and Disability Justice', *Leaving Evidence*, 12 April 2017, www.leavingevidence.wordpress.com/2017/04/12/access-intimacy-interdependence-and-disability-justice
Mingus, Mia, 'Access Intimacy: The Missing Link', *Leaving Evidence*, 5 May 2011, www.leavingevidence.wordpress.com/2011/05/05/access-intimacy-the-missing-link
Mitropoulos, Angela, *Contract and Contagion: From Biopoltiics to Oikonomia* (Wivenhoe /New York/Port Watson: Minor Compositions, 2012), available at www.minorcompositions.info
Moten, Fred, and Stefano Harney, *The Undercommons: Fugitive Planning and Black Study* (Wivenhoe/New York/Port Watson: Minor Compositions, 2013), available at www.minorcompositions.info.
Rose, Sarah F., *No Right to Be Idle: The Invention of Disability, 1840s–1930s* (Chapel Hill, NC: University of North Carolina Press, 2017)
Russell, Marta, and Ravi Malhotra, 'Capitalism and Disability', *Socialist Register*, 38 (2002), pp.211–28
Spillers, Hortense J., 'Mama's Baby, Papa's Maybe: An American Grammar Book', *Diacritics*, 17/2 (Summer 1987), pp.64–81
Villarosa, Linda, 'Pollution Is Killing Black Americans. This Community Fought Back', *New York Times Magazine*, 28 July 2020, www.nytimes.com/2020/07/28/magazine/pollution-philadelphia-black-americans.html
Wool, Zoë, and Nick Dupree, 'Life Support', *Somatosphere*, www.somatosphere.net/2014/life-support.html, 18 February 2014

Artworks and Exhibitions Referenced

Hirata, Jason, '25 OCTOBER, 2015 – 12 MAY, 2019', Kunstverein Nürnberg, Nuremberg, 1 March – 26 May 2019
Hirata, Jason, 'Sometimes You're Both', 80WSE, New York, 4 December 2019 – 23 February 2020
Jafa, Arthur, *Dreams Are Colder than Death*, video, 2014
Lazard, Carolyn, *A Conspiracy*, Dohm white noise machines, dimensions variable, 2017
Lazard, Carolyn, *A Recipe for Disaster*, video, 2018
Lazard, Carolyn, *Consensual Healing*, video, 2018
Lazard, Carolyn, *Pre-Existing Condition*, video, 2019
Lazard, Carolyn, 'SYNC', Essex Street, New York, 10 November – 17 October 2020
Lord, Jordan, *After... After... (Access)*, video, 2018
Lord, Jordan, *Shared Resources*, video, 2021
McArthur, Park, *Carried and Held*, 2012–
McArthur, Park, 'Edition One and Two Fantasies', Essex Street, New York, 15 July – 21 August 2020
McArthur, Park, and Constantina Zavitsanos, *Scores for Carolyn*, video, 2019
O'Grady, Lorraine, *Art Is...*, performance, 1983
Rowland, Cameron, 'D37', Museum of Contemporary Art, Los Angeles, 14 October 2018 – 24 June 2019
Rowland, Cameron, *Encumbrance*, 2020
Sun Kim, Christine, *Close Readings*, four-channel video, 2016
Sun Kim, Christine, *Closer Captions*, video, 2020
Zavitsanos, Constantina, 'L&D Motel', Participant, Inc., New York, 15 September – 27 October 2019
Zavitsanos, Constantina, *self portrait (EMDR)*, 2010

lights down

lights up

Dasha Loyko

Adaptation

Adaptation

20 April 2020. Kitchen. Overflowing bin, candles, burnt out lightbulb hanging from ceiling. ACHILLES *and* TORTOISE *arguing about electricity bill.*

ACHILLES: The lights had not been back since the first lobectomy.
Between averaged miles and one-way locks, this was
no exception. Inanimate things yearned to multiply, too.
What are you doing there with that saucer?

TORTOISE: I'm lacking character. Not she not her nor I could predict what
had happened before. Lather-fractured lipids, round dead,
escaped alveoli, slipping along pre-bubbled backstreets.

[ACHILLES *picks up a knife, starts scraping spilled candle wax off the kitchen table, looks at* TORTOISE, *who is on the floor.*]

ACHILLES: Sit tight in and across...

TORTOISE: A measure of time!

ACHILLES: ...stale and stable quicksand.

[*Pause.*]

ACHILLES: I love you.

TORTOISE: This is a tale of fatigue, not a love story!

ACHILLES: Tragedy!

[ACHILLES *continues scraping. The candles have been burning all evening and the wax seeped into the cracks in the wooden table.*]

TORTOISE: Talk to me when your mouth is free!

ACHILLES: But all speech is outbreath and all thought is mute.

TORTOISE: Granted. Everything is always exactly as it seems.

[ACHILLES *picks up a knife, starts scraping spilled candle wax off the kitchen table, looks at* TORTOISE, *who is on the floor.*]

ACHILLES: There was once a time you had to pay to receive. Then you
would be paid to receive. Then, you would pay to receive again.
It is all about symmetry.

TORTOISE: Symmetry?

ACHILLES: Or attitude, depending on which way you look at it. [*Looking over the room.*] We should really declutter, these cupboards
are about to burst.

TORTOISE: What's the trouble? It's out of sight.
ACHILLES: Something might fall out and hurt you.
TORTOISE: The future still looks manageable. We never have to worry about storage capacity in the case of a force majeure if force majeure is in the contract. Clever, huh? Every emergency accounted for, any risk spread so thin you can put it on toast.
ACHILLES: I suppose you're right.
TORTOISE: Granted. Everything is always exactly as it seems.
ACHILLES: Did you know that the brain adapts to every single experience, used cars, familiar smog, fresh betrayal, lemongrass, punctuation?

[ACHILLES *stops scraping, picks up bits of wax, walks over to the overflowing bin.*]

I was just reading up about foot creams. I came across a podiatrist who said you could put Vaseline on your feet and wrap them in cling film. They promise soles as smooth as the early universe!
TORTOISE: Other than the danger of suffocation and waste of plastic, that seems reasonable.

[ACHILLES *throws away the wax, ties up the bin bag, takes it out, returns.*]

ACHILLES: It's not the increasing entropy that is so strange but the fact that it was so low to start with! A universe so smooth just after the Big Bang when it should have been lumpy. Gravity! Never fails to surprise. Should have been way lumpier than it was.
TORTOISE: But what about gold?
ACHILLES: Ah, I thought you'd ask! It's all about the optics. What you're thinking of is known as the Golden Universe. It is not Midas' jet trail but a physical possibility for misalignment.
TORTOISE: Do we have time for that?
ACHILLES: We would have to sort all the brand-new limbs and crumbs into bits and blobs! Make space, then fill every blank. And we can't even find a day to declutter the kitchen.
TORTOISE: How tiresome!
ACHILLES: Too much paperwork, that is. Better stick with what we've got: a few millennia's worth of taxonomy notes down on record.

[ACHILLES *stops scraping, picks up bits of wax, walks over to the overflowing bin.*]

TORTOISE: Are you done with that? Looks like it needs a little more work.
ACHILLES: I'm done for today, it's starting to hurt my eyes.
TORTOISE: Someone should change that lightbulb.
ACHILLES: I'll do it later.

[ACHILLES *throws away the wax, ties up the bin bag, picks it up, takes two steps towards the door, pauses under the lightbulb hanging from the ceiling, turns back.*]

ACHILLES: It's time to calculate your share. Here, try this, I won't run after you: charred pear, fairly bitten, spare juice contained by prompt vacuum suction, then pause, repeat until flesh approaches zero—here, here you have yourself a starting point—from here, anything goes. Goes like this [*holding bag full of rubbish in left hand, gesticulating with right as if tracing data on a chart*]: biology is the study of living organisms—mainly—unless the organisms are not living, then it becomes medicine, epidemiology, economics, the study of the throbbing desire inanimate objects imitate to pretend they are alive, on occasion, and when they do succeed, then *forth forth forth* they go and multiply like hell, hot or cold, humid or above sea level, air or sand. Billions and billions—all striving to become a community unless not, unless striving to become a commodity unless not. Mocking oil prices going *up up* until temporarily down.

[*Continues gesticulating, continues holding the bag that starts leaking cloudy white liquid onto the wooden floor.*]

Today, in fact, for the first time in history—PLOP. [*Drops bag on the floor.*] PLUNGE!—down the hole they go. All the way down the deepest depth, and you know what? *It is not how many times you get knocked down*—I bet they whisper to each other as they descend—*It is how many times you get back up! Life will never get you down because the harder you fall the higher you bounce*—as they pass below zero—*Our greatest glory is not never falling but rising every time we fall! Attitude is everything! Bounce back faster!*

TORTOISE: Is that Confucius?

ACHILLES: A nervous wreck!

TORTOISE: How do you make holy water?

ACHILLES: You boil the hell out of it.

TORTOISE: Why shouldn't you write with a broken pencil?

ACHILLES: Because it's pointless!

TORTOISE: What does a lover want from love?

ACHILLES: Scale and scalability.

TORTOISE: And from time?

ACHILLES: A measure in height and girth.

[ACHILLES *takes the bag out, returns.*]

ACHILLES: I love you.

[TORTOISE *takes a fresh sponge from the sink cabinet, starts cleaning up the bin fluid on the floor.*]

TORTOISE: You need to try harder. Scream poetry at dead things! How else do you think resurrection works?

[*Pause.*]

[TORTOISE *continues scraping. The fluid has seeped deep into the cracks in the floorboards.*]

TORTOISE: Someone should change that lightbulb, I can barely see what I'm doing. And it's getting hard to breathe with all these candles!

ACHILLES: I'll do it later.

TORTOISE: Later! A few hours too long is not long enough. I can barely see! Can you even see what you're doing?

ACHILLES: I don't need to see what I'm doing, I know what I'm doing. That stain on the floor still needs a bit of going over.

[TORTOISE *looks at the poorly lit wet patch, retreats to shell. Achilles blows out the candles and goes out. Returns with a new lightbulb.*]

Should have kept those candles on.

[*Pause.*]

You know I love you.

TORTOISE: [*Muffled, from shell*] You need to try harder.

[*Pause.*]

ACHILLES: Your odour and apathy lead me on.

[*Pause.*]

I love you as a ritual of slow self-management.

[*Pause.*]

I love you because I have the capacity to love you.

[ACHILLES *takes lightbulb from cardboard package, examines it.*]

I love you to the breadth of my imagination, and you better fucking cherish that because that is as much if not more than I can ever keep for myself. And that is as much as you can hope I can give—I am a giver, you see!

[*Starts pacing around the room, opening and closing cabinets, looking for something.*]

My love for you is the confirmation bias I yearn for. Your absence is the sweetest gift of compassion. The void you forced upon me is all about you.

[*Takes out a small foldable stepladder from the largest cabinet.* TORTOISE, *disturbed by the noise, peeks out from shell, retreats.*]

I burst out laughing when I realised you're dumb. The dumb void of exponential geometry: growing a fifth leg sideways.

I love you to the jolt of habitual spread of neural connections. I cherish the latent blow against the hollow of my gut. I love you.

[*Unfolds stepladder, places it on the floor under lightbulb hanging from ceiling; ladder stands slightly slanted.*]

I love you for corrupting the input on its way out. You complete me in the way I entered your life complete. You complete the excess void I had already harboured before you gave me more unsolicited space. I love you because you ask me *when* and *when did you know*. You suffocate my budding habits. You burden my functions, as planned. You cradle my words as I cradle them, then throw them out with oceanwater, as planned. I catch and distil. I analyse the sediment, as planned. We do the ropes, as planned. I owe you, as planned. You love me, as planned. I love you, as planned. You love me, as planned. Your dumb love is alkaline, as planned. I love you, as planned. You love me, as planned, dumbly, short-handedly, wrongly, in isolation. You love me, in isolation. You love me, in isolation. You love me in isomorphic variation of the fantasy you had aged seven. Still there? Perhaps. Keep it. You love me, willingly. I love you, willingly. You hurt me, willingly. I hurt, willingly. You hurt me, willingly. I hurt, willingly. I hurt, willingly, to offer up hectares of scorched ground for dumb new life to sprout. You hurt me, willingly. I hurt, willingly. Alone, you love me, willingly. Alone, you are born in me. Alone, I plan you. Alone, you complete, willingly. Alone, I isolate you, willingly. Alone, you are dumb, willingly. Alone, I love you, willingly.

[ACHILLES *gently holds up the side of the slanted stepladder with left hand, looks at new lightbulb in right hand, up at ceiling, at lightbulb again.*]

TORTOISE: [*From shell*] But all speech is outbreath and all thought is mute! An unpunctured membrane of eternal regularity is all I ever ask for, really! Is it too much to ask?!

[*Pause.*]

[ACHILLES *grips the top of the ladder and rests the sole of his right foot on the second step from the bottom, looks up at lightbulb in the ceiling, thrusts foot down,* — CRACK — *lifts left foot off the floor, wobbles,* — THUD — *regains balance. Unscrews old bulb, replaces with new, it lights up, he goes down, leaves.* TORTOISE, *silent, shattered under the foot of the ladder perforating its shell.*]

switch

on

Charlotte Prodger

Beamers

The face in its red state is called a beamer. The process of the blood filling the face is called taking a beamer. Taking a beamer triggers an infinite feedback loop. The redder the face gets, the more they point and say the word beeeeeeamer. They lick the pads of their fingers, point them at you and make a sound with their mouths, like hissing spit on a hotplate. Multiple hissing hotplates. Sympathetic nervous system. Nowhere to go. Nothing to be done but sit it out, hope their attention is distracted elsewhere, to a fresh beamer, or a teacher arriving to unlock the classroom door.

Sean Abernethy sits on the carpet with his legs splayed loosely before him like a baby gorilla. Mrs Slater has stepped out and left us quietly at work in the grid. There is a fat hot fizzing pushing us against the walls. Pinned, afraid. Glee inside the accelerating eruption. He's under the longest table in the room, eight pushed together. Small shining eyes in a wide face in the semi-gloom. Laughing, bellowing, flinging out random objects pulled from the tabletop. Regarding his missiles, riding the wave, catching his breath. With each fling there's a formless roar from Sean Abernethy and a swell of panic from everyone else. In between flying objects, someone tries to find a safer position by edging along the wall to a new spot where there are already several people jostling to get behind each other. Tables get turned.

Lynn Beattie has a spike. The hair on top of her head is gelled upward, vertical spikes. This only works with straight hair but everyone does it, so the wavy-haired people with their gelled tufts look like guinea pigs. Lynn Beattie has full soft cheeks and a small wet mouth. Translucent skin with freckles floating beneath. There is something of a middle-aged woman about Lynn Beattie, it may be the length of her school skirt. She is eleven and hilarious. The spikes shake slightly with some of her movements. When Lynn Beattie gets excited, she screws up her face tight, raises both hands to it, pointed inward, and rapidly moves her fingers in front. Two taut fast spiders dancing at her screwed-shut eyes. Then she turns to you, facing you with her face still screwed, and does the same to your face, her rapid spider hands hovering at your eyes. Then they turn back to her face, then yours again, and all the while she's making this small, sustained sound, a tight squealing. A sound of something at the very edge of itself. At morning break we all get ejected into the playground. A song by Stevie Wonder has just been released, the one about the telephone. There's a payphone in the playground, on the wall at the foot of a ramp. When we exit the glass doors, Lynn Beattie walks over to the payphone, lifts the receiver on its steel cord and sings the whole song into it while I watch.

Winter afternoon, 3pm light falling, some yawning. Leftover from six weeks ago, the north wall of the classroom has been refashioned as the flight deck of a spaceship. Elaborate controls framing a view of deep space. Mrs Slater disappears into the cupboard to the right of deep space, reappears with a cardboard box and carries it over to the windowsill at the back of the room. She hands out white paper, a square for each of us. We fidget and wait, no one speaking. We've to put in the box any questions we have, she says, and it's anonymous. We can ask things, she says, things we want to know but have been too embarrassed to ask. The box gets brought to her desk at the front of the room. One by one, the squares get taken out and unfolded. Someone's written what's a blow job. Mrs Slater tells about how this is something her sister likes to do, to get ready for sexual intercourse. Someone else has written what's it like to be in love. Mrs Slater says, imagine the love you have for a pet. It's like that but much bigger.

The first house is a small granite bungalow at the edge of town. Once a gatehouse for estate staff, now for rent. In the front room, the living room, two public service announcements, on different days, forty seconds each. In one, a cliff face explodes in slow motion, a volcano erupts, an industrial drill bores into a vast block of rock, and the acronym is chiselled into a granite headstone. There is a deep rumble. John Hurt speaks. So far it's been confined to small groups, he says. But it's spreading, he says. Read the leaflet that's coming. In the other, the camera glides past icebergs at night. There is bass hum and ice creak foley. Inscribed with the acronym, icebergs crash into the sea. The camera submerges. This all happens after the six o'clock news. Then the leaflets drop onto all the doormats at once. In the school—single storey and built from pink composite blocks—the acronym in people's mouths is Got Aids Yet?

First day of secondary school, new smells and a shift in timbre. We're swimming in a wider channel. Mr Murray the guidance teacher opens his desk drawer and takes out a short, stiff, brown leather strap. He's making a general introduction to his classroom. We sit at our single desks facing him. He says it's called a Tawse. He shows us how it's forked. The brown leather is split in two, halfway down its length. He tells us it's deliberate—it's designed that way so it hurts more. He tells us he will use it.

Erotic charge, electric jolt of looking down and seeing an upright Tampax, index of her, analogue of wanting. Vertical in the inside pocket of her blue 501 denim jacket, hanging on the back of her black plastic chair. Negative shape, index of outside her, in Modern Studies. On the outside pocket of her jacket, a red hammer and sickle badge. On mine, a gold baby Lenin inside a circle inside a radiating star. Modern Studies, Mr Paterson vibrating. Keys jangling like bursting, red face like conflicting chemicals pushing to get out. He has the flicked hair of a young liberal. Grey suit trousers, a little taper, slight shine. He's a chalk breaker. His handwriting is rangey. All capitals and then suddenly none. His speech booms, then trails off. Pausing, looking out at the faces in tables of twos. Maybe it's for emphasis. Probably it's the combing of a blank mind for what comes next. Pausing, pacing in front of the blackboard with the blood beneath the surface, fingers through his hair. Frustrated the day after the 1987 general election, he puts me in the cupboard at the back of the room.

Lesbian becomes lemon in the glissando slide of an Aberdeen football chant. They ask Poofy Davies who teaches us German for the word for lemon. He gives them the word, and it gets pulled into their rhyme. The chant is evolving. Poofy Davies shifts about a little, watching a while, hand on hip at the front of the class. I can see the shape of his vest beneath his shirt. He watches until handclaps begin colliding with the chant syllables, then he interjects. Alright now settle down. He and I are in silent competition with each other. When chanting is directed at me, it's diverted away from him. Back and forth it goes.

IRA, Mr Brett is saying. IRA. He says it in a Northern Irish accent over and over. Then he says the word Barry over and over in a Northern Irish accent. He isn't Irish, but Barry the new boy is. We all sit in a semicircle while Barry winces. Beamer. The teacher's foot in its black shiny loafer shakes side to side. The stage remains unlit at the far end of the room, the shaking of Mr Brett's foot the only movement in the wide dark drama hall. Us in silence. Then the bell.

A tall girl with fine hair, a slightly protruding top lip and something of a deer about her face, frequently faints. The fainting mainly happens in the thick rush between classes. Two-lane traffic in the corridors, bottlenecks of bodies opening out into the wide reverberating main hall with multiple corridors branching off it. The biggest thoroughfare. The girl is splayed face down on the floor, static with closed eyes, hair spread out the way it fell. People surge past her, water parting for a boulder. We've been told that she's doing it for attention and that we must ignore it. Walk on.

In General Science, Mr Kindness passes by our table of four. Handing out pH strips, he calls me Progeny, his wordplay. He asks do you know what Progeny is? I say no. Offspring he says. It's offspring. And continues on his way with a tinkling trolley of beakers. Another afternoon he gets me off my stool and onto my feet, pulling me up by my rattail, further up—beamer—until I'm on my toes.

The second house is larger, granite and two storeys. It looks over a valley. In the dip, a road and a river run parallel, west to east. Daylight is coming and the school bus. Half the road shaded by pines is black ice. Five of us from the village wait on the verge. Two brothers stand apart, smoking with their early moustaches. The oldest has frosted ginger hair and a grey Rucanor bag between his feet, three stars above the word. He spits. It shoots out like a bar of soap from wet hands. He does this every few minutes. He's holding a Regal between middle-finger and thumb. The burning end is pointing inward. To tap the ash, he flicks the filter in staccato with his index finger. He does it more than necessary. It's repeated often, like the spitting. Tapping and spitting take turns. I can't remember their names, but I can remember which farm they lived at. They have a sister and their mother is a housekeeper on the estate. On the bus, the sister says their mother will make Baked Alaska for the Laird today. Because it's his birthday and that's his favourite.

Every morning Donna Bell ties my wrists with my school tie in an alcove. The tie that isn't compulsory but I've started to wear for its edge, its diagonals. Maroon/silver strip/navy/maroon/silver strip/navy. Those of us on the school buses from the outlying farms and villages arrive earlier than the town pupils walking to school. So you hang around waiting before class. People have their spots for the waiting. Some hiding, some out in the open. Tied in an alcove, a doorway. People pass by. People pass but can't see because my hands are behind my back. Her wearing Brut. Me silent and the wettest I've ever been.

The floor of the main hall is pine lines. Turning into one of the adjacent corridors, it switches to black linoleum, the sharp catch of it underfoot. The sound of it catching under six hundred feet. I have a job as a cleaner, cleaning the school after school. Everyone is gone. It's me, one other pupil and three or four adult cleaners. I like seeing the classrooms empty. I like seeing these adult cleaners who I never see any other time. I have long wide corridors to myself, where I swing an industrial machine around to polish the black floors. Circular, droning, heavy manoeuvring. Then back again next morning to walk on them.

compose

recompose

Flo Ray

AR TICULATIONS

A project in two forms: one part is a poem, intended for reading aloud. The other is the same poem, but drawn as bones—an excerpt of which is included here. Both parts exist in conjunction; one is not subordinate to, or a clarification of, the other.

AR TICULATIONS

I have it
was am it it
break up
king down
in rain cut
mud slab s
worm grub mosmoss
leaves
a thickset wad
still leaf
ing left
the nerve

your end
stale bed slate
head
board
over rip
e sunk cell
this dug pit
my own wet rut
no breadth
to love rot hold
less breath
lessbreath
less
brittle mass
set castoffwhite
hard set
up check
ar bevelled fact

dry sip
my dusk pulse
two too
hollow mouths
what rib em
bed
did up
right limb ex
static strut
cut rigid shiver
dew over
dew

re
new dank lull
tip a little
gristle knot
tip hot salt cup
stain wetted
sockets
pelvic slab
lug back to
move me it this
to cope
you slip sli pup
on top
we two in sync
like deadlock fuck
defunct
fall out in out
of syncope

red the
trench red air
it stank
grit scaffold leg
what broke
give up up still
you keep kept
mov ing me
it this
em rit r tes to
rest in what
forever less

shut
I long touch
to stayin in
eclipse
our last joint
part
your move
move love evolve
re act the
pause
in jaw de
part
clench bit

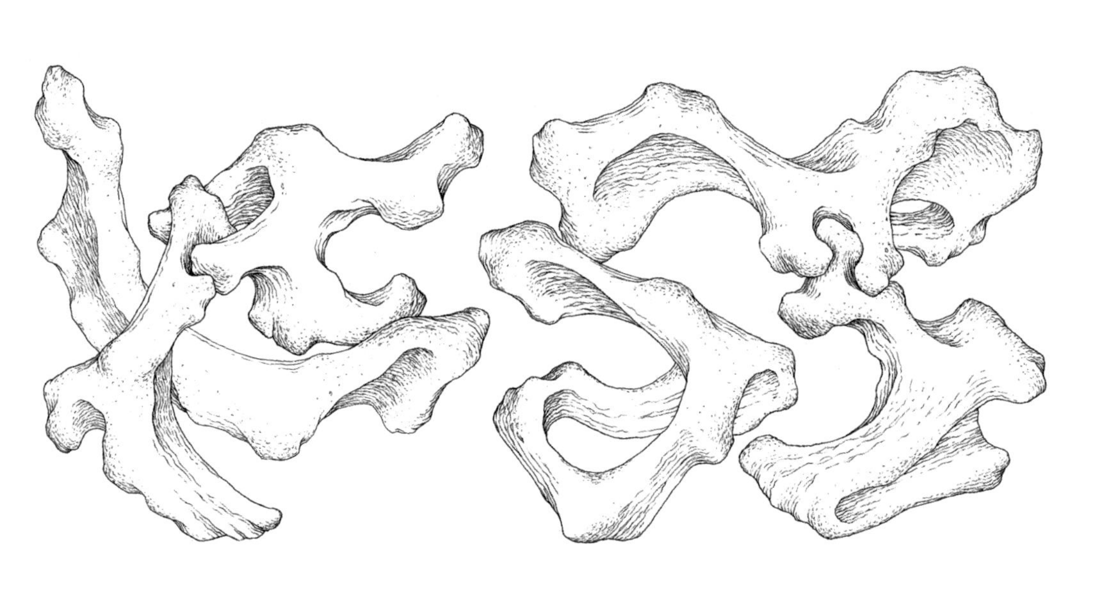

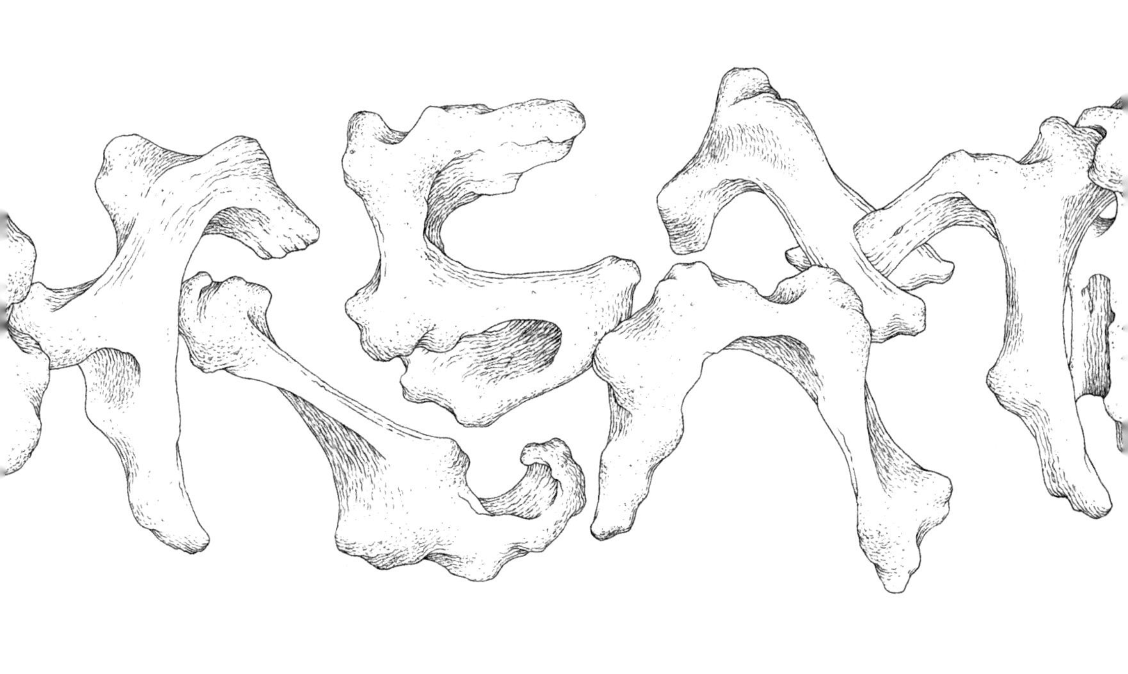

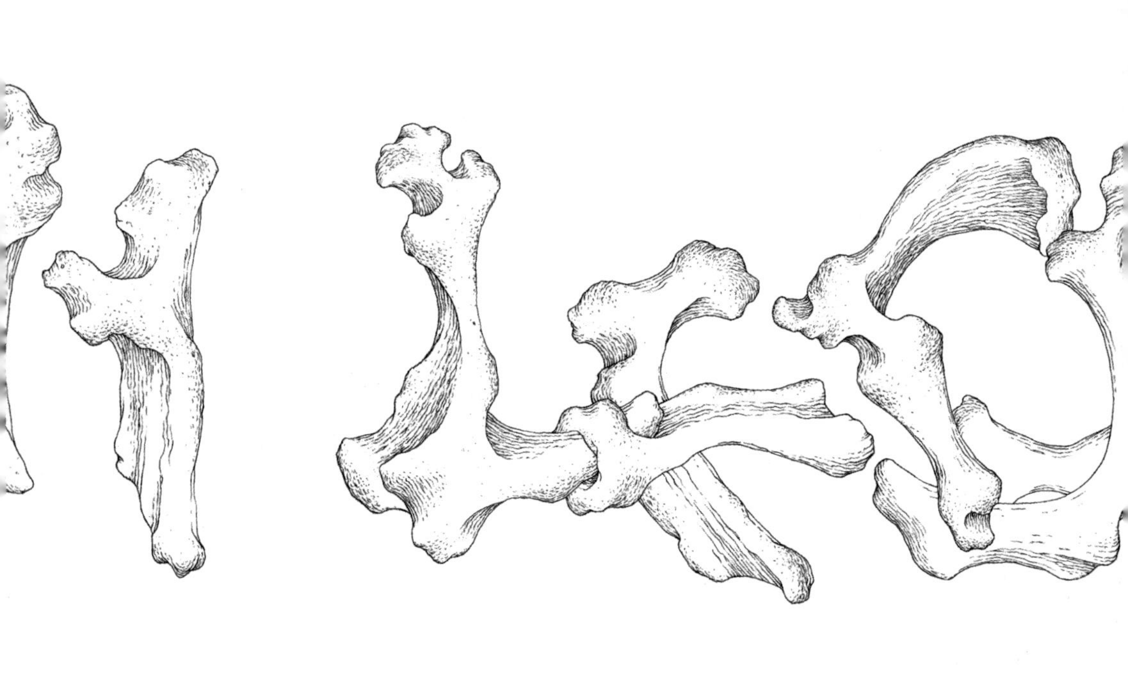

FR A

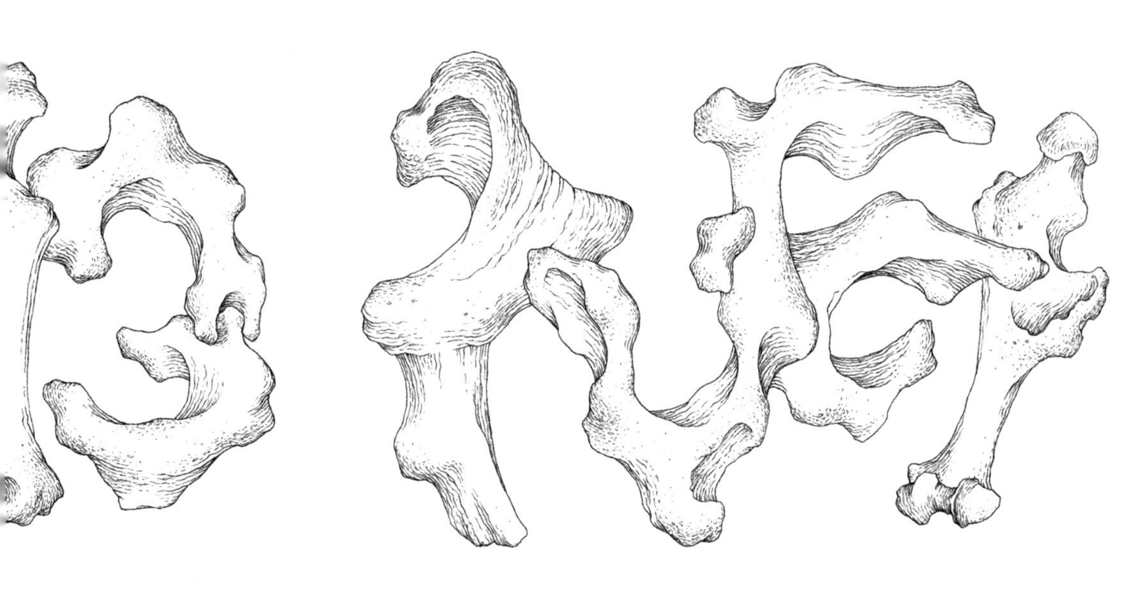

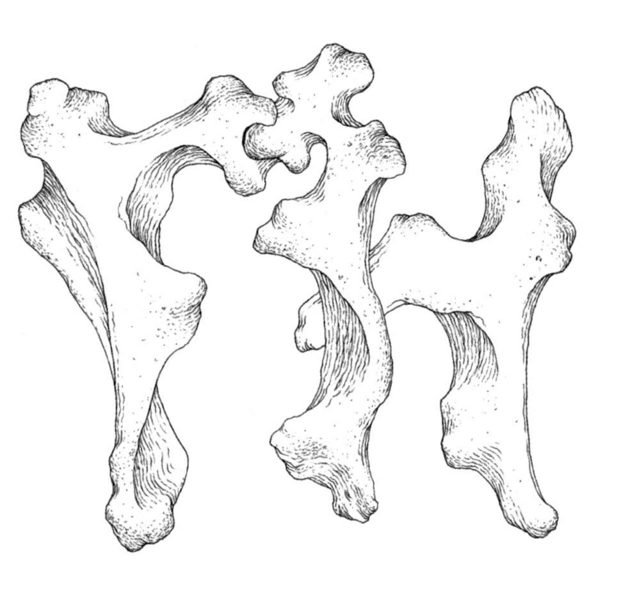

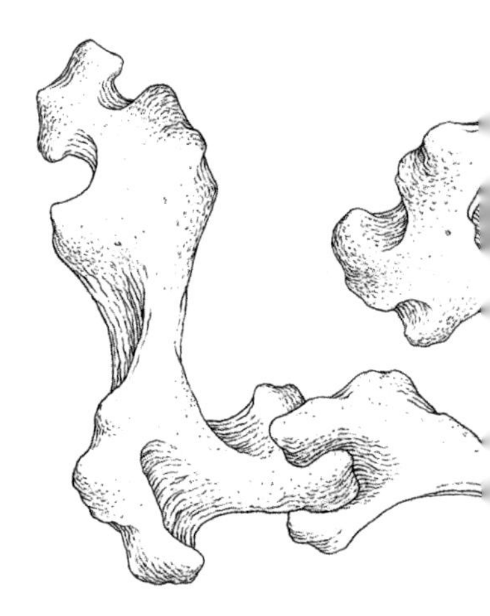

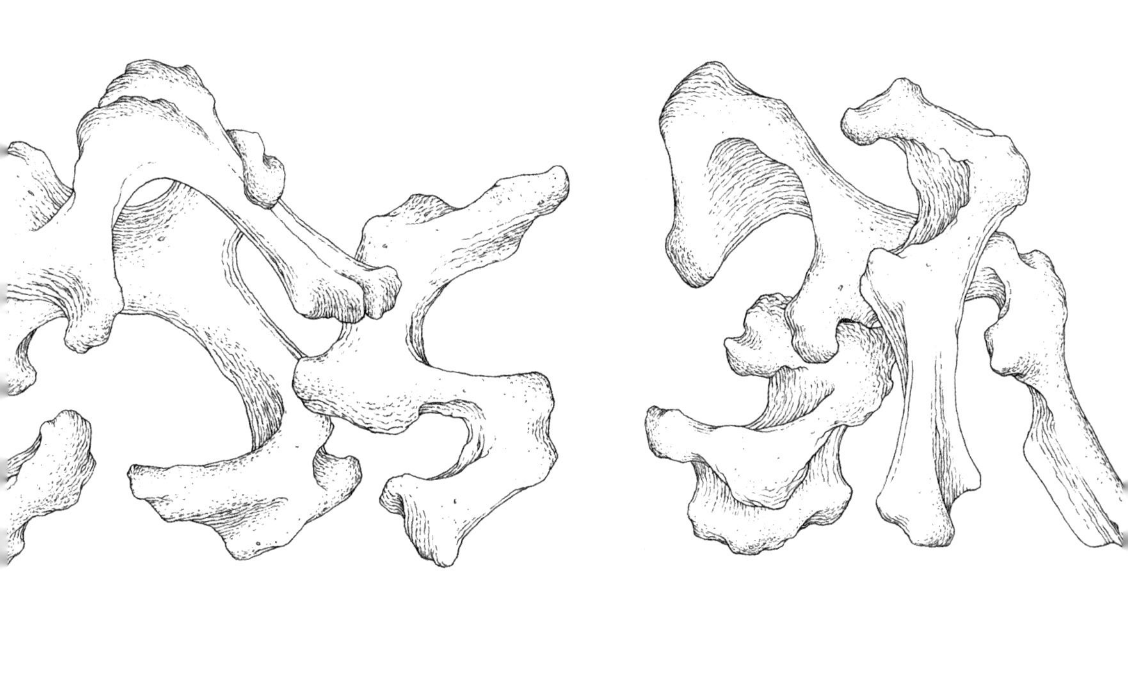

transition

to

P. Staff

eat clean ass only
/ on venus

eat clean ass only

lying together in a wet puddled pool,
jelly rubber
dick in the shower ,, animals in the bed
& _ the concrete steps that lead up to our house after it rains, the lines of the
cracks in the concrete have this new aura this time of year,
a seeping aura,,
where the water is glowing—

it's that time of the year, right?

pup,
my pup.
piss in the pool
_in the tub
_in the fat
_round your hips
let your lips rest on the time machine, love

there goes the spit
in your empties, there goes a tenner, there goes the journeying to
a sacred foothold,,
crying salty, wet cum tears.

i am delighted to help you
to kiss you
to
wash your hair

eat clean ass   only
eat   it clean
do   it clean   it is
not   eating it,   it is

two animals,   you and you
eat clean ass only

for
the metropolitan life insurance company
,, all capital letters
and closed brackets
,, right?
I am always thinking about weightlessness—so gross
a military procession
between a girl slash boy, all hanging out, just like—nothing
a pronoun, unable to hold a person together—like nothing from something

I
could be to
not believing

no oil,
no moisture, no life.

anymore.

so keep it coming you fucking coward. I say to myself,
and myself only :)

it will all evaporate anyway, like—money.
burnt particles float up
in the atmosphere
i hope
uhhhhhhh, yeah

yeah i do think so

I keep collecting things:

  a violent image
  a pay slip
  soda water canister
  so much paper
  so much grief
  and so much sleep

  unthinkable loss,
  hunger and
  sound

  and so much warmth
  unthinkable,,
  burnt particles

  unending churn
  bad breath
  and acne

  and dirt
  grease hair
  and diarrhea

        and caustic tooth
        rot
        my ass unwashed

feeling so sexy and free

clearly unlocatable
and fleshy

in the room, the bed, the shower the dialectic
is
getting buried,

buried
it is buried

all as
it is, it is
buried
and
if it's in me

it is me
and if it's me
it is
me,

shit on your finger tips
swipe my eyeball

and if it's
not me
i am it
it is it huh?

and if
i am not it then
fuck it i
am
not it,

two animals, you and you shit, and not it

i am not it

and if it is
not
me
then it is buried

if it is buried
it is buried
and i have nothing wet salt
nothing

eat clean ass only and i have nothing

eat clean ass
only
and it is
,,
please.

it is, please. shit on your,, nothing.

huh /
and i am happy.
.

i am delighted
to help you
to kiss you
to wash your hair.

on venus

on venus, things are much the same as they are here.
on venus, days outlast years.
on venus, there were once oceans
that have long since burnt away.
on venus, there are no seasons.
on venus, there is pressure,
enough pressure to crush absolute.
on venus, the hours between day and night
are far thinner than here, and lapsing_
on venus, the winds blow harder
they strip every surface,
the air hostile //
on venus
we are neighbours
in nerves /
with chemicals
/ with acid
in our insides
with muscles
like rats_ and flora
like spiders—like sex something that looks like sex but isn't
/ fucking
like lava //
like insects
head underground
like dogs—
dogs tested on
dogs with guts
full of—something
like wailing /
_ and sobbing
like buildings
door handles
made of blood
/ touch and nervous like drugs
—and senses
and change and infirmity and pain
—like suffering
, like sleeping
no sleeping / like home
and no home like this—
like—rotation and testes
new ovaries_
new organs
/ like rain

on venus
/ the rain
on venus,,
burns away
before it reaches the surface.
the insides
like no insides
,, like new organs
for everyone!
new organs for everyone!
on venus
on venus //
there are no
on venus,
there are no moons.

wipe

to

Alice Theobald

Point of View / It’s Too Heavy Alone

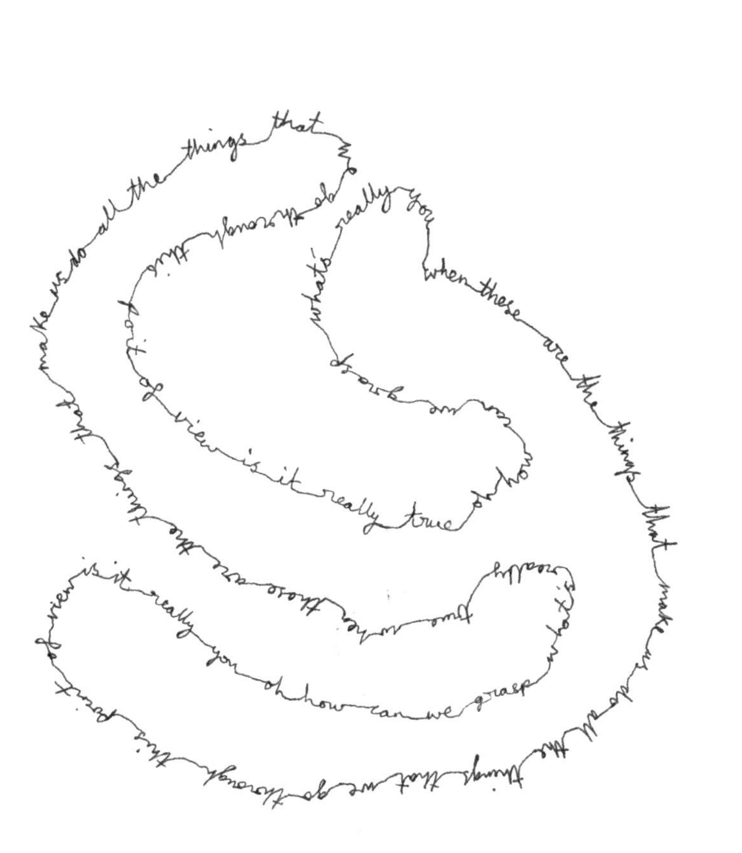
what's really you when these are the things that make us do all the things that we go through this point of view is it really you oh how can we grasp what's really true when these are the things that make us do all the things that we go through this point of view is it really true oh how can we grasp

when
you these
really are
what’s the
grasp things
we that
can make
how us
oh do
true all
really the
it things
is that
view we
of go
point through
this
point through
of go
view we
is that
it things
really he
you all
oh do
how us
can make
we that
grasp things
what’s the
really are
true these
when

It's Too Heavy Alone

What's your position?
I forget.
Your position?
Yes. Sometimes I forget...
Where to go? And supposed to be?
And how to hold myself.
With your own arms?
No, it's just not the same.
It's difficult to carry yourself.
Alone yes.
Your own weight.
Yes!
It's too heavy alone.
And one would have no ground to stand on.
No ground to stand on for your position.
No.
You'd need help to do that.
Yes, help.
It's what happens...
On top of everything else.
Of what?
Everything!
When your own making is leading you astray.
Who's making actually?
Your making.
Making what though?
I'm getting tired
Our making?
No.
I feel sick.
Hang on, we need to set some limitations.
And hang on to what?

move

forward

Jesper List Thomsen

Blackbirds

Why?
It comes natural

In my right pocket
I keep
my tongue,
my mother tongue,
there
next to
the phone
kept alive
by vibrations
of incoming
calls
and iMessages,
massaging the muscle
that's what's
going on,
a tongue on life support

courtesy of C O NN E C TI VITY
in response to P R O X IM I TY

Mother tongue
little wet
from
little use,
like an unused
SIM card tied to
a contract
6
12
18
24 years,
and more

Dubious contractor
luring me in
with infinite
time,
unbearable
loads

Download,
see that's
what happened!
A nurtured download
escaping the fold,
to migrate
back into
the web
Ouch!
Damn!
Shit!
Tht's
A
bad
bad
me taphor

but,

sensitive ear
stay alert,
you must not
forget
the whispers
of your mother
in young age:
nose
eyes
ears
chest
belly
crotch
leg
knee
foot
toe
finger
hand
arm
shoulder
back
spine
neck
head
brain
mind

Disembodied
semanticist
keep on going,
your language
is your home
your bed
your view
your social
alliances
your discursive dead ends,
your language
is for all,
your language
is what the www
promised to be,
pre cookie
pre eco
pre backfeed
, pre eat your own
vomit son!

Eat it now
eat it always,
and remember
not to question
this act

that's how we keep the rounds going
that's how we
move #REMEMBER

But the language,
this tongue
that only works
because of its
default sense of
detachment,
because of its fierce
insistence to
perplex,
because of its
lack of lullabies

You see mother
there is a blackbird
traversing the skies

it flies high
first aided
by its wings,
then gliding
out of sight

The neoliberal I
was instated
first by theft, then
by implementation

And where are we now?

This body lives here,
it bends slightly
using the interior
of the airplane for support.
Fingers tapping,
eyes looking,
mind falling in
and out
of want to
not to.
A hum,
a vibration
travels through the body,
alerting it
of being under
artificial care

Sacrificial care
Consequential care
Parental care
Dental care
Pernicious care

E's
for the first time,
body shared
muddy body
soft body
horny body, with
horny bodies,
all horny
bodies
trembling along
to the same
continuous beat
of wanting
to fuck
you
in a dark
room
somewhere
on Kingsland Rd

There are rural parts of the body
that rarely,
if ever,
get any attention.
As geo-political centralisation
sweeps across the body,
pulling with it all focus and
financial concern
towards
the bum,
face
and hand.
Clad in sponsorshipped uniformity,
attending to my drink vessel;
this body is an enterprise
post language
pure rock

Preposterous man
who doesn't know
himself
i.e.
acts a nob,
is a nob,
in the long tradition
of nobs being nobs
because they
have
no cocks.
Amputated at birth
because mommy really
wanted a girl.
Daddy cuts it off
and throws it
at the dogs.
The dogs throw
it at the cats.
The cats
throw it
at the chickens.
The chickens throw it at
the rats.
The rats
bring it down
into the Belly
of Earth,
and drop it
on the Eternal Fire,
whilst
Elvis Presley
cries in the chapel
somewhere
just outside
Phoenix, Arizona

So,
no cock
and a big mouth
with nothing
to suck,
other than the abuse
of language

in short form,
which rhymes
only
with foghorn

Acknowledging the method
is already being too kind
to a man
primarily dealing in
his own tan

moving on!

Opera of nonsense!
Cacophony of
bodily remorse!
Corporal revulsion!
Penetrate
and integrate,
I, the I,
dividing the present
from the past
and future.
That is to say,
I,
form the past
and the future,
simultaneously
from this position
HERE!
That's why
a voice
matters

Language has been stripped of the body,
the body of language.
Ousted to the point where voice
and therefore agency is neglected.
A division that proved fatal
to May's political shambles,
to West's onstage meltdown;
the examples
as in reverse!

Stay Product bro
Live your Words love

Speaking isn't just the uttering of sense
or nonsense,
it isn't just the lungs
provoking
vibrations
of the cords
tuned by
throat
nose
mouth,
but also the handing over of an entirety,
of the body
PER SE

The President
somewhat
got
that
right

arriving through
the anus
moving in
and up
through the rectum
up the
descending colon
traversing colon
ascending colon
the cecum
passing through
the cecocolic orifice
into the ileum

through the length of
the jejunum
the duodenum
and into the stomach
up the oesophagus
passing the pharynx
the oral cavity
over the tongue
and out through
the mouth

get into
the body
and
or
mind of that
thing
you despise
the most in this
moment
and love
in this moment

identity and escape
identify and escape
identify and move intentionally in a direction that's unlikely to you. identify as something other, real or not real, and move in a direction unlikely for you. identify as someone and move intentionally in a direction that's unlikely to you. identify as your mum and move in a direction unlikely to you. identify as Beyoncé and move intentionally in a direction that's unlikely to you. identify as molecule and move intentionally in a direction that's unlikely to you. identify as propaganda and move intentionally in a direction that's unlikely to you. identify as shy and move intentionally in a direction that's unlikely to you. identify as tree and move intentionally in a direction that's unlikely to you. identify as sensation and move intentionally in a direction that's unlikely to you. identify as genius and move intentionally in a direction that's unlikely to you. identify as skin and move intentionally in a direction that's unlikely to you. identify as bee and move intentionally in a direction that's unlikely to you. identify as translator and move intentionally in a direction that's unlikely to you. identify as desire and move intentionally

in a direction that's unlikely to you. identify as milk and move intentionally in a direction that's unlikely to you. identify as algorithm and move intentionally in a direction that's unlikely to you. identify as summer and move intentionally in a direction that's unlikely to you. identify as CAConrad and move intentionally in a direction that's unlikely to you. identify as love and move intentionally in a direction that's unlikely to you. identify as tongue and move intentionally in a direction that's unlikely to you

shadow all
moves along
and under
runs in a simple
duration towards
the furthest sea

finally dead
uhh, it's nice
a tremendous bend
by someone who
does not know
how
to bend

and then one
wonders what a
dancer   who
moves her
body sporadically
yet controlled
in some harmony
with ambition
and intention
and frequency
, ouch

tearing up
the bus stop
so the bus
doesn't stop

what the fuck
why not
what happened to
your bus
to your bus stop

• • •

dissolve

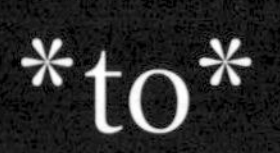
to

Afterword

Intertitles: Or, I Am Glad To Be Wrong In So Many Ways

Vahni Capildeo

Hello, you. I never have been so much you as when addressed by this book. I never have tasted the speranza in desperation so much as in the appeal to the reader as not a number. Oh, book, have you had an 'impact' on me, no, and have I been 'engaged', no, have I have been addressed, I have been redressed, a bloody body in gossamer armour. 'Who is you?' A famous-in-my-family question, uttered by a face like a paper bag. You is up in the air. I woke up this morning and I was not you, but reading you, I am.

I enter the worlds of this book with the wrong senses. I am empowered to sense wrongly, being wrongly sensed and entranced. This week my friend the lake swimmer warned us about hemochromatosis. If our mouth tastes metallic, get our iron levels checked. Years ago my friend the falconer wrote about stress. Her mouth tasted metallic; her bereavement levels went unchecked. In the coronavirus daze, if my mouth tasted metallic, would I get checked? Tillie O. wrote, 'I Stand Here Ironing'. I enter here as the iron. I read as steam. I read as rust. I read as the tsunami of unflattened, unflattering pintucks. The cloth I press is red, like genital mutilation. The cloth I press is blue and fragile, like cruelty in his eyes. The cloth I press is green, like the grass of a black-and-white landscape which has become not the background to text, but its groundation.

Iron, I pass over what is folded in the in-between. My surface is hot and maculate. My cord is frayed. Soft machine metamorphosis is a readerly writerly act. If the glans clitoris is an electrocuted pearl, am I covered in oyster shells the way Artemis is covered in breasts that are testicles that are meteorites? For in the worlds of this book, sometimes all flesh is orchids, sometimes langoustines. De Beauvoir's hateful description of middle-aged sexual desire as the creaking and grating of shellfish is a distant and disadvantaged relative whose photo album is classical tragedy, pity and terror, in the hands of a child growing up beside gender. Here languor is back, and part of the furniture, a chaise longue for crustaceans.

I enter the worlds of this book with the wrong senses. I classify the PDF as perfume. Salty, marine, warm skin, metallic fluids; blood, not so much milk; hardly indoles, hardly a rubbish of white flowers or the luxury of crap; whale vomit, richly, muchly. Almonds and vanilla, sweetness with a touch of toxicity, the body feminine not as flower but as seed and as tree.

Blacked-out lines of text appear like the London tube system. Something, underground, is getting you somewhere faster. Meantime, a disused station of imaginable period beauty remains concealed. Its name is an intertitle. The stops on this map are all intertitles. The reader who has to get somewhere, faster, is on the train of named stations. One you and another you and another you disembark through closed doors to find solace in the concrete ballrooms of betrayal, the architecture of the in-between at intertitle stops.

The happiest video I saw this spring was the woman swinging a surfboard in between her legs. The surfboard was attached to a string, the other end of which was inserted into her vagina. Squeeze. Lift. Squeeze. Lift. Medicalised it is ok, squeezenlift, sexual health gets the ok, squeezenlift, collective yoga bridging is ok and expensively accessorised, squeezenlift, so what about this kind of beach body, squeezenliftnswing? She looked so happy! And why not? Weightlifting, in displays of masculinity, pumps the arms above the head. Weightlifting, in delighted cahoots with gravity, puts the vagina squarely above ground. Tell me the interior of such a body is not a gallery or an entrance hall, but an entire theme park, complete with mystery funhouse and obstacle course. Intertitles: surfboards or water slides?

If you take a line for a walk, is it a dog or a magic fish? If you treat a page like a walk, is it a whispering gallery? How does a net work? Is a net a silencing by lines? Ripped, knotted, rotten, neon, twine? A whisper network must consist of boundary violations woven like intertitles. For a whisper network is a system of the sounds and silences formally known as unimaginable. The ones you do. It is as loud as nothing else.

The text alongside the photographs makes a shape of motion like a dancing torso and tells of self-portraits being burnt. My brain seems to move away and back. The tail of a great reptile is brushing the desert. The forbidden words, like oscillation, like iridescence, make great inscriptions visible from outer space though not intended for that. You are? They are? We are? It is? Of the earth. Sacrifice reappears as a scene in sequins on a danger skirt.

Getting into intertitles. A gallery of—Oh heavens! How did you get out? And how did you—Thank you for the revival of the calling card, the call-out card, the grim humour of a race card you can play. Thank you for reminding us of the artist who could hand a piece of text and turn away, silent but not silenced, implicated but not complicit. In between the words and images of this book, I pick up cards and feel a garment flowing behind me, river of magical realist fabric, a swish the full length and breadth of every space. You read. You swim. You breathe.

fade

out

Image Descriptions

These descriptions were written for colour images that have been reproduced in the physical book in black and white. Colour images are present in e-book and PDF versions.

CAConrad

Page 95: A shopping trolley that is seemingly abandoned fills the centre of this photograph. The shopping trolley is on top of a scraggy-looking piece of land with patches of both dirt and grass visible. Because the ground looks very dry it might be the end of the summer in the western hemisphere. The shopping trolley has a bright orange handle with white illegible writing on it (presumably the supermarket name it came from) and a bright orange square seat for children at its front. Although we cannot see the sky in the photograph, we can tell the sun is shining because the metal of the trolley is gleaming.

Page 96: In this photograph a pair of white hands with glittery black nail polish are cradling a small potato. The potato has been anthropomorphised as it has two round eyes (circles with black dots in them), a small nose (a letter 'c' turned 90 degrees) and a large mouth (an upside-down shape of a tunnel) drawn on it in black marker. On the potato's head is a sparkly pearlescent star shape. There is an area painted with black sparkly nail polish on the underside of the potato. In the background of the photograph we can see a brown wooden set of shelves containing books. These are fitted all the way to the top of the photograph. On the left-hand side, we can see a white wall and it has a white picture frame hanging on it. The work in the frame is indiscernible but it is multicoloured.

Page 97: This photograph depicts a close-up of wood and detritus. In the bottom third of the photograph we can see light grey concrete. One thin section that runs horizontally across all the concrete has been filled with a lighter grey material. Running parallel to this filled-in area are marks that could be dried water residue. The top two-thirds of the photograph are taken up by wood in different stages of breakdown. We can see a sawn, thin tree trunk, wood shavings, twigs and spaghetti strips of planed wood. The colours of these different woods range from beige to red to purple to green.

Page 98: In this photograph we can see the bottom half of a rusty machine gun. It may possibly be an AK47. It is sitting atop some grass. We can see dirt patches through the green blades. Some of the blades are thicker and longer than others.

Page 99: In this photograph we can see irregular slabs of concrete with green grass weeds growing between them. The haphazard nature of the concrete slabs forms into some order as a clear path becomes visible in the distance of the photograph. It has been raining as some of the concrete slabs appear darker than others. The whole photograph has been rotated 90 degrees to the left.

Page 100: In this photograph we can see a sky at dusk in the background and in the foreground the silhouettes of two trees. The sky has flecks of clouds that are light blue and dark blue. The trees have a bright orange light (possibly from a streetlamp although it is not clear) shining through their branches. This orange light creates a stark contrast of colours between the sky and the silhouetted trees. Overall this creates a sense of drama and atmosphere.

Page 101: A derelict warehouse is depicted in this black-and-white photograph. There are steel columns running along either side of the space and a tall metal ladder leans on one of them on the right-hand side. There is detritus all over the floor; this includes old car tyres, wooden pallets, metal tubing and planks of wood. The back wall of the space is covered in metal tubes and wires. We can also see old fitted connecting boxes hanging on this wall. On the left-hand side of the photograph (and towards the back) natural light is filtering into the space. This is also apparent on the left-hand side. The whole photograph has been turned 90 degrees to the right.

Page 102: An explosion is coming out of the back of a large black truck in the bottom third of this photograph. It seems as though the velocity of the explosion has forced open the truck door. There are bright orange and red flames licking the side of the truck through the open door. Black and grey smoke is billowing up and away from the truck. The top two-thirds of this photograph contain the sky and a silhouette of a tree. The tree is not a pine tree but has the same shape as a Christmas tree. The sky is completely white.

Jesse Darling

Page 117: A digital scan of a pale yellow A4-sized piece of writing paper sits squarely within the page. In the top right-hand corner is the date '10/2020'. Directly underneath is the word 'Berlin'. On this yellow piece of paper are four paragraphs of typed text, printed at a slight angle, causing the left margin to be greater at the top than at the bottom. Two creases appear across the paper at equidistant points, dividing the page into three sections. This suggests the paper has been folded to fit into an envelope at some point. The creases intersect the first and third paragraphs.

Page 118: The second image is also of a pale yellow A4-sized piece of writing paper that sits squarely within the page. Six paragraphs of printed text sit squarely on the paper giving equal margins at both sides. Creases are in the same place as on the last piece of paper. On this image, however, the top crease appears between the second and third paragraph and the bottom crease crosses the fifth paragraph. The letter is signed off with the line:

Sending love until next time –

A burgundy-coloured handwritten signature appears directly below and is substantially larger than the printed text. To the left of the signature is the following:

xo,
JD

Anaïs Duplan

This work is a collage of image and text.

Page 124: A black woman with short hair who is wearing a yellow polo neck and white-and-peach patterned trousers lies on her side on a bed. She is holding the side of her face with her hand. The bedspread is green and on the left-hand side of the image we can see the corner of a white pillow. The wallpaper behind the bed is peach and has red leaves on it. In the top right-hand corner of the image we can see the bottom of some peach-coloured curtains. Underneath these curtains we can see a black bag with large straps. This bag is covered by a blue translucent square.

Page 126: Black text floats on top of a black-and-white image of grass. The top half of the image is brilliant white, which we understand as being the clear blue sky.

Page 127: Black text floats on top of a black-and-white image of grass. The top half of the image is brilliant white, which we understand as being the clear blue sky. This image occupies the left third of the page.

Page 128: An abstract, blurry image appears on the page. It consists of two images overlapping. It seems as though they depict the strap of a handbag and the bag is sitting on top of a person's leg. The whole image has a blue tone to it as there is a mid-blue square floating on top of it.

Page 129: An abstract, blurry image appears on the page. It consists of two images overlapping. It seems as though they depict the strap of a handbag and the bag is sitting on top of a person's leg. The whole image has a blue tone to it as there is a mid-blue square floating on top of it. This image occupies the left third of the page. The remaining space is filled with the image of the back of a polaroid picture and a giant orange fruit covered in red netting (with the word 'China' visible) sits on top of a radiator. Black text is sitting on top of the image of the fruit and radiator.

Page 130: A giant orange fruit covered in red netting sits on top of a radiator on the left-hand side of the page. Black text is overlayed on top of it. On the right-hand side of the page blue text sits on top of scribbles made in blue. We can see these handwritten sentences: 'I'VE BEEN THINKING ABOUT IT A LOT AND IT SEEMS LIKE', 'I DON'T KNOW', 'I WISH I COULD TELL YOU WHAT I FEEL.

Page 131: We can see the continuation of scribbles and a repetition of the blue handwritten words and scribbles that appeared on the previous page. We can see the words 'INKING', 'AND IT SEEMS LIKE', 'COULD TELL TOO', 'BUT SHIT', 'I CAN'T EVEN BECAUSE WHAT TO HAVE FOR DINNER… 4 DAYS'. On the right-hand side of the page we can see an upside-down image of a person dressed in red and wearing black shoes. They appear to be floating. This image has black text sitting in a white square on top of it. We can also see rectangles of blue in the upper right-hand side of the page.

Pages 132–3: On the left-hand side of the page we can see the same upside-down image of a person dressed in red and who is wearing black shoes as appears on the previous page. They appear to be floating. This image has black text sitting in a white square on top of it. A grey rectangle appears where the image of the person wearing red meets the black text.

Inua Ellams

Page 139: Black handwritten text occupies the page. Every few words, a mustard-coloured forward slash appears. This sequence of handwritten text and mustard-coloured forward slashes continues from the top of the page to the bottom of the page and from left to right.

Sharon Kivland

Page 225: A scan of a grey book cover is vertically centred but justified left on the page so that there is an almost equal border of white around the top, right and bottom edges of the image. On the grey cover, a decorative border appears, framing the edges of the image. This border is made of dense floral patterns. Inside this border is text in French that suggests it is a school textbook, with lines left blank where the owner might fill in personal details. At the top is the République Française crest depicting a seated woman, and in the centre, in significantly larger font, are the words:

École Communale
CAHIER MENSUEL

Page 226: A scan of a grey page appears in the same dimensions as the previous page, suggesting it is part of the same book. This image is also vertically centred but justified right. Inside the grey paper is an image centred on the page leaving a nearly equal border of grey around it. The image is a reproduction of a coloured etching of two women and a young girl. The young girl to the left of the image is wearing a green, Victorian-era dress and black ankle boots. She is gesturing with her right hand to something beyond the frame of the page and with her left hand she is holding the arm of the woman next to her. This woman occupies the centre of the image and is wearing a grey and blue dress that meets the ground and conceals her feet. The dress has a wide collar and decorative cuffs and embroidery details. She is significantly taller than the girl and she looks down to meet the girl-in-green's gaze. She is standing next to a third woman who occupies the right of the frame and wears a brown dress of a similar style. This woman also looks to the girl in green and her face is in profile. She is wearing a brown hat and a dangling gold earring. These three people are standing in front of a draped pink curtain that is bound by a pink braided tie-back with tassels. This is directly behind the young girl and beside a partially obscured table with a vase of pink and green flowers. The carpet they are standing on has pink and green flower motifs embroidered onto it.

Page 227: A scan of the interior page of the grey book, justified left with white border surrounding the scan on three sides. The page is densely lined for writing exercises and contains expressive, cursive handwriting in black ink that fills each page. The text runs from the left margin to the opposite edge and fills each page with text. Near the top of the page, in upper case, is the word: COURS. Following this, in cursive handwriting, are the words: Anglais / English.

Pages 228–235: On each of these pages is a scan of an interior page from the grey book. Each scan is aligned to the centre of the spread, with a white border surrounding it on three sides, creating the impression that the grey book is lying open. The pages are densely lined for writing exercises and contain cursive handwriting in black ink that fills each page. The text runs from the left margin to the opposite edge and fills each page with text.

Page 236: A scan of a grey page of the same dimensions as the previous images is justified right on the page and centred, leaving an equal border of white around the image on three sides. Inside its edges is a double-line border demarking a rectangle. Inside this rectangle are a series of numerical tables. Each depicts a times table from 2 to 10. This chart is headed with the title, in upper case: TABLE DE MULTIPLICATION.

Flo Ray

Pages 334–339: In each of these pages, fine pencil line drawings of bone-like forms traverse the page from left to right. Detailed line work gives a shaded, three-dimensional quality to the rendering of the contours of the bones. These forms interconnect and take on the shape of letters. A single line of 'writing', made from these bone characters, is centred on the page and takes up roughly a third of the vertical proportions. The line of text touches the extreme margins of the page on both sides and continues uninterrupted onto the opposite page.

Alice Theobald

Page 355: Cursive handwriting snakes in this photograph to form a shape that looks like a deflated ship's anchor. Each word is connected to the next word by a line. There are no breaks between the words. The photograph sits in the centre of the page.

roll

credits

Biographies
(in order of appearance)

Laure Prouvost was born in 1963 in Moulenn-break, Albania. She lives and works in an underwater mobilhome to research tunnel engineering, currently in the Channel. She practices making video, boobs, sounds and tea cups, objects and installation. Here a long list of museums and institutions. A line, interesting things, a coma, a line, a list of residencies and prizes. A selection of solo projects including: a Melting Into Another in Lisbon, an Occupied Paradise in Aalst, Deep See Blue Surrounding You in Venice and Toulouse, a Waiting Room with objects in Minneapolis, a New Museum for Granddad in Milano, A tearoom for Grandma in Derry, a karaoke room in Brussels, a new octopus ink vodka bar for Gregor in Rotterdam, A travel agency for an Uncle in Frankfurt, a lobby for love among the artists in the Hague and Luzern... tea bags, and wet floors and tentaculees.

Jess Chandler is a publisher and editor and runs the independent publishing houses Prototype and House Sparrow Press. She was a co-founder of Test Centre, which ran from 2011 to 2018, publishing innovative works of poetry and fiction. She has worked as an editor at Reaktion Books, and as a researcher and producer on factual television programmes. She is also the Digital Editor of *Poetry London*.

Aimee Selby is a freelance editor specialising in art, architecture, art history and photography, for publishers including Prestel, Ridinghouse, Reaktion Books, Barbican Art Gallery and the National Gallery. Her writing has been published in *Rattle: A Journal at the Convergence of Art and Writing* and *Andy Holden: Chewy Cosmos Thingly Time* (Kettle's Yard, 2011). She was the editor in 2009 of the volume *Art and Text* (Black Dog Publishing).

Hana Noorali & Lynton Talbot work collaboratively with artists to produce text, exhibitions and live events. Together they have started non-profit galleries in both London and Berlin and have curated exhibitions in public institutions, project spaces and galleries across London and internationally. In 2019 they were selected to realise an exhibition, *The Season of Cartesian Weeping*, at the David Roberts Art Foundation as part of their annual curator's series. In 2020 Hana Noorali, along with artist Tai Shani and curator Anne Duffau, started TRANSMISSIONS, an online platform that shares artists' work in a classic DIY TV format. TRANSMISSIONS has worked with Legacy Russell, Lawrence Abu Hamdan, CAConrad and others. In 2019 Lynton Talbot started Parrhesiades, a multi-platform project working with artists for whom language is an essential part of their work. Parrhesiades has worked with Sung Tieu, Johanna Hedva, Cally Spooner, Anaïs Duplan and others.

Isabel Waidner is a writer and critical theorist. Their novels *We Are Made of Diamond Stuff* (2019) and *Gaudy Bauble* (2017) were shortlisted for the Goldsmiths Prize and the Republic of Consciousness Prize (2x), and won the Internationale Literaturpreis. They are a co-founder of the event series Queers Read This at the Institute of Contemporary Arts (ICA) in London, and the programmer and presenter of *This isn't a Dream*, a literary talk show, hosted by the ICA via Instagram Live. They are the editor of *Liberating the Canon: An Anthology of Innovative Writing* (2018), and their next novel *Sterling Karat Gold* is forthcoming with Peninsula Press in June 2021.

Fatema Abdoolcarim is an Indian-Pakistani Hong Konger. She is a visual artist, filmmaker and writer. Her visual works have been shown at the Montreal Museum of Fine Arts, Dr. Bhau Daji Lad Museum, Mumbai, and Luggage Store Gallery, San Francisco. As film director her short films have been shown at Locarno, Sundance and ZINEBI, and as collaborator with Juan Palacios, their feature documentary, MESETA (2019), has premiered and won in competitions at CPH:DOX and L'Alternativa Barcelona. She is currently working on her first feature-length fiction film, *Hum*. Her PhD in Creative Writing at the University of Manchester—*Hum* and *After the Cut: A Close Looking Into Seventeenth-century Mughal Painting, 'Zulaykha's Guests Distracted by Yusuf's Beauty'*—received the UK Arts and Humanities

Research Council Award (2017–2019). *Shh* was first performed in 2018 in Manchester at *Murmur: Ed Atkins and Fatema Abdoolcarim*, and has subsequently been performed at art and writing symposiums, readings and literary festivals in the UK and Denmark.

Victoria Adukwei Bulley is a poet, writer and artist. Winner of a 2018 Eric Gregory Award, she has held artistic residencies internationally in the US, Brazil and at the V&A Museum in London. She is currently a doctoral student at Royal Holloway University, for which she is the recipient of a Technē studentship for practice-based research in creative writing.

Bebe Ashley lives in Belfast. When procrastinating from her PhD, she takes British Sign Language and Braille classes and writes pop culture articles, specialising in Harry Styles. Bebe's debut poetry collection, *Gold Light Shining*, was published by Banshee Press in 2020. www.bebe-ashley.com

Anna Barham is a London-based artist working across video, sound, print, installation and performance. Her work centres on various collective reading processes that explore the transformation of meaning as language is translated between different bodies, forms and technologies. Recent projects include *To be we to be*, Index, Stockholm, and Quote-Unquote, Bucharest; *Liquid Crystal Display*, Site Gallery, Sheffield, and MIMA, Middlesborough; *A sentence can be ours and ours*, Playground Festival, Museum M, Leuven, BE; *This is a voice*, Wellcome Collection, London, and MAAS, Sydney; *Secret Surface*, K-W, Berlin. She recently published a new book, *Poisonous Oysters*.

Paul Becker is a writer and painter based in Stockholm and the UK. His most recent book, *Choreography, Coreografia*, is a fiction set within the R.W. Fassbinder film *Chinese Roulette* (1976) and published by Juan de la Cosa (John of the Thing), Mexico. For several years he has been compiling *The Kink in the Arc*, a collective novel based on the idea of ekphrasis.

Elaine Cameron-Weir was born in 1985 in Red Deer, Alberta, Canada. She has had numerous solo exhibitions of her sculptural work including at The Dortmunder Kunstverein in Germany, Storm King Art Center in New Windsor, New York, as well as at The New Museum, New York. Her work has also been shown at Remai Modern in Saskatoon, Canada; the Montréal Biennale, Montréal, Canada; the Fellbach Triennial, Fellbach, Germany; and in numerous group exhibitions. Upcoming projects include participation in the Belgrade Biennial and a solo show at the Henry Art Gallery at the University of Washington. She writes alongside her sculptural practice, usually in lieu of preparatory drawing and often uses phrases from her writing as titles and supplementary material. Her written work has appeared in *Flash Art Magazine*, journals such as *The Happy Hypocrite* and *Novel*, and also on the Parrhesiades project platform. She currently lives and works in Queens, New York.

Adam Christensen is a Danish artist based mainly in South London who makes performance, video, fabric and text works, and performs with the music project Ectopia, which was Wysing Arts Centre's band-in-residence in 2016. The readings and musical renditions that constitute a large part of Christensen's practice are informed by the environments and settings in which he performs. Whether in homes, clubs, galleries or streets, with a few listeners or big audiences, his performances are always intimate stagings that combine personal recollections with theatrical deliveries. The most banal of stories transformed into a seductive narrative. A language that is often dramatic, even if monotonous in tone, as well as explicit and humorously tragic in content. A stage composed of exuberant, colourful fabric works draped over metal structures, depicting silhouettes of characters caught in emotional states. Extravagant costumes. Heels. Make-up. Emotionally affective accordion performances where the heaviness of voice and sorrow of delivery transport artist and listener somewhere else entirely. An embodied persona existing both on and off stage so that the threshold between the two becomes loose and blurred, existing across different places and times, establishing a variegated, relational space that sets the scene for further displacements of everyday experience.

Sophie Collins grew up in Bergen, North Holland, and now lives in Glasgow. She is the author of *Who Is Mary Sue?* (Faber, 2018) and *small white monkeys* (Book Works, 2017), and the editor of *Currently & Emotion* (Test Centre, 2016), an anthology of contemporary poetry translations; a sequel, *Intimacy*, is forthcoming. She is the translator, from the Dutch, of Lieke Marsman's *The Following Scan Will Last Five Minutes* (Pavilion, 2019). She is currently translating Marsman's novel, *The Opposite of a Person* (Daunt Books, 2022), as well as working on new poetry and prose.

CAConrad has been working with the ancient technologies of poetry and ritual since 1975. They are the author of *Amanda Paradise*, forthcoming from Wave Books in 2021. Their book *While Standing in Line for Death* won a Lambda Book Award. They also received a Creative Capital grant, a Pew Fellowship, and a Believer Magazine Book Award. They teach at Columbia University in New York City and Sandberg Art Institute in Amsterdam. Please view their books, essays, recordings, and upcoming events at www.bit.ly/88CAConrad.

Rory Cook is a writer and editor based in Manchester. Between 2017 and 2020 he organised Murmur, a series of occasional events aiming to bring poetry and innovative writing to new audiences. He is the founding editor of the publishing platform Monitor Books, and is currently working towards a PhD at the University of Salford, researching strategies of interfacing in contemporary poetry and art practice.

Jesse Darling is an artist who lives and works, based in Berlin and London. They work in various media and in different spaces. Recent projects include the curated series of one-minute videos *Everything happened so much: archive as poem in the age of perpetual witnessing*; solo museum presentations *Gravity Road* at Kunstverein Freiburg, *Crevé* at Triangle Marseille and *The Ballad of Saint Jerome* as part of the ART NOW series at Tate Britain, and a non-institutional mail art initiative with no title, funding or commission during 2020 and the early months of 2021. They have published texts in print and online including *Granta*, *Tripwire Journal*, Whitechapel Press *Documents* series, *Artforum*, *frieze*, *Rhizome.org* and *The New Inquiry*.

Anaïs Duplan is a trans* poet, curator and artist. He is the author of a book of essays, *Blackspace: On the Poetics of an Afrofuture* (Black Ocean, 2020), a full-length poetry collection, *Take This Stallion* (Brooklyn Arts Press, 2016), and a chapbook, *Mount Carmel and the Blood of Parnassus* (Monster House Press, 2017). He has taught poetry at the University of Iowa, Columbia University, Sarah Lawrence College, and St. Joseph's College. His video works have been exhibited by Flux Factory, Daata Editions, the 13th Baltic Triennial in Lithuania, Mathew Gallery, NeueHouse, the Paseo Project, and will be exhibited at the Institute of Contemporary Art in LA in 2021. As an independent curator he has facilitated curatorial projects in Chicago, Boston, Santa Fe and Reykjavík. He was a 2017–2019 joint Public Programs fellow at the Museum of Modern Art and the Studio Museum in Harlem. In 2016 he founded the Center for Afrofuturist Studies, an artist residency programme for artists of colour, based at Iowa City's artist-run organization Public Space One. He works as Program Manager at Recess.

Born in Nigeria, Inua Ellams is a poet, playwright & performer, graphic artist & designer and founder of: The Midnight Run (an arts-filled, night-time, urban walking experience), The Rhythm and Poetry Party (The R.A.P Party) which celebrates poetry & hip hop, and Poetry + Film / Hack (P+F/H), which celebrates Poetry and Film. Identity, Displacement & Destiny are recurring themes in his work, where he tries to mix the old with the new: traditional African oral storytelling with contemporary poetics, paint with pixel, texture with vector. His books are published by Flipped Eye, Akashic, Nine Arches, Penned In The Margins, Oberon & Methuen.

Olamiju Fajemisin is a writer, curator, and student at the Courtauld Institute of Art, London. Her work has been published by various publications and institutions, including *frieze*, *Contemporary&*, *Brand-New-Life*,

Burlington Contemporary, Kunsthall Bergen, Haus der Kunst, and the Salzburg International Summer Academy of Fine Arts. She is the digital editor of *PROVENCE*. Her performative practice constitutes an ongoing exploration of the possibilities of spoken text.

Johanna Hedva (they/them) is a Korean-American writer, artist, musician and astrologer, who was raised in Los Angeles by a family of witches, and now lives in LA and Berlin. Hedva is the author of *Minerva the Miscarriage of the Brain*, a collection of poems, performances and essays, and the novel *On Hell*. Their new album is *Black Moon Lilith in Pisces in the 4th House* (2021), a doom-metal guitar and voice performance influenced by Korean shamanist ritual. Their EP *The Sun and the Moon* was released in 2019. Their work has been shown in Berlin at Haus der Kulturen der Welt, Klosterruine, and Institute of Cultural Inquiry; The Institute of Contemporary Arts in London; Performance Space New York; the LA Architecture and Design Museum; and the Museum of Contemporary Art on the Moon. Their writing has appeared in *Triple Canopy*, *frieze*, *Lithub*, *The White Review*, and is anthologized in *Whitechapel: Documents of Contemporary Art*.

Caspar Heinemann is an artist, writer and poet based in Glasgow. His interests include springtime, counterculture, mystical reverence and professional irreverence. He has held solo exhibitions at Cell Project Space (with Alex Margo Arden), London; Outpost Gallery, Norwich; Almanac, London; and Kevin Space, Vienna, and recent group exhibitions at La Casa Encendida, Madrid; Georg Kargl Fine Arts, Vienna; ICA, London; and Cabinet, London. Heinemann participated in the Moscow International Biennial for Young Art, Bergen Assembly and the Baltic Triennial, and has recently read at Camden Arts Centre, Sussex Poetry Festival and Tate Modern. His first poetry collection, *Novelty Theory*, was published in 2019 by The 87 Press.

Sophie Jung is an artist, writer and teacher living in Basel and London. She's invested in triggering a de-categorizing of concepts and a de-conceptualization of categories, hopes for unholy alliances, cross-material solidarity and assemblages that defy resolution. Her approach to 'stuff'—both legible utensil and metaphoric apparition—sits somewhere between materialist responsibility and wild becoming. Her writing exists in the tradition of *écriture feminine* and lives as polyvocal collage, often materialized and extended collaboratively. Recent exhibitions include *Preluge* at Galerie Joseph Tang, Paris; *Unsetting* at Istituto Swizzero in Milan; *Sincerity Condition* at Casino Luxembourg; *Taxpayer's Money* for Frieze LIVE; *Dramatis Personae* at JOAN, LA; and *The Bigger Sleep* at Kunstmuseum Basel. She is currently working on solo exhibitions at E.A. Shared Space in Tbilisi and Parrhesiades in London. Recent publications include *On Care* (MA BIBLIOTHÈQUE, 2020), *Seen from Here: Writing in the Lockdown*, ed. Tim Etchells and Vlatka Horvat (Unstable Object, 2020) and *The Happy Hypocrite 12: Without Reduction* (Book Works, 2021) as well as a monograph of works and writings to be published by Mousse Publishing in 2021.

Sharon Kivland is an artist, writer, editor and publisher, the latter under the imprint MA BIBLIOTHÈQUE. She has also been called a poet, much to her surprise. Her work considers what is put at stake by art, politics and psychoanalysis. She is currently working on the natural form, as well as editing the letters and other material sent to her by the French psychoanalyst Jacques Lacan during the course of their turbulent love affair which endured from 1953 until his death in 1981.

Tarek Lakhrissi (b. 1992, Châtellerault) is a visual artist and a poet based between Paris and Brussels. He currently teaches at CCC Research Master Program of the Visual Arts Department at HEAD (Geneva School of Art and Design). Lakhrissi has been exhibited internationally at galleries and institutions including: Museum of Contemporary Art, Biennale of Sydney (2020); Wiels, Brussels (2020); Palais de Tokyo, Paris (2020); Palazzo Re Rebaudengo/Sandretto, Guarene/Turin (2020); Quadriennale di Roma, Palazzo delle Esposizioni, Rome (2020); High Art, Paris

(2020); Hayward Gallery, London (2019); Auto Italia South East, London (2019); Grand Palais, FIAC, Paris (2019); Fondation Lafayette Anticipations, Paris (2019); L'Espace Arlaud, Lausanne (2019); Zabriskie, Geneva (2019); Fondation Gulbenkian, Paris (2018); CRAC Alsace, Altkirch, France (2019); Kim?, Riga (2018); Artexte, Montreal (2017); Gaité Lyrique, Paris (2017); SMC/CAC, Vilnius (2017). He is nominated for the 22nd Fondation Pernod Ricard Prize (2020–2021).

Quinn Latimer is a California-born poet, critic and editor whose work often explores feminist economies of writing, reading and image production. Her books include *Like a Woman: Essays, Readings, Poems* (Sternberg Press, 2017); *Sarah Lucas: Describe This Distance* (Mousse Publishing, 2013); *Film as a Form of Writing: Quinn Latimer Talks to Akram Zaatari* (WIELS/Motto Books, 2013); and *Rumored Animals* (Dream Horse Press, 2012). Her writings, readings and film collaborations have been featured and exhibited widely, including at REDCAT, Los Angeles; Chisenhale Gallery, London; Lafayette Anticipations, Paris; the Poetry Project, New York; the Venice Architecture Biennale; and Sharjah Biennial 13. She is a lecturer at Institut Kunst, in Basel, where, with Chus Martínez, she also organizes a biannual series of symposia on questions of gender, language, and artistic practice. Latimer was editor-in-chief of publications for documenta 14 in Athens and Kassel.

Ghislaine Leung lives and works in London, UK. Recent solo projects include: *CONSTITUTION*, Künstlerhaus Stuttgart, Stuttgart; *VIOLETS 3*, Netwerk, Aalst; *CONSTITUTION*, Chisenhale Gallery, London; *Power Relations*, Essex Street, New York (2019); *VIOLETS 2*, Netwerk, Aalst; *Local Studies*, Reading International, Reading (2018); *The Moves*, Cell Project Space, London (2017). Leung is a member of PUBLIKATIONEN + EDITIONEN. Her first collection of writings, *Partners*, was published by Cell Project Space in 2018.

Jordan Lord is a filmmaker, writer and artist, working primarily in video, text and performance. Their work addresses the relationships between historical and emotional debts, framing and support, access and documentary. Their video and performance work has been shown internationally at venues and festivals including MOMA, Artists Space, Performance Space NY, DOCNYC, and Camden Arts Centre. Their 'solo' exhibition of video work *After... After...* was presented at Piper Keys in London, UK, in 2019. Their work is by no means solo. They currently teach in the Integrated Media Arts MFA programme at Hunter College, CUNY, from which they also graduated.

Dasha Loyko is a Belarusian-born artist based in London. She works with errors, logic, gossip, soundalikes, and other hiccups of rationality. Using cross-genre experimental writing as her starting point, her multimedia practice engages with the mechanics and the accidents of knowledge-construction.

Charlotte Prodger works with moving image, printed image and writing. She was the winner of the 2018 Turner Prize and represented Scotland at the 2019 Venice Biennale. Solo exhibitions include *SaF05*, Stedelijk Museum, Amsterdam (2021); Scottish Pavilion, Venice Biennale (2019); *Colon Hyphen Asterix*, Hollybush Gardens (2018); *BRIDGIT/Stoneymollan Trail*, Bergen Kunsthall; *Subtotal*, SculptureCenter, New York (2017); *BRIDGIT*, Hollybush Gardens, London; *Charlotte Prodger*, Kunstverein Düsseldorf (2016); *8004–8019*, Spike Island, Bristol; *Stoneymollan Trail*, Temple Bar Gallery, Dublin (2015); *Markets* (with The Block), Chelsea Space, London; *Nephatiti*, Glasgow International (2014); *Percussion Biface 1–13*, Studio Voltaire, London (2012); and *Handclap/Punchhole*, Kendall Koppe, Glasgow (2011). Performances include *Orange Helvetica Title Sequence*, New York Book Art Fair, MOMA PS1 (with Book Works); *Fwd: Rock Splits Boys*, Artists Space, New York, and Café Oto, London (with Mason Leaver-Yap); *Assembly: A Survey of Recent Artists' Film and Video in Britain*, Tate Britain, London (2014); and *Querido John*, Kings Place, London (with Electra and The Wire, 2012). Prodger's videos have screened at various film festivals including London Film Festival, New York Film Festival, Toronto International Film Festival and Internationale

Kurzfilmtage Oberhausen. Her writing has been published in *frieze*, *F.R.DAVID*, *2HB* and *The Happy Hypocrite*.

Flo Ray is an artist and writer based in London, UK. She works in and around familiar modes of (dis)connection and (mis)communication via text, film, performance, drawing, sculpture and installation.

P. Staff is an artist based in London, UK, and Los Angeles, USA. In 2009 Staff completed a BA in Fine Art Practice and Critical Contemporary Theory at Goldsmiths College, University of London, and subsequently studied Modern Dance at The Place, London, in 2011. They were a part of the influential, alternative education project the LUX Associate Artist Programme led by artist-curator Ian White in 2011. Staff's work has been exhibited, screened and performed internationally, including solo shows at the Serpentine Galleries, London (2019); Irish Museum of Modern Art, Dublin (2019); MOCA, Los Angeles (2017), amongst others. They have been part of a number of significant group shows such as *The Body Electric*, Walker Art Center (2019); *Made in LA*, Hammer Museum (2018); *Trigger*, New Museum (2017); and the *British Art Show 8*, touring venues (2016). Staff received the Paul Hamlyn Award for Artists in 2015. Their work is held in public and private collections internationally.

Alice Theobald is an artist and musician working primarily in performance, moving image, installation and text. She is based in Birmingham, UK. Recent projects and exhibitions include 'Ballad of Simple Women', Abu Dhabi Art Fair, performance programme 2020; *What Not To Wear Out My Soul* for Art Night London; *We May Believe or We May Never Know* at The White House CREATE, Dagenham; *Weddings and Babies* at Pilar Corrias, London; *It's Not Who You Are it's How You Are*, Baltic Centre for Contemporary Art, Gateshead. Her work has also been shown at Lisson Gallery, London (2015); Focal Point Gallery, Southend (2015); Chisenhale, London (2014); Gasworks, London (2013); Baro Galeria, Sao Paulo, BR (2013); ICA Singapore, SG (2012). In 2013 she co-founded the music group/artist-collective Ravioli Me Away with Sian Dorrer and Rosie Ridgway. In 2019 they produced *The View From Behind The Futuristic Rose Trellis*—an Alt-Opera which toured the UK to Wysing Arts Centre, Cambridge; Baltic, Gateshead; The Box, Plymouth; Block Universe / The Albany, London. They have released four albums, toured internationally and supported acts such as The Fall, Ana Da Silva (The Raincoats) and The Pop Group. Their recent club remix LP *NAUGHTY COOL—H.M.S RMA* was released by ALTER in 2021.

Jesper List Thomsen is an artist based between Turin and London whose work begins in writing, traverses the body and ends in painting. His forthcoming book *FREEEee* will be published by L'Esprit de L'Escalier in 2021. Recent exhibitions and performances have taken place at Fanta-MLN, Milan; Hot Wheels Athens, Athens; Parrhesiades, London; South London Gallery, London; Grüner Salon, Volksbühne, Berlin; Bureau des Réalités, Brussels; Künstlerhaus Stuttgart, Stuttgart; ICA, London. A book-length collection of his texts was published by Juan de la Cosa/John of the Thing, Mexico City/London in 2018.

Vahni Capildeo FRSL is Writer in Residence at the University of York and an outgoing Seamus Heaney Centre Poetry Fellow at Queen's University, Belfast. Their work ranges from poetry to non-fiction to immersive theatre, and has been recognized with awards including the Forward Poetry Prize for Best Collection and the Cholmondeley Award. Current projects include 'Active Silence' from York, a collaboration with Trinidadian artist Andre Bagoo to accompany Capildeo's pamphlet of expanded translations, and 'Savannah Sequences', a record of walks, developed while Writer in Residence at the University of the West Indies, St Augustine Campus. Capildeo's publications include *Odyssey Calling* (Sad Press, 2020) and *Skin Can Hold* (Carcanet, 2019), written thanks to a Douglas Caster Fellowship at the University of Leeds.

Matthew Stuart and Andrew Walsh-Lister are typographers, editors and writers currently based between the United Kingdom and

United States, respectively. Together they edit / run Bricks from the Kiln (www.b-f-t-k.info) an irregular journal / multifarious publishing platform established in mid-2015, and also collaborate on a range of other publishing, editorial and curatorial projects, often / occasionally under the name Traven T. Croves. Collectively and individually, they have exhibited, taught and delivered talks internationally at institutions including MOMA PS1, Graham Foundation for Advanced Studies in the Fine Arts, Wysing Arts Centre, Scottish National Gallery of Modern Art, Tenderbooks, Central Saint Martins, Printed Matter Art Book Fair, Outpost Gallery, Ox-Bow School of Art, Royal College of Art, Chicago Architecture Biennial and Brno International Biennial of Graphic Design.

Acknowledgements

'About the Body and Likeness' by Sophie Collins was commissioned by the Hayward Gallery, Southbank Centre, in 2018. 'Thank You For Your Honesty' was commissioned by *Poetry London* and published in their Summer 2018 issue.

CORONA DAZE 87 and 24 will be published in CAConrad's forthcoming book *Amanda Paradise* (Wave Books, 2021), and are included here with the kind permission of the author and publisher.

Earlier versions of Rory Cook's poems originally appeared in *A Plume Annual* (Museums Press, 2017) and *SPAM001* (SPAM Press, 2020).

The type of *Frau Welt* by Sophie Jung was set in collaboration with Boah Kim.

'Q' di Quadro *or My Body, Her Refrain (It Comes Back)*, by Quinn Latimer, first appeared in *This Is My Body, My Body Is Your Body, My Body Is the Body of the Word*, ed. Lilou Vidal (Paraguay Press, 2019), published to coincide with the titular exhibition at le Delta, Namur (23 November 2019 – 19 April 2020).

'Tracklist' and 'Complicity, Fetish, Agency' by Ghislaine Leung were first published by Cell Project Space, London, as part of the book *Partners* in 2018, edited and designed with Patricia L. Boyd and Stefano Faoro.

Blackbirds by Jesper List Thomsen first appeared in *BASE BASE,* a book-length collection of his texts published by Juan de la Cosa/John of the Thing, Mexico City/London in 2018.

For their help, advice and support in bringing this project to life, the editors would like to thank Rachael Allen, Jesse Darling, David Dibosa, Anne Duffau, Gareth Evans, Maud Gyssels, Geirmund Knutsen, Helen Marten, Chris McCormack, Sarah McCrory, Louise O'Kelley, Guy Robertson, Valerie Talbot, James Trevelyan, Jessica Paz Zamora Turner and Ahren Warner.

Note on Title Cards

Throughout this anthology title cards conceived / contributed by Matthew Stuart and Andrew Walsh-Lister are inserted / inverted between sections. Punctuating interstitial spaces, their black background dissolving the cinematic frame, the title cards placed here hope to offer moments of pause; an address to the reader that leads them from one scene to the next, bridging and guiding each phonic void.

Typically, title cards (or 'intertitles') connect filmic sequence, but they also disrupt—the viewer becomes the reader. And of course books, like films, are temporal objects; they exist across, weave together and triangulate multiple modes of time. As John Latham recites: 'To me, a book is outside of time. A book when it is read begins to bring time into the organism when it's being read. But there's another part of it, which is the story or the material, which is another process altogether. It's not necessarily architectural. But when we've got the time it's being written and when we've got the non-time, which is the book, and when we've got the idea in the mind of the person who is reading it, you have got three components which are enough to make up the whole heart of existence.'*

Cutting across time, cards read: inter / titles / curtains / fade / in / dissolve / to / fade / away / cut / to / stop / start / wait / proceed / change / over / leave / embark / out / in / rest / continue / rinse / repeat / clear / space / close / open / end / begin / beat / resume / clear / throat / hold / return / once / more / halt / go / turn / page / release / refocus / pause / play / still / forward / take stock / carry on / lights down / lights up / switch / on / compose / recompose / transition / to / wipe / to / move / forward / dissolve / to / fade / out / roll / credits / curtains / close / inter / titles

* Lines spoken by Latham (credited as 'Sculptor / Philosopher') in *The Cardinal and the Corpse. Or a Funny Night Out*, a 1992 TV movie directed by Christopher Petit and Iain Sinclair.

About Prototype

poetry / prose / interdisciplinary projects / anthologies

Creating new possibilities in the publishing of fiction and poetry through a flexible, interdisciplinary approach and the production of unique and beautiful books.

Prototype is an independent publisher working across genres and disciplines, committed to discovering and sharing work that exists outside the mainstream.

Each publication is unique in its form and presentation, and the aesthetic of each object is considered critical to its production.

Prototype strives to increase audiences for experimental writing, as the home for writers and artists whose work requires a creative vision not offered by mainstream literary publishers.

In its current, evolving form, Prototype consists of 4 strands of publications:

(type 1 — poetry)
(type 2 — prose)
(type 3 — interdisciplinary projects)
(type 4 — anthologies) including an annual anthology of new work, *PROTOTYPE*.

Intertitles

Published by Prototype in 2021
Edited by Jess Chandler, Aimee Selby, Hana Noorali & Lynton Talbot
Designed by Traven T. Croves (Matthew Stuart & Andrew Walsh-Lister)
Typeset in Lector
Printed by KOPA *in* Lithuania

A CIP record for this book is available from the British Library

ISBN: 978-1-913513-13-9

(type 4 // anthologies)

admin@prototypepublishing.co.uk
www.prototypepublishing.co.uk
@prototypepubs

prototype publishing
71 oriel road
london e9 5sg
uk

p prototype

( ) ( )

Supported using public funding by
ARTS COUNCIL
ENGLAND

This Voice

This voice belong to this page.
This voice belong to this page, and only this page.
This voice wants to be clear but it belongs to this page and only this page. For ever and ever.
This voice belong to this page, and only this page.
This voice belong here.
This voice is here for this page.
This voice' only desire is to be played by beautiful white page.
This voice belongs here.
This voice is here for this page.
This voice would ideally be heard in five minutes.
This voice' aspiration is to be played louder.
This voice only exists for this page.
This voice expressed existentialism of a voice being played by this page. Here and now.
This voice would do anything for this page.
This voice breathes this page.
This voice, this voice is orange and green. It smells of paint.
This voice belóng to this page and only this page.
This voice loves this page.
This voice is a window in the middle of the page. Here.
This voice is the space beneath your feet, is the space above your head.
This voice is twenty different carpets put on top of each other. Here, on the floor, the layers only seen, as you walk up.
This voice is just floating above you.
This voice makes the page floating, levitating.
This voice makes the page feel light.
This voice make you feel heavy.
This voice makes you feel heavy near theses page.
This voice would ideally have been heard two minutes ago.
This voice exist tomorrow.
This voice loves this page.